HISTORICAL DICTIONARIES OF RELIGIONS, PHILOSOPHIES, AND MOVEMENTS
Edited by Jon Woronoff

1. *Buddhism,* by Charles S. Prebish, 1993
2. *Mormonism,* by Davis Bitton, 1994
3. *Ecumenical Christianity,* by Ans Joachim van der Bent, 1994
4. *Terrorism,* by Sean Anderson and Stephen Sloan, 1995
5. *Sikhism,* by W. H. McLeod, 1995
6. *Feminism,* by Janet K. Boles and Diane Long Hoeveler, 1995
7. *Olympic Movement,* by Ian Buchanan and Bill Mallon, 1995
8. *Methodism,* by Charles Yrigoyen Jr. and Susan E. Warrick, 1996
9. *Orthodox Church,* by Michael Prokurat, Alexander Golitzin, and Michael D. Peterson, 1996
10. *Organized Labor,* by James C. Docherty, 1996
11. *Civil Rights Movement,* by Ralph E. Luker, 1997
12. *Catholicism,* by William J. Collinge, 1997
13. *Hinduism,* by Bruce M. Sullivan, 1997
14. *North American Environmentalism,* by Edward R. Wells and Alan M. Schwartz, 1997
15. *Welfare State,* by Bent Greve, 1998
16. *Socialism,* by James C. Docherty, 1997
17. *Bahá'í Faith,* by Hugh C. Adamson and Philip Hainsworth, 1998
18. *Taoism,* by Julian F. Pas in cooperation with Man Kam Leung, 1998
19. *Judaism,* by Norman Solomon, 1998
20. *Green Movement,* by Elim Papadakis, 1998
21. *Nietzscheanism,* by Carol Diethe, 1999
22. *Gay Liberation Movement,* by Ronald J. Hunt, 1999
23. *Islamic Fundamentalist Movements in the Arab World, Iran, and Turkey,* by Ahmad S. Moussalli, 1999
24. *Reformed Churches,* by Robert Benedetto, Darrell L. Guder, and Donald K. McKim, 1999
25. *Baptists,* by William H. Brackney, 1999
26. *Cooperative Movement,* by Jack Shaffer, 1999
27. *Reformation and Counter-Reformation,* by Hans J. Hillerbrand, 1999
28. *Shakers,* by Holley Gene Duffield, 2000
29. *United States Political Parties,* by Harold F. Bass, Jr., 2000
30. *Heidegger's Philosophy,* by Alfred Denker, 2000

Historical Dictionary of the Shakers

Holley Gene Duffield

Historical Dictionaries of Religions,
Philosophies, and Movements, No. 28

The Scarecrow Press, Inc.
Lanham, Maryland, and London
2000

SCARECROW PRESS, INC.

Published in the United States of America
by Scarecrow Press, Inc.
4720 Boston Way
Lanham, Maryland 20706
http://www.scarecrowpress.com

4 Pleydell Gardens, Folkestone
Kent CT20 2DN, England

British Library Cataloguing in Publication Information Available

Library of Congress Cataloging-in-Publication Data

Duffield, Holley Gene, 1934–
    Historical dictionary of the Shakers / Holley Gene Duffield.
        p.   cm.   — (Historical dictionaries of religions, philosophies,
and movements ; no. 28)
    Includes bibliographical references.
    ISBN 0-8108-3683-1 (alk. paper)
    1. Society of Friends—History Dictionaries.   2. Quakers Biography
Dictionaries. I. Title. II. Series.
BX7611.D84   2000   99-38149
289′.8′03—dc21   CIP

Most especially to my Pamela (whose auburn hair and green eyes might suggest that she is hellish, but whose profusion of love and kindness and humility demonstrate far otherwise and distinguish her among human beings) and to twin yellow Labs Emmy Sue and Shaker Wells and to all the other members of my dear family: Mark, Jake, Cramer, Matthew, Jennifer, Little Person, Charlie, Casey, Jane, Paul, Pivo, Tim, Gretchen, Erin, Fluffy, and Popcorn.

Contents

Series Editor's Foreword

With at most 20,000 people ever having participated to one extent or another, the Shakers are definitely the smallest group included in this series on religions, philosophies, and movements. Yet small causes can have disproportionately large effects, and that is certainly the case for the Shakers. Although very few of them remain, they still are known far and wide. Their positions on many important issues—including communitarian lifestyle, communistic economy, self-reliance and the value of labor, certainly also piety and obedience to God, to say nothing of gender relations—are worthy of closer study. Relatively few have been converted entirely to their worldview over their religion's 225-year history in America, but the number who have been partially convinced or at least influenced by their belief system is legion.

This *Historical Dictionary of the Shakers* is a rather special form of testimony to them. It is not a general description, let alone an analysis, of the Shakers and Shakerism. Rather, it focuses on numerous aspects, including their social and economic organization, their religious practices and theology, and more commonplace matters such as their clothing and dwellings. It presents significant Shakers, from the sect's founder, Ann Lee, to those who contributed most to its early expansion and later development, and on to the remaining few. The entries provide a real feel for the Shakers since they frequently draw on contemporary commentaries by them, or about them, by Shakers, former Shakers, and outside observers. A broader basis is provided in the introduction to this volume, and the time element is encapsulated in the chronology. The bibliography is of particular importance, presenting a still-flourishing literature and showing that views can vary starkly depending on one's perspective.

It is not an easy task to present the Shakers suitably, a group once virulently criticized that later became the "darlings of American popular culture," as the author shows. That is probably why he logically brings in the views of many other observers of yesterday and today. Holley Gene Duffield thereby gives us a very nuanced picture of the Shakers, to whom he has devoted much time researching and writing. His knowledge enables him to introduce us to a very exceptional people.

Jon Woronoff
Series Editor

Chronology

1736   **Ann Lee**, the principal founder of **Shakerism**, born on February 29, in Manchester, England.

1758   Ann Lee joins **James** and **Jane Wardley** in their religious society.

1762   Ann Lee marries **Abraham Stanley**.

1772   Ann Lee receives revelation that the source of all evil is indulgence in sexual intercourse for sensual pleasure.

1774   Arrival of the first **Shakers** in America at New York Harbor on August 6.

1776   Shakers gather at their first common home in Niskayuna (later named **Watervliet**), New York. Approximate membership: eight.

1780   Shakers open their gospel to the public. **Joseph Meacham**, the father of institutional Shakerism, joins the Society. Approximate membership: 10–12 (Evans et al., *Compendium* 37).

1781   In May, Ann Lee and some of her followers begin a 28-month missionary journey through Massachusetts and Connecticut.

1783   On September 4, Shaker missionaries return to Niskayuna.

1784   **William Lee**, Ann's biological brother and one of the early leaders of the sect, dies on July 21. Ann Lee dies on September 8. James Whittaker succeeds her in leadership.

1785   Shaker gospel closed to the public.

1787   At **New Lebanon**, New York, Shakers establish the first of 24 highly structured communal **villages**. Watervliet (Niskayuna), New York, village formally established. James Whittaker, the last of the original English leaders, dies on July 20. Joseph Meacham and **Lucy Wright** are his successors in leadership—the Shakers' first native American liturgical team. Shakers hold their first communal dinner after gathering into "gospel order" at New Lebanon on December 25.

1790   **Hancock**, Massachusetts, village established. **Enfield**, Connecticut, village established. Publication of Joseph Meacham's *A Concise Statement*.

1791   **Harvard**, Massachusetts, village established.
1792   **Tyringham**, Massachusetts, village established. **Canterbury**, New Hampshire, village established.
1793   **Shirley**, Massachusetts, village established. **Enfield**, New Hampshire, village established. **Alfred**, Maine, village established.
1794   **Sabbathday Lake**, New Gloucester, Maine, village established.
1796   Joseph Meacham dies on August 16. Lucy Wright becomes principal **lead** of the Shakers.
1798   Shakers reopen their gospel to the public at about this time.
1799   Approximate beginning of the so-called **Kentucky Revival**.
1803   Approximate total membership: 1,603 (Robinson, *Concise History* 57).
1805   Shaker missionaries arrive at Turtle Creek, Ohio, on March 22.
1806   **Union Village** (Turtle Creek), Ohio, village established. **Watervliet**, Ohio, village established. **Pleasant Hill**, Kentucky, village established.
1807   **South Union**, Kentucky, village established.
1808   **Gorham**, Maine, village established. Publication of **Benjamin S. Youngs**'s *Testimony of Christ's Second Appearing.*
1810   **West Union,** Indiana, village established.
1816   Publication of **Rufus Bishop** and **Seth Youngs Wells**'s *Testimonies.*
1817   **Savoy**, Massachusetts, village established.
1819   Gorham, Maine, village closes.
1821   Lucy Wright dies on February 7. Publication of first *Millennial Laws* (then called *Orders and Rules of the Church*).
1822   **North Union**, Ohio, village established.
1823   Approximate total membership: 4,000 (Green and Wells, *Summary View* 84).
1824   **Whitewater**, Ohio, village established.
1825   Savoy, Massachusetts, village closes. Approximate total membership: 3,400 (White and Taylor, *Shakerism* 152).
1826   **Sodus Bay**, New York, village established.
1827   West Union, Indiana, village closes. Publication of Seth Youngs Wells and **Calvin Green**'s *Testimonies.*
1828   Approximate total membership: 2,632 (Robinson, *Concise History* 57).
1830   Publication of Green and Wells's *A Brief Exposition.* **Frederick W. Evans**, perhaps the best-known Shaker of the latter half of the nineteenth century, joins the Society.
1836   Sodus Bay, New York, village closes. **Groveland,** New York, village established.

1837   Beginning of the decade in the movement called **Mother Ann's Second Coming**.

1839   Approximate total membership: 5,000 (Robinson, *Concise History* 57).

1842   New principles developed during Era of Manifestations.

1843   Frederick W. Evans becomes **elder** of **Novitiate Order** (a.k.a. Gathering Order or North Family) at New Lebanon, New York.

1847   Spirits depart from the Shakers.

1858   Approximate total membership: 4,500 (Evans et al., *Compendium* 32–37).

1860   Approximate total membership: 6,000 (Dixon, *New America* 319).

1863   President Abraham Lincoln exempts Shakers from fighting in the Civil War.

1869   Evans publishes *Autobiography of a Shaker.*

1871   Inauguration of Shaker monthly journal.

1874   Approximate total membership: 2,415 (Nordhoff, *Communistic Societies* 117; Hinds, *American Communities* 81).

1875   Tyringham, Massachusetts, village closes.

1889   North Union, Ohio, village closes.

1892   Prominent Shaker **Harvey Eads** dies.

1893   Frederick Evans dies.

1895   Groveland, New York, village closes.

1896   **Narcoossee**, Florida, village established.

1898   **White Oak**, Georgia, village established.

1899   Publication of monthly journal ceases.

1901   Approximate total membership: 600 (MacLean, *Shakers of Ohio* 111).

1902   White Oak, Georgia, village closes. Religious services closed to the public.

1904   Publication of **Anna White** and **Leila S. Taylor**'s *Shakerism: Its Meaning and Message.*

1907   Whitewater, Ohio, village closes.

1908   Shirley, Massachusetts, village closes.

1910   Watervliet, Ohio, village closes. Pleasant Hill, Kentucky, village closes.

1911   Narcoossee, Florida, village closes.

1912   Union Village, Ohio, village closes.

1917   Enfield, Connecticut, village closes.

1918   Harvard, Massachusetts, village closes.

1922   South Union, Kentucky, village closes.

1923 Enfield, New Hampshire, village closes.

1931 Alfred, Maine, village closes.

1938 Watervliet, New York, village closes.

1940 Approximate total membership: 100 (Andrews, *Gift to Be Simple* 6).

1947 New Lebanon, New York, village closes.

1959 **Shaker Central Trust Fund** established.

1960 Hancock, Massachusetts, village closes. Around this time, the Sabbathday Lake community appears to be admitting new people.

1961 **Delmar Wilson,** last male Shaker to sign the **Church Covenant,** dies. Publication of the *Shaker Quarterly* begun.

1965 The **Lead Ministry** at Canterbury closes the Church Covenant.

1971 Establishment of the **United Society of Shakers, Inc.,** a nonprofit organization, at Sabbathday Lake.

1974 Shaker Bicentennial in the United States of America.

1990 **Mildred Barker**, a prominent twentieth-century leader of Shakerism, dies.

1992 **Ethel Hudson**, the last Shaker at the Canterbury village, dies.

1999 Sabbathday Lake continues as the only viable Shaker village. Six members: four **sisters** and two **brothers**.

Introduction

These are the heirs of heaven,
And thither they are bound:
The likeness here is given,
The people can be found.
With Christ they are partakers,
Tho' formed of flesh and blood,
And you may call them Shakers,
These people are of God.

Richard McNemar, Shaker

Today, a very widespread misunderstanding about **Shakers** and **Shakerism** persists. In reference to both of them, the past tense often is employed erroneously, as in "Who were the Shakers?" and "What was Shakerism?" The truth is that the United Society of Shakers, the most recent appellation by which the group is known, is extant; however, it exists only at the **Sabbathday Lake** community, New Gloucester, Maine. Four **sisters** and two **brothers** compose the community.

The Shaker pilgrimage in America began inauspiciously on August 6, 1774, when **Ann Lee** (sometimes spelled Lees), an Englishwoman, landed at New York Harbor. She was accompanied by **Abraham Stanley** (or Standerin), her husband; **William Lee**, her brother; **Nancy Lee**, her niece; **James Whittaker**; **John Hocknell** and his son **Richard Hocknell**; **James Shepherd**; and **Mary Partington**. Contrary to the Shakers' high hopes of spreading their gospel in America, as early as 1776 the small, seemingly unnoticeable band had begun to incur frequent persecution for several reasons.

One problem faced by the immigrant "**Shaking Quakers**," as they were often called at the time, was that their arrival coincided with the American Revolution. To the small sect's political detriment, while colonial patriots were dying trying to dissolve the political bands connecting them to Britain and to establish a democratic republic, the Shakers remained pacifistic, a practice that aroused suspicion among patriots on various occasions, particularly since they had newly arrived from the land of the enemy. Specifically, the Shakers were accused of being spies for the British military, which resulted several times in unlawful ill treatment of them and once even in the incarceration of a few of their number in 1780.

In addition to the small sect's politics regarding its new country, its peculiar religious principles and practices, which lingering Calvinists and staid Congregationalists and Baptists could not abide, also generated early antagonism toward the group. For one thing, a female had founded and was leading the heterodox sect—probably not a unique but certainly an unusual circumstance at that time. "Mother Ann," as Ann Lee was called by her followers, also was the subject of a fantastical allegation by the sect: she was believed to be the person in/through whom the **Christ Spirit** was making its Second Advent—Christ Jesus, Christ Ann. Furthermore, so-called orthodox Christians and other people who engaged in natural human carnality questioned the logic of the group's practice of **celibacy** (albeit, exercise of the principle had been united with Christianity from the religion's inception). Although the consequence of universal celibacy is termination of the human species, such is not a problem for the spirit-developing Shakers, for they believe that the carnal human is on a plane of existence that is a great deal lower—and, hence, greatly less significant—than that of the spiritual human. For the remainder of the eighteenth century and throughout the nineteenth century, development of the Shaker counterculture was regarded with apprehension by factions of the mainstream culture. By the early nineteenth century, already a body of literature—a good deal of it by Shaker **apostates**—reflected the often-severe antagonism between the sectarianism of "**the world**" and that of the Shakers.

Even after the continual dire reduction in the membership of the United Society of Shakers (or the **United Society of Believers in Christ's Second Appearing**, one of the sect's "official" names) which began prior to the Civil War, when the mainstream culture's concerns about the possible harmful influence of Shakerism might reasonably have abated to virtual nonexistence, the orthodox society continued to harbor negativity about the **Believers**. Among other ways, this attitude was expressed in the imaginative literature created by non-Shakers. For example, in "A Shaker Romance" (1895), by Charles Sherman Haight, the narrator charges that Shakerism is "a perfect refuge for tired humanity" and that the Society is nothing more than a "living grave" and a place of "durance vile." Furthermore, Shakers lead "solitary, loveless lives" filled with "never-ending monotony," and they "lack all possible ambitions and personal hopes" (625, 627).

Eventually, about two years after their immigration and "after passing through many trying scenes" (Green and Wells, *Summary View* 23), the Society's members founded a common home. Upon their arrival in America, without means of subsistence, most of the pilgrims had to fend individually with whatever laboring skills they had. Fortunately for them, John Hocknell had enough wealth to purchase a tract of wilderness in an area called Niskayuna (later the site of the **Watervliet village**), about seven miles northwest of Albany, New York. After Hocknell returned from England with his family in December 1775, the Believers began to convert the wilderness into a settlement. They took up residence in the woods in September 1776. To the Believers' great woe, however, in almost exactly eight years, Ann Lee, the Shakers' charismatic leader, would die there.

While working diligently for over three years to improve their material comforts in the wilderness, the Shakers waited uneasily for the augured increase in their membership and rued its delay. Of course, as a consequence of its practice of celibacy, the Society produces no "cradle" Shakers, so to speak; thus, it always has been totally dependent upon "**gathering**" or "**in-gathering**" (synonymous terms denoting the recruitment of new members) to increase the numbers of Believers. "There were three religious revivals that assisted in the promotion of the growth of Shakerism. The first of these was in 1779 . . . which broke out at New Lebanon . . . New York" (MacLean, *Shakers of Ohio* 10). During the course of this regional revival, the Shakers "began to be known and visited by great multitudes, many of whom embraced their testimony" (Green and Wells, *Brief Exposition* 22). Among them was **Joseph Meacham**, a former Baptist minister, soon to become "Father" Joseph and the Society's first native American leader.

During the next seven years following this initial in-gathering, four other events especially significant to the shaping of Shakerism occurred. First, from May 1781 to September 1783, Ann Lee and a contingent of other Believers were away from Niskayuna to preach their gospel in Massachusetts and Connecticut. They were persecuted constantly; nevertheless, they added members to their faith. Thus, they contributed greatly to the spreading of Shakerism in several parts of New England. Next, William Lee, Mother Ann's younger brother and an influential leader, died in July 1784. Despite the gravity of his loss to the development of Shakerism, a "still heavier trial" for the Believers was "the loss of the visible presence and protection of their dearly beloved Mother, [who] resigned her soul to God" just two months later (Green and Wells, *Summary View* 29). (Speculation exists that the deaths of both William and Ann resulted largely from the beatings they had received during their recent journey.) Finally, James Whittaker, the last of the leaders who came to America with the sect, died in July 1787, after less than a mere three years of directing the Society. However, during his short tenure, he promoted practices and principles, such as strict **obedience** to church leaders, that were to become instrumental in the evolution of institutional Shakerism. Upon his death, the Society became virtually all American. About Joseph Meacham, Whittaker's successor, Mother Ann had said, "It will not be my lot nor the lot of any that came with me from England, to gather and build up the church; but it will be the lot of Joseph Meacham and others." Further, "Joseph Meacham is my firstborn son in America; he will gather the church into order; but I will not live to see it" (quoted in Green and Wells, *Summary View* 42).

Proceeding from the unifying efforts of Whittaker, who preached to scattered Believers throughout New England during much of his leadership, Father Joseph Meacham devised and organized the Shaker communal (or communitarian or communistic) societies, along with **Lucy Wright**, whom Meacham chose as co-leader and who would succeed him as the principal **lead** after his death. According to one chronology, the primary impetus for this arrangement was the necessity to establish **union** among the widespread Believers: "for a further increase of gospel order . . . they should be brought into a nearer connection together, and thereby be enabled to serve God in a more united capacity, as members of the body of Christ in a church relation" (Green and Wells, *Summary View* 58). Beginning with the establishment of a permanent community at **New Lebanon** (later Mount Lebanon), New York, in 1787, which immediately evolved into the center of Shaker union, the Shakers had created 10 other villages by 1794: one more in New York, Watervliet (a.k.a. Niskayuna, 1787); four in Massachusetts, **Hancock** (1790), **Harvard** (1791), **Tyringham** (1792), and **Shirley** (1793); one in Connecticut, **Enfield** (1790); two in New Hampshire, **Canterbury** (1792) and **Enfield** (1793); and two in Maine, **Alfred** (1793) and Sabbathday Lake (1794). The total population by this time was around 2,500 members.

In about 1785, the Society ceased public profession of its faith until around 1798 in order to devote all its energy to its protection and internal development. After reopening its gospel to the public, Shakerism was received sufficiently well to allow the Society to organize 11 more communities by 1836: one more in Maine, **Gorham** (1808); one more in Massachusetts, **Savoy** (1817); two more in New York, **Sodus Bay** (1826) and **Groveland** (1836); two in Kentucky, **Pleasant Hill** (1806) and **South**

Union (1807); four in Ohio, **Union Village** (1806), **Watervliet** (1806), **North Union** (1822), and **Whitewater** (1824); and one in Indiana, **West Union** (1810).

The so-called **Kentucky Revival**—"the wild carnival of religion" (MacLean, *Shakers of Ohio* 61)—beginning approximately at the commencement of the nineteenth century, was another religious event that was immensely serendipitous to the increase of the Society's membership. The revival seemed to be the realization of another of Mother Ann's prophecies: "The next opening of the gospel will be in the southwest; it will be at a great distance, and there will be a great work of God" (quoted in Green and Wells, *Summary View* 42). Having knowledge of the revival, the Society was prompt to seize the opportunity to increase membership. From New Lebanon, on the first of January 1805, three missionaries were dispatched to open the Shaker testimony of salvation to the revivalists. **John Meacham, Benjamin S. Youngs**, and **Issachar Bates Sr.** walked about 1,200 miles before beginning their preaching in Kentucky, Ohio, and Indiana around March 22, conversing with and relaying their gospel to all who would listen.

Greatly as a result of their and other Believers' endeavors on behalf of the Shaker gospel, by 1824, enough people "of all classes and various denominations, the high and the low, the rich and the poor [had] flocked together" to create the seven western Shaker settlements (Green and Wells, *Summary View* 83). According to Shakers in 1848, with the addition of the western communities, "the number of believers contained in all the Societies . . . exceeds 4000," not counting "numbers who have recently received faith, but are not yet gathered into the established Society" (Green and Wells, *Summary View* 84). The Shaker population was nearing its pinnacle.

Concurrent with the development of the western communities was the **administration** (*see* GOVERNMENT/ADMINISTRATION) of Mother Lucy Wright, who succeeded Meacham after his death in 1796 and who led the Society for 25 years, until her death in 1821. When she led with Meacham, "the principles in regard to property and order in general were fully carried out and *established*" (Evans et al., *Compendium* 183.) When she was the principal **lead** herself, one of the more significant tasks she assumed was to ensure the uniform development and practice of Shakerism in the eastern and western societies—a task that entailed, among other things, setting standards of conduct to be followed by all Believers wherever they might be, instituting uniform clothing, and providing academic education: Shakers were to act alike, look alike, and talk alike, as if all

Shakers were one Shaker whom all "the world" might see anywhere, anytime.

Partly as a result of Mother Lucy's efforts to deal with the behaviors of the relatively quick influx of new members from various backgrounds and widely different sections of America, and, ironically, mainly as a result of her death (so alleges Brewer, *Shaker Communities* 40), the first seminal regulatory Shaker text, *Orders and Rules of the Church at New Lebanon, August 7th, 1821,* was issued in 1821. When revised and reissued in 1845, the title became *Millennial Laws or Gospel Statutes and Ordinances adapted to the Day of Christ's Second Appearing* (hereafter, the abbreviated title *Millennial Laws* refers to both the 1821 and 1845 texts). This first book of regulations was gathered largely from the traditional verbal instructions of the **elders**, which had varied somewhat from village to village. Now, all Believers everywhere had a common guide for standards, regulations, orders, and doctrines. At the time of the death of Mother Lucy, then, Shakerism seemed to be healthy, to have an unlimited future, and to be as defined as it ever could be. The Society enjoyed order, security, and prosperity.

However, germination of the bases of its decline was under way. Shaker leaders were cognizant of and much alarmed by detrimental conditions, such as an increase in **backsliding** by young members:

> They exerted a constant pressure on Elders and leaders, for more liberty and indulgence in their worldly tastes and selfish desires; they did not believe in so much self-denial and restraint as was enjoined by the laws of the community and the example of the older members. (White and Taylor, *Shakerism* 228)

Apparently, partly as a consequence of such situations, August 16, 1837, "began a remarkable period in Shaker history, a decade or more of strange manifestations" (Andrews, *People Called Shakers* 152). Believers refer to the period by names such as the "Era of Manifestations," "Mother's Work," or "**Mother Ann's Second Coming**." Among other uncommon events during this time span, occurring because long-departed Believers residing in the spirit world were much concerned about the welfare and progress of the Society, these spirits allegedly visited Shaker villages in an effort to renew the members' spirituality and to increase their understanding of what being in union with the Christ Spirit really means.

For more than 10 years, Shakers engaged in "strange" behaviors, such as shaking uncontrollably, whirling, singing never-before-heard songs, speaking strange languages, writing messages and books that they supposedly were normally incapable of composing, having visions of heavenly places, talking to dead elders and various dignitaries, creating special holy places for worship, and receiving invisible **gifts** from invisible entities. To some observers, including some suspicious Shakers themselves, behaviors became so absolutely absurd that they were thought to be detrimental to the progress of the Society. Thus, ironically, the "fresh tide of spirit power [that] flooded the life of the societies" (White and Taylor, *Shakerism* 228) and supposedly strengthened them might have ministered also to Shakerism's decline.

An example of an intelligent neophyte and potential lifelong Shaker lost to the Society during this "remarkable period" was **David Rich Lamson**, a self-appointed social reformer, who, along with his family, joined the Hancock, Massachusetts, society in 1843 "in search of the people of God" (Lamson, *Two Years' Experience* 18). He was soon so appalled at what he witnessed that he bolted after two years and became a severe judge of the Shakers—"that singular and mysterious people" (Lamson, *Two Years' Experience* 15). Fortunately, Lamson cared enough about the world to publish the truth as he saw it. For example, regarding the so-called gifts and divine revelations allegedly manifested at Hancock during his stay there, Lamson recorded this passage:

> A majority of the members . . . believe that all which professes to be revelation, and is sanctioned by the elders, is really such. And every time they see any of these manifestations of whirling, jerking, shaking, twisting, winking, &c., it begets in them a degree of awe and religious fear. . . . [T]his takes place at almost every meeting. And they meet to worship about five times a week. By this means, they are brought into the most perfect submission to their Lead, the elders and ministry. It is the worst kind of slavery. The mind is enslaved by means of this superstition. (92)

Despite any losses in membership due to strange behaviors, the Society of Shakers undoubtedly experienced its "greatest glory during the first half of the nineteenth century" (Horgan, *Shaker Holyland* 4).

Undoubtedly, also, since that time, Shakerism has had to endure a continuous and radical decline in membership that began just prior to the Civil War. Even before the war, four settlements had desisted. By 1889, three more were closed. During the first two decades of the twentieth century, nine additional communities were abandoned. In 1974, on the bicentennial of Shakerism in America, of the total of 24 settlements formally established by the Shakers, only the ones at Canterbury, New Hampshire, and Sabbathday Lake, Maine, were operational, but both communities were being assisted economically by historical societies and benevolent organizations and individuals. However, Canterbury itself was no longer occupied by a Shaker after Sister **Ethel Hudson**, aged 96, died on September 7, 1992. Excepting the short-lived and meager-membered communities organized in Georgia and Florida during the late 1890s, no significantly successful community was established after Groveland, New York, in 1836.

Why Shakerism has been in a seemingly moribund state for about 150 years has received much investigation and speculation. Non-Shakers as well as Shakers themselves have proffered causes. Generally, these fall into two classifications: intrinsic and extrinsic. Marguerite Fellows Melcher, for example, who attempted the first comprehensive history of the Shakers by a non-Shaker with her *The Shaker Adventure* (1941) posits that "external disasters" imposed on the Society by the outside world did not "constitute a fundamental reason for the decline of Shakerism." Rather, "the seeds of decay and death had been sown in the spirit. The first cause, of course, was abatement of original zeal." Among other internal causes was "ineffectual leadership" (246, 247, 252).

Conversely, **Shakeresses Anna White** and **Leila S. Taylor**, who created the last attempt by Shakers themselves to write a comprehensive statement of the Shaker pilgrimage with their *Shakerism: Its Meaning and Message* (1904), virtually ignore internal problems as a cause of membership decline. To them, Shakerism began suffering mainly because of the overwhelming effects of the numerous and rapid transformations in American culture following the Civil War:

> A race freed from bondage was to be civilized and educated or remanded to a worse than chattel slavery . . . a continent hitherto almost unknown was to be explored, settled and controlled; political parties, aristocracies of money, brains and enterprise were to be born, or strangled in the birth; benevolences, charities, improvement of conditions in houses and schools, streets and sewers, races and incipient nations, opening of railroads, mines and cities, absorbing and assimilating huge masses of crude and undeveloped humanity from all the nations of the world—these were the tasks which he—the man of America—found awaiting him. The question of his soul's salvation or the gaining of Heaven became absurdly irrelevant. This outward activity to the neglect of the inner nature had its effect in the decadence of spirituality. The conception of sacrificing personal freedom or ambition, for the service of Christ or the Kingdom of Heaven, became . . . remote. Churches of the old order suffered; Shakers of the new order diminished in numbers. (205–206)

Still other historians of the Shaker pilgrimage offer a plethora of specifics regarding the decline. For example, some focus on economic matters that Shakers had no power to combat:

The advance of modern machinery which was supplanting hand labor, the growing use of concentrated foodstuffs, and the change in medicine from bulky doses of herb concoctions to tabloids, the innumerable factories being built to turn out thousands of spools, brooms handles, and the articles which formed the nucleus of the Shaker industries, which relied wholly on hand labor . . . these oncoming conditions were . . . seen . . . by the discerning. (Sears, *Gleanings* 278)

Whatever the causes of the Society's loss of membership and despite all efforts, especially by so-called progressives during the last several decades of the nineteenth century, to restore its former healthy condition, with the closing of the Hancock, Massachusetts, community in 1960—about 100 years after the peak of the Society's membership—only 2 villages remained operative. Now, as a new millennium approaches, only Sabbathday Lake is viable.

Apart from the Shakers' failure to attract more than just a few new Believers, several internal "political" problems have been their lot in the latter half of the twentieth century. For instance, the death in 1961 of Brother **Delmar Wilson** left the Society with no males. Since the tradition of institutional Shakerism had been that only males could hear the confession of males, logic dictated that no male could ever again join the Society. Allied with this problem was the closing of the **Church Covenant** in 1965. The **Lead Ministry**, then located at Canterbury, New Hampshire, decided, in effect, that the United Society of Believers in Christ's Second Appearing would live out its life through the remaining covenanted Shakers. However, Shakers at Sabbathday Lake, Maine, not only have continued to induct males but also to induct females, none of whom can sign, at least theoretically, the traditional Church Covenant and become a **Church Family** Shaker—a bona fide **True Believer**. The rift between Canterbury Shakers and Sabbathday Lake Shakers ended "officially" in 1990 with the death of Eldress **Bertha Lindsay**, the last member of the Canterbury Shaker ministry and the last of the long line of ministry succession by Americans inaugurated by Joseph Meacham.

Without opposition, the remaining Shakers fashion Shakerism as they please. They are co-led by Brother **Arnold Hadd** and Sister **Frances A. Carr**, who in 1948 became the last Shaker of the Maine community to sign the Church Covenant. In a sense, she and Sisters **Minnie Green** and **Marie Burgess**, who also joined the Society before the closing of the covenant in 1965, are the last "real" or "old" Shakers—terms that somewhat agitate the community because the members themselves make no such distinction: Shakers are Shakers.

Due largely, no doubt, to the efforts of scholars and to a lesser degree to works of imaginative literature featuring Shakers, during the last 50 years especially, non-Shakers' interest in Shakers and Shakerism has become extraordinary. For one thing, as witnessed by an ever-enlarging bibliography (increasing virtually every day), they have been examined by such a myriad of people from such a myriad of angles that one must wonder whether in this, the third century of Shakers in America, anything about the Society remains to be said. For example, explored extensively have been the Society's **industries** and **economy**, its communistic organization, its practice of **gender parity**, its benevolence and its generosity, its brand of Christianity, its **songs/poems**, its architecture, its aesthetics, its future, its contributions to the cultural heritage of the United States, and its love and peace and kindness alleged to have made the world a far, far better place than it otherwise might have been had Shakers not existed.

For another thing, the general attitude of the mainstream culture toward Shakers and Shakerism has ameliorated to the point of seeming to be virtually totally benevolent and concerned. By the tens of thousands yearly, Americans (and a good many foreigners, too) visit Shaker museums, belong to Shaker historical societies and study groups, visit the few museum villages, read articles and books (such as this one) about Shakers, and see films and television programs about Shakers; and the more ardent of them even hope somehow, someday actually to meet a real Shaker, so they pilgrimage to the **Chosen Land** (i.e., Sabbathday Lake, Maine), hoping to be in the presence of Sisters Frances, Minnie, Marie, and **June Carpenter**, as well as Brothers **Wayne Smith** and Arnold Hadd.

The current homage (not to be construed merely as charity but also as genuine friendship) now paid to the Shakers and, in turn, the Shakers' appreciation of it (along with mutual affection for their friends) are clearly reflected in the following passage from the "Home Notes" section of the *Clarion* (Winter 1998), written by Sister Frances:

> Among our good friends who visited during September were the Ponds, who were able to join us for the noon meal—an all too brief visit. Also, the McCaskeys stopped in on their way back to Deer Isle. Having these friends visit proved to be a real boost to the kitchen of Chosen Land as the Ponds gifted us with a turkey, ham and chicken and the McCaskeys brought a special treat of lobsters and crab. . . . We are humbled and overwhelmed at the outpouring that came to us from friends from all over. Each card and Christmas letter is read and enjoyed by all. Every gift of fruit (so welcome during the cold of a Maine winter) is relished, and each and every gift, be it candy, nuts or other edibles, books, or financial help for work here at Chosen Land

evokes feelings of gratitude, not only for the gifting itself but for the love and friendship which prompted the giver. So often at times of giving one looks for special words and ways to express feelings of gratitude when perhaps, in Shaker tradition, a simple "thank you" will do.

One modern historian declares that "Americans have taken this small society into their hearts and their homes. They have adopted the Shakers as 'family.' . . . Once feared, hated and persecuted, now the Shakers are the darlings of American popular culture" (Stein, *Shaker Experience* 422–423). In other words, "the world" is now fast friends with the Shakers: it goes to **Meeting** with them, gives money to them, restores their only viable village, picnics with them, has photographs taken with them, hugs and kisses them, invites them to lecture and to discuss, and honors them. It seems to adore them. Now, at long, long last, when the Society is smaller than it was when it made the first step of its pilgrimage in America, the Shakers seem to have become very, very dear—at least to the people pursuing knowledge of and developing an appreciation for their cultural heritage.

NOTES

1. Note that Shakerism and its membership are often referred to by various names, including: Believers, the Church of Christ's Second Appearing, the Community of Shakers, the Millennial Church, Shaking Quakers, the Society of Shakers, True Believers, the United Society of Believers in Christ's Second Appearing, the United Society of Believers, the United Society of Believers in the Second Appearing of Christ, the United Society of Shakers, in addition to simply Shakers. As such, whenever these terms appear throughout the dictionary—in full or shortened form, such as "the Society"—they should be understood as being synonymous with Shakerism's adherents and members throughout the movement's history. When a particular context or time period in the history is designated by one appellation or another, the text clarifies this point.

In terms of typography used throughout, one should also be aware that boldface type indicates references to individual entries in the dictionary; italic type is reserved for alternative spellings of a main entry and other names by which the main entry is known.

Finally, although "Shaker/Shakeress" is indeed a main entry herein, all instances of the word "Shaker" and its variations are not necessarily set in boldface, unless they refer to the main entry itself—that is, unless they are used as nouns to denote individual male/female members of this religious sect.

2. Note that in Shaker parlance, "southwest" is used to denote a different region than is usually meant by the U.S. Southwest, namely the states of Arizona, New Mexico, and so forth. Rather, to the Shakers, the "southwest" is used to denote the region southwesterly of New England, where the majority of their villages lay—specifically, Ohio, Kentucky, and Indiana. As such, whenever the word appears lowercased throughout the dictionary, the reader should be aware that the Shaker geographical definition is meant. A similar distinction is made between the "West" of the United States as a whole and the "west" in the Shaker context (i.e., all areas situated near the westernmost point of the sect's extension).

The Dictionary

-A-

ADMINISTRATION. *See* GOVERNMENT/ADMINISTRATION.

ADVENT. An alternative term for **novitiate**, as in, "[At **Union Village**, Ohio,] we found a number of Advents, both brethren and sisters" (Morrell, "Account" 43).

AFRICAN-AMERICAN MEMBERSHIP. Although the membership of the Shaker sect always predominantly has been Anglo-American and European, the leaders of the Society of **Shakers** apparently never have engaged in discrimination against applicants simply because of different cultural and racial origins. However, only one African American, **Rebecca Cox Jackson**, has ever attained a powerful position in the Shaker **government**. She was appointed **eldress** (*see* ELDER/ELDRESS) of the **Philadelphia Family** about the middle of the nineteenth century.

Among observers of the Shakers, Charles Nordhoff notes the presence of small numbers of African Americans in Shaker **villages** in the 1870s. Prior to the Civil War, the Society held an adamant antislavery position, often succoring runaway slaves passing to somewhere else. Probably, especially in the more northern villages, some of the slaves stayed to become members. Certainly, after the war, some chose **Shakerism** as their faith. In any case, the total number of African-American Shakers in the movement's history seems to be far less than 100.

ALFRED, MAINE (1793–1931). *Spiritual name: Holy Land.* One of the earliest and longest-lived communities, Alfred was located in York County, about 30 miles southwest of Portland. Three **families** were gathered initially. In 1823, the community had about 200 members, but by 1875, only 2 families and 70 members remained.

> The decrease began to be rapid about thirty years ago [1845], when the founders, who had become very aged, died off, and new members did

1

not come in sufficient numbers to take their places. Two thirds of the present members were brought into the society as children, many being brought by their parents. (Nordhoff, *Communistic Communities* 180)

Among the fascinating tales involving the earliest **Shakers** of the inland Alfred area (before the community was officially organized) is that of a sea and river voyage taken by them in August 1784 to Niskayuna, New York, to see, unbeknownst to them, an ill and soon-to-die **Ann Lee**, who had had a vision of their visitation.

> On their return, they encountered a terrific storm and fully expected their little craft [*The Shark*] would go to the bottom. [Sister] Dana Thombs saw in a vision Mother Ann, calm and smiling, with uplifted hands, breathe peace upon the troubled waters. . . . Soon after their return the news of Mother Ann's decease reached them. Carefully comparing times, this sister found that her vision of Mother Ann occurred about six hours after her departure from earth. (White and Taylor, *Shakerism* 94–95)

With its seed, cloth, and lumber production, among other business ventures, Alfred was also an industrious **village**. Unfortunately, it "had a history of several fires which undoubtedly contributed to some of the major changes in industries." Although the sawmill had burned in 1841, during the 1870s and 1880s, the **brethren** were involved in large scale lumbering operations for businesses of **the world**, delivering to one lumberman, for example, "four hundred and forty thousand [board feet? of] white pine lumber for which . . . [they were] paid . . . $3.50 per thousand" (Barker, "History of 'Holy Land'" 46, 48).

With an ever-increasing strain on financial resources resulting from decline in membership—which left the commune with an insufficient labor force not only to maintain the daily requirements of the community but also to earn capital for it—the remaining Alfred family joined with the **Sabbathday Lake** family in May 1931.

ALLEN, CATHERINE (18?–1922). One of several "progressive" members of the North Family of **New Lebanon**, New York, who in the latter part of the nineteenth century and first decades of the twentieth sought to reform not only the Society but also **the world**, thus moving away from the traditional Shaker position of **separation from the world**—of letting it run its course. Shaker reformers fancied themselves as instruments of change for the betterment of society in general, of American society in particular. Among her untraditional activities within the Society, Sister Catherine, a member of the omnipotent **Lead Ministry** from 1908 until her death, organized the Self-Improvement Society, devoted to developing the intellectual and aesthetic character of **sisters** (*see* BROTHER/SISTER). Her extra-Shaker projects included advocating reforms in areas such as women's rights and suffrage, involvement in political affairs, temperance, and animal rights.

Her belief in the value of the Shaker way to the world is expressed in the introduction to one of her essays published in 1902. Note her use of "our," for example:

> In this time of our nation's crisis, in fact the crisis of the world, when savage competition bids fair to destroy, not only itself, but what remains of our Republic, industrial and social problems are attracting universal attention; and we find an awakened interest in many leading minds to know more of the quickening impulse, sustaining power and practical results of the organization which has for more than a century been held together on the basis of religious communism. (*Century of Communism* 2)

ALLICE, MOLLY (17?–?). *Alt. sp.: Allis.* "The first woman [to join the Society] after the testimony was publickly opened" on May 19, 1780 (Green, "Biographical Account" 26).

APOSTATE. *A.k.a.: defector, dissenter, ex-Shaker, seceder, turnoff.* **Shakerism** has abounded with defectors, mostly during the nineteenth century (and it suffered an apostasy as recently as 1994). Because **Shakers** "freely dedicate and devote themselves and their services, together with all their temporal interest, to the service of God, to be forever consecrated to pious and charitable uses," Shaker chroniclers often refer to apostates in rather reproachful language: "whoever deliberately violates his faith, and withdraws or separates himself from the Church . . . can be viewed by the faithful in no other light than as a reprobate" (Green and Wells, *Summary View* 63).

Some dissenters have been so disenchanted and embittered by their experiences with the Shaker organization that they have promulgated vitriolic criticism of it. Among the more dramatic presentations of allegations against the Society are those rendered by **Valentine Wightman Rathbun Sr.** (*Some Brief Hints, of a Religious Scheme,* 1781), **Amos Taylor** (*A Narrative of the Strange Principles, Conduct and Character of the People Known by the Name of Shakers,* 1782), **Thomas Brown** (*An Account of the People Called Shakers,* 1812), and **Mary Marshall Dyer** (*A Portraiture of Shakerism,* 1822). Among other charges levied against the Shakers by such apostates is that they practice witchcraft and hypocrisy and that they will eventually destroy Christianity and the United States with their despotism.

In contrast, some other apostates have been rather complimentary in their accounts of their experiences with the Shakers. Among these is **Hervey Elkins**, who lived with the Shakers from the age of 14 to 29 years. In the epilogue of his *Fifteen Years in the Senior Order of Shakers* (1853), he renders a laudatory assessment of the people he chose to leave because of his own "malady of . . . mind." He says, for example, that Shakers are

> favored with . . . a call to suppress the passions, to subdue the will, to correct the affections and refine the heart; a call to gather and cherish those noble attributes and sublime qualities, which Paul has so faithfully delineated as the fruits of the spirit; to discard superstition and repudiate idolatry; to turn away their minds from the low pretexts and small arguments elicited and urged in opposition to the cross of Christ, to that nobler and more consistent logic which advocates the more appreciable glory of that higher destiny and better sphere of action, which afford health of body, strength of intellect, and vivacity of soul; to turn their eyes from that philosophy and wisdom, which knows no influence but the judgement and will of man, to that wiser and better philosophy, which teaches us to renounce all to obtain a life in Christ, and a resurrection of the soul from the dead . . . and who, *I* ask, would be ashamed of such a call as this? (130–31)

The opportunity to be members of the Society and, thus, to consecrate their lives to God is regarded by the Shakers to be a **privilege**. Once this privilege is violated, seceders or turnoffs must appeal for reinstatement or "another privilege," as evidenced by a journal entry of Tuesday, November 13, 1855, by Sally Harris: "Today Francis Shain returned back begging for another privilege[;] he was sent away. . . . He therefore went and returned Monday the 19th when a privilege was granted him and he was set to work" (Harris, *Journal* 79).

Although the curious always have come and gone, not until late in the **administration** (*see* GOVERNMENT/ADMINISTRATION) of Father **Joseph Meacham** did the first significant defections occur after the **Believers** had been gathered into communities:

> Some among the members had not surrendered their self-will, but insisted on their own way. . . . The Elder of the Children's Order led in the apostasy, which lasted for a few months. The Youth's and Children's Orders were then combined and in the spring of 1796 were dissolved altogether. . . . Father Joseph encouraged the faithful by the repeated assertion that if but five souls were left they would have the promise of the kingdom as revealed by Mother. (White and Taylor, *Shakerism* 102–103)

AVERY, GILES (1815–1890). Among the **Shakers** from the time he was four years old, when his parents joined the Society, "Giles was one of the most gifted **Brothers** in the Shaker order, and was prominent in both temporal and spiritual interests" (in Avery, *Autobiography* 20). **Elder** Giles served 30 years as a member of the **Lead Ministry** in **New Lebanon**, New York, and was one of the more sophisticated members of the Society, as manifested, for example, by the intellectual quality of his writings on a variety of subjects. The many remembrances of and tributes to him on the occasion of his being "translated" to spirit life are evidence of the respect other Shakers had for him.

Contrary to his fellow Shakers at New Lebanon, such as **Frederick W. Evans** and, later, **Catherine Allen** and **Anna White**, who advocated reform in the Society and in its relationship with non-Shaker culture, Avery was traditional and conservative, maintaining, among other things, that the individual alone was responsible for himself/herself: "Every soul must work out its own salvation by practicing the self-denials of Jesus, aided by baptisms of the holy spirit of Christ; an influx of the saving power of the divine Creator! Salvation is not otherwise found" (Avery, *Sketches* 16).

-B-

BACKSLIDING. A **Shaker** "backslides" when he/she no longer progresses in spiritual development—no longer **travels** in the gospel. Instead, he/she returns to or adopts worldly ways. One mode of backsliding with which the Shaker organization has had to contend constantly is the exercise of the seemingly ever-present inclination of the genders naturally to be attracted to each other physically and romantically. Among other ploys, virtual total spatial separation of males from females—such as via separate entrances to buildings—was designed by leaders of the sect to inhibit "unprofitable" relationships between **sisters** and **brothers**. However, entries on absconders in Shaker journals (such as those of the West Family of **Pleasant Hill**, Kentucky, during the 1840s and 1850s) testify that males and females found ways to circumvent separation strategies. Backsliders were regarded with such disdain that even the ones allowed to remain in or return to the community of Shakers were regarded as inferior to **True Believers**.

BACKSLIDING ORDER/BACK ORDER. A seceder (or at least a man who thought a bit about becoming a **Shaker**) reported in 1821 that a special **order** (or **family**) existed for

> those who have had faith and the privilege of hearing the gospel, but have turned from it; and afterwards have returned and acknowledged their error and confessed their sins. All such are placed in an order by themselves, having lost, as they say, their travels with those who remained faithful. (Brown, *Account* 58)

The fact of the existence of such an order also was testified to by another Shaker **apostate** in 1828. He alleges that **Joseph Meacham**, well aware of the inability of some people to maintain their faith, created a Backsliders' or Back Order, whose name reflects "the conduct of the members, and their degree of inferiority. . . . All members, who secede, are sent on their return, into this order" (Haskett, *Shakerism Unmasked* 152–153).

BAIRD, DANIEL (18?–?). A member of the **North Union**, Ohio, community, Daniel was a notable and prolific inventor. His most famous innovation was a "soft" metal—an antifriction alloy of pewter and tin—that came to be called "Babbitt Metal" (mainly as a result of patent infringement litigation involving the inventor Isaac Babbitt and another party).

BAPTISM. Regarding this much-disputed matter—a "watery war"—in the Christian religion, **Shakers** reject the use of literal water in the baptismal rite, contending that it has nothing to do with the baptism of Christ in Jesus (or of anyone else):

> The baptism of CHRIST is not the baptism of water, but of the HOLY GHOST. . . . Thus it appears evident that the baptism of CHRIST is a spiritual work . . . the true baptism of the water of life washes and cleanses the soul from all pollutions of sin. It is a purifying operation of the elements of the HOLY SPIRIT. (Green and Wells, *Summary View* 283–284)

To one auditor, this position is in the mainstream of Shaker thought: "Indeed, it not be consistent with their [Shakers'] general mode of interpreting the Scriptures, to admit of any ordinance but what is of a spiritual nature, or to admit of a literal interpretation of any of the ordinances" (Bates, *Peculiarities* 87).

BARKER, (RUTH) MILDRED (1898?–1990). Sister Mildred entered the Society at the **Alfred**, Maine, community, and moved to the **Sabbathday**

Lake, Maine, community when she was seven years old. Among other duties, she served as caretaker of the young **sisters** (*see* BROTHER/SIS-TER), for whom she developed the Girls Improvement Club (GIC). Similar to the Self-Improvement Society inaugurated earlier by Sister **Catherine Allen**, the GIC aimed at extending the intellectual and aesthetic opportunities of the girls by "a special emphasis on literary work, study, and concentration" (Carr, *Growing Up Shaker* 105). **Frances A. Carr**, current **lead** of the Shakers, was one of Sister Mildred's pupils and has said of her, "Sister Mildred, without a doubt, lived the Shaker life more completely than anyone I had ever known" (Carr, *Growing Up Shaker* 130). In addition, she contributed much to the knowledge of the Shakers' musical culture, and she supported the development of what is now the Shaker Library at Sabbathday Lake—a major holder of primary materials.

Besides serving the community as **trustee** beginning in 1950, she was instrumental in what might be called a "revival" at (and of) Sabbathday Lake. Her opposition to the closing of the membership covenant in 1965 by the **Canterbury** ministry (then the **Lead Ministry**), was evidenced by, among other ways, her support for the membership of **Theodore E. Johnson**, not only the first "new" Shaker **brother** after the closing but also the only brother for quite some time following the death of **Delmar Wilson** in 1961.

During the three decades prior to her death, Sister Mildred was the undisputed spiritual leader and spokesperson of extant **Shakerism**. She spoke and wrote extensively about Shaker history and tenets, which, along with her engaging personality, made her a celebrity of sorts among people of **the world.** No doubt, the public's surge of interest in things Shaker during the last half of the twentieth century was partly generated by this very likeable and fascinating figure.

BATES, ISSACHAR, SR. (1758–1837). Born in Hingham, Massachusetts, to parents who were Presbyterian, Issachar, "altho . . . a mischievous boy, . . . thought much about God" (Bates, "Sketch" 101). At age 17 he became a fifer in the American Revolution, and at age 43 he became a **Shaker**, apparently after having thought enough about God to believe that the Society was doing His/Her work. About five weeks after a visit to **New Lebanon**, which "was not much over an hour: for we did business quick, I eat quick, & talked quick, & heard quick, and started home quick; for I was quickened," Issachar returned to New Lebanon and confessed his sins in August 1801. However, when he returned home, "Not one in my own family; nor in the neighborhood; nor within 70 miles, but were opposed to me. And the children in the streets that used to reverence me when I was a [Baptist] preacher; now mocking me" (Bates, "Sketch" 150–151). Despite early familial opposition, his wife confessed her sins about 14 months later, and Issachar and most of his family moved to the community in **Watervliet**, New York in 1803.

Brother Issachar's major contribution to the dissemination of the Shaker gospel began "on the 1st day of january [*sic*] 1805, at 3 o'clock in the morning." After he had been judged by the ministry to be "man enough . . . to leave . . . [his] family once for all, & all . . . [his] friends in these parts: & hasard . . . [his] life in that wild part of the world [the Shaker southwest] for Christ's sake, & for the sake of them poor souls whom God is preparing for salvation," Issachar, **John Meacham**, and **Benjamin S. Youngs** began a 1,233-mile journey to the southwest that concluded on March 22, 1805—2 months and 22 days later—at the home of **Malcolm Worley** (then a **New Lighter**) at Turtle Creek, Ohio, the eventual site of **Union Village** (Bates, "Sketch" 152–153). The missionaries were instrumental in helping to establish the seven Shaker communities in the west—at one of which, **Watervliet**, Ohio, Brother Issachar served as **elder** until 1832, a position he did not want because, among other reasons, a number of the members there "were very active in running over their leaders—& this I dreaded" (Bates, "Sketch" 27).

According to his own calculation, he had traveled 38,000 miles by 1811, most of it on foot, "and in every place I have been mobbed and persecuted; & have been called by almost every base name that could be thought of; & my life threatened as often as any dogs" (Bates, "Sketch" 20). Despite a long history of such tribulations, when he was "recalled in his old age to Mount Lebanon, he withdrew with great reluctance from his hard-won fields in the west" (White and Taylor, *Shakerism* 135).

In the estimate of one chronicler of Shaker history, Issachar Bates Sr. was the Society's "most indefatigable missionary to the 'Southwestern territory' . . . in ten years . . . converting eleven hundred people to **Shakerism**" (Melcher, *Shaker Adventure* 267).

BATES, PAULINA (1806–1884). Sister Paulina joined the Society in 1825 at **Watervliet**, New York, where she twice served as **eldress** (*see* ELDER/ ELDRESS), of the South Family beginning in 1848 and of the Second Family beginning in 1871. During the time of **Mother Ann's Second Coming**, she received a **gift** to write and edit material from the spirit world. In 1849, a two-volume collection of such material was published at **Canterbury** as *The Divine Book of Holy and Eternal Wisdom*, which, among other things, bluntly reproached members for straying from the basic principles of **Shakerism**.

Among her other contributions to spreading the Shaker gospel was her role in fostering the **Philadelphia Family** by being among the ministry and elders who endowed **Rebecca Cox Jackson** in 1858 with the power and authority to establish the **family** officially. Also, she has been regarded as "instrumental in maintaining [the] Shaker mission to the Philadelphia sisters from 1872 [to] 1873" (Williams, *Called and Chosen* 157).

BELIEVER. A name synonymous with and commonly used instead of the general "**Shaker**," a Believer (sometimes deemed a **True Believer**) is a covenanted member of the Society, that is, a **Church Family** Shaker, a bona fide Shaker. This label originates from one of formal names of the movement, the **United Society of Believers in Christ's Second Appearing.**

BIBLE. The **Shakers** use both the Old and New Testaments of the 1611 King James Version of the Scriptures. The text is available to all members for study and is used in **Meeting**, usually being read from or alluded to by the **elders** conducting the worship services.

BISHOP, JOB (17?–?). One of the earliest American **Shakers**, "Father Job" (as he was sometimes called) had been in the presence of **Ann Lee** and, thus, was among those who rendered published **testimonies** (collected by Brother **Rufus Bishop** and edited by Brother **Seth Youngs Wells**, among others) on her behalf against charges of drunkenness and other immoral behavior. In 1792, he was appointed a **lead** of the **bishopric** composed of the **Enfield** and **Canterbury** communities in New Hampshire.

BISHOP, RUFUS (?–1852). Among other contributions to developing the Shaker gospel, Brother Rufus began in 1812 to collect **testimonies** of the life and character of Mother Ann and the first **elders** as a means to counteract charges from **the world**, primarily, that the earliest **Shakers** in America, far from being admirable, actually engaged in clandestine, lewd, and immoral behavior. These testimonies (and others similar to them) were published (and edited) at various times throughout the nineteenth century. Generally, they delineate the first Shakers as kind, upright, and sincere, among other attributes.

Whether it was his good fortune or his bad, Brother Rufus was a member of the **Lead Ministry** during the period of **Mother Ann's Second Coming** (1837–1847)— the most unusual and fantastical decade in Shaker history. In 1849, he was appointed senior elder of that body.

Estimates of his character and effectiveness vary, but none, perhaps, is more authentic than the following one by a Shaker who knew him personally:

His mind, . . . which saw clearly and at a glance the strength or the infirmity of men, which decided at once without hesitation or repeal, was admirably fitted to lead in whatever department of life destiny should assign him. But his gentleness, kindness and humility—his reliance upon a power above, for guidance in all the spiritual affairs of the church, better qualified him for a leader of a theological sect. (Elkins, *Fifteen Years* 19)

BISHOP, TALMADGE (17?–?). One among the unsatisfied **New Light** Baptists of a short-lived revival beginning in the summer of 1779, Brother Talmadge, in the course of seeking salvation elsewhere, accidentally found **Ann Lee** and her small sect at Niskayuna, New York, in the spring of the following year. He was so satisfied with their religion that he achieved the distinction of becoming "the first man who set out to obey the [Shaker] gospel in America" when it was opened to the public on May 19, 1780 (Green, "Biographical Account" 26).

BISHOPRIC. A small group of communities, such as **Harvard** and **Shirley**, Massachusetts, spatially close enough to share an administration (*see* GOVERNMENT/ADMINISTRATION) or ministry, usually two **elders** and two **eldresses**. Bishoprics were devised by **Joseph Meacham**.

BLANCHARD, GROVE (17?–?). Brother Grove spent close to six decades (approximately from 1814 to 1871) in administrative positions. He served in the ministry of **Harvard**, Massachusetts, and as head of the Harvard/**Shirley bishopric**. In 1840, he made a notable defense of the Shaker principle of not supporting war in any way when he presented to the Massachusetts legislature a tally of over $40,000 in pensions owed to but refused by **Shakers** who had served in the army during the American Revolution. The Shakers' refusal to accept the large amount of "blood money" impressed a sufficient number of legislators to defeat a proposition that would have forced Shakers to pay military taxes if they did not serve in the armed forces. *See also* PACIFISM.

BLINN, HENRY CLAY (1824–1905). Elder Henry entered the Society in 1838 at **Canterbury**, New Hampshire, where he eventually became head of the ministry and was, along with **Frederick W. Evans** and **Harvey L. Eads**, among others, one of the leaders of the Society in the middle and late nineteenth century. Perhaps his greatest service to the Shaker gospel was effected through his writing and editing, which he did for nearly 60 years.

He was a "true historian . . . [with] a chaste and graceful style" (White and Taylor, *Shakerism* 325), who advocated a return to the **Shakerism** of the past. In his 24-page *The Life and Gospel Experience of Mother Ann Lee* (1882), for example, he expressed his belief "that the original principles on which Shakerism had been founded remained sufficient," and in his retelling of the story of the first **Shakers** through the **testimonies** of some of them, he "featured a fundamental tension between the Shaker gospel and the values of the world" (Stein, *Shaker Experience in America* 333).

As editor of the Shaker journal the *Manifesto* (*see* LITERATURE) from 1882 to 1899, which was dedicated to stating simply the religious views (among other things) of the Shakers, Elder Henry had and took the opportunity to express his traditionalist position. Among other ways, he did this by including a plethora of tributes to Mother Ann—three, for example, in the September, October, and December 1899 issues. The one in September, written by Eldress **Emma B. King**, declares that "the crowning feature of the life of Mother Ann was her loyalty to principle" (138)—a statement that does indeed support Blinn's desire to maintain the values of the past.

BRETHREN. *A.k.a.: brothers.* Shaker males.

BROTHER/SISTER. Prefixes of address to each other adopted by the Shakers, apparently because they describe the nature of the ideal or spiritual relationship between males and females—son and daughter of the **Father/Mother Deity**. More generally, the terms also denote simply a male/female Shaker.

BROWN, THOMAS (1766–?). At age 32, Brown, "one of those men who are found in all ages and lands, a man with a spiritual hunger, seeking a faith to satisfy it," visited the Shakers at Niskayuna, New York, seven miles from his home in Albany (Symonds, *Thomas Brown* 51). However, after several years of apparently trying to accept **Shakerism** as the instrument by which he could save his soul, the intelligent and refractory

Brown concluded that he could not abide, among other things, the Shakers' principle of absolute **obedience** to the **elders** and their contention that the Second Coming (*see* MILLENNIUM) had been effected by **Ann Lee**.

Brown's significance to the study of the Shaker pilgrimage is his *Account of the People Called Shakers* (1812), wherein he somewhat disingenuously says, "I have refrained from expressing my belief of this people, their doctrines or practices, in this work, or making digressions on what I have written, but have left the reader to form his own conclusion" (361).

Although he claims that he was a member of the Shakers for about seven years, he apparently did not sign the **Church Covenant**, which, strictly speaking, makes him not a genuine Shaker **apostate**, although he generally is regarded as one.

> It is due to truth to say that he was never considered as a member at all. . . . He was generally considered by those in the Society who knew him, a suspicious character, and one in whom very little confidence could be placed. . . . [H]e appeared to delight in displaying his talents and boasting of his beats in religious disputation. He seemed not to care on which side of the argument he engaged. (Wells, *Thomas Brown* 4)

BURGESS, MARIE (19?–). Besides Sisters **Minnie Green** and **Frances Carr**, Sister Marie is the only other **Shakeress** (*see* SHAKER/ SHAKERESS) extant who joined the group before the **Church Covenant** was closed in 1965. Along with all the other present-day members, she resides in the community at **Sabbathday Lake** in New Gloucester, Maine.

BURNETT, MICAJAH (1791–1879). A member of the **Pleasant Hill**, Kentucky, community for 70 years, Brother Micaja, as well as serving as a widely traveled buyer and seller for the village,

> became the master carpenter, architect, and town planner of Pleasant Hill . . . and lent his services on occasion to other communities. . . . The East Family House, built in 1817, was the first of the large dwelling houses to be constructed on the present village road. It is a massive brick structure built in a T shape, three and one-half stories high in the front with two floors in the back. Double entrance doors and separate staircases . . . were used in all the dwelling houses to facilitate the separation of the sexes. The sisters resided on the right side of the house and the brethren on the left. Their "retiring room," located in the front and middle of the buildings, [was] large enough to accommodate three or four beds, a chest of drawers, and several chairs, and [was] used only

for sleeping. The twenty-three surviving buildings in the restored Shaker village . . . stand today [1970] as a monument to him. (Thomas, "Micajah Burnett" 600, 605)

BUSHNELL, RICHARD (?–1873). The first of six children who, along with their mother, joined the **Shakers** (over the very strong objection of the father), Richard served the North Family of **New Lebanon**, New York, as a **deacon,** a second **elder,** and a **trustee.** In the estimate of two Shaker chroniclers, he

> was a spiritual father of the purest and holiest type, beloved by his family and held in highest confidence and esteem in the whole region where his life was spent. He did much to build up the North Family, and much of the comfort and prosperity of their later years is due to the self-denying labors and economics of this noble father. . . . [H]e employed every means in his power to earn a livelihood, often denying himself the necessities of life for the sake of the family. (White and Taylor, *Shakerism* 144)

-C-

CANTERBURY, NEW HAMPSHIRE (1792–1992). *Spiritual name: Holy Ground.* Situated in Rockingham County, "this society is located on gently rising ground, overlooking most of the surrounding country, high up on the Canterbury hills, twelve miles northeast of the beautiful City of Elms—Concord, the capital of the State" (White and Taylor, *Shakerism* 90). The community had about 45 members in 1792, about 80 in 1796, about 200 in 1823, and about 300 in 1850, but it was in decline by 1875, when it had 145 members in 3 **families.**

For most of the nineteenth century, Canterbury was an enterprising and prosperous community. Among other things, it manufactured wool and flannel cloth, the famous "Shaker cloak" (or "Dorothy cloak") for women, gloves (some of silk and fur), a washing machine (one of the few inventions that the **Shakers** ever patented and one that won a gold medal at the Centennial Exposition in Philadelphia in 1876), brooms, lumber, herbal medicines, maple sugar products, and butter and cheese. However, by the turn of the century, the Canterbury **economy** was suffering from a situation common to Shaker communities:

> Most of the industries in which the societies in past years found lucrative employment have been taken from them by the industrial develop-

ments and monopolies of recent times; and while their large possessions of real estate have greatly diminished in productiveness, with the farm lands of smaller holdings, taxation has steadily increased. (White and Taylor, *Shakerism* 318)

An abridged twentieth-century chronology of the events of this community (provided by Shaker Village, Inc.) is as follows:

1916	Membership consists of 2 **brothers**, 47 **sisters**, one 61-year-old male who remained for 7 years, and 12 females younger than 21.
1933	Canterbury Shakers begin selling Shaker artifacts to collectors and museums.
1938–1939	The last two Canterbury brothers, Arthur Bruce and Irving Geenwood, die.
1950	Membership in the Canterbury Shaker community consists of 16 sisters between the ages of 46 and 83.
1957	The **Lead Ministry** moves to the Canterbury site. The ministry votes to close the covenant membership of all Shaker societies.
1969	Shaker Village, Inc., a nonprofit corporation, is established to preserve and interpret the Canterbury Shaker village.
1988	On June 11, Lead Minister **Gertrude Soule** (b. August 19, 1894), dies.
	Members of the **Church Family** are Eldress Bertha Lindsay (b. July 27, 1897) and Sister Ethel Hudson (b. June 4, 1896).
1990	On October 3, Eldress Bertha dies.
1992	On September 7, Sister Ethel, the last Canterbury Shaker, dies. **Sabbathday Lake**, Maine, becomes the only Shaker village still peopled with members.

CANTERBURY APOSTATES. Apart from individual dissenters who promulgated material about **Shakerism**, several groups of them during the 1840s entertained **the world** with stage performances of Shaker **songs** and **dances**, among other things. Perhaps none of them was more impertinent than the alliance one Shaker journalist calls the "Canterbury apostates" (or "Eastern reprobates"). While at **Union Village**, Ohio, on July 9, 1847, the journalist records that the group "rode thru the village as undaunted as ever Judas of old did. They threw a number of their handbills into the dooryard and on one of them was written with a pencil, that they expected to be here on the following sabbath" (Morrell, "Account" 51).

One of the company's handbills for a performance at the American Museum in New York City, for example, announces that "the celebrated and far-famed Chase family, from Canterbury, N[ew] H[ampshire]," featuring ex-**Shakeress** Miss L. A. Chase, will perform "Shaker singing, dancing, shaking, whirling, &c." in "real Shaker costume." Among other expositions, Miss Chase, "with unheard of bodily powers," will "whirl round like a top, fifteen hundred times," a "wonderful feat [that] has never failed to call forth shouts of applause, and excite the wonder and admiration of the millions who have seen it" (Patterson, *Shaker Spiritual* 402).

Not all of the public was receptive to such performances. For instance, citizens in Cincinnati took offense, as recorded in this newspaper passage:

> Can there be found in Cincinnati an audience who could so far forget themselves as to encourage by their presence a set of sturdy lubberly felons, who for pay will consent to tickle the ears and gratify the sight of the groundlings, with the same sounds and the same actions, which scarcely a year ago they offered to their maker as holiest incense? (Quoted in Morrell, "Account" 55)

CARPENTER, JUNE (19?–). One of the two additions to the Shaker sisterhood after the closure of the **covenant** in 1965, Sister June is also the youngest female in the **Society**. (The other new and younger female member apostatized in 1994.)

CARR, FRANCES A. (1927–). The last **Shaker** in the **Sabbathday Lake**, New Gloucester, Maine, community to sign the **Church Covenant** before it was closed in 1965 by the **Lead Ministry** in **Canterbury**, New Hampshire, Sister Frances functions as the current **lead** of the **Society** (albeit, she does not employ the honorific appellation "Eldress"). She is extremely active and sophisticated in writing and speaking about **Shakerism** past and present. Her feature article "Home Notes" (reporting on current affairs of the **family**) regularly appears in the *Shaker Quarterly* and the *Clarion* (the latter a publication of **Friends of the Shakers**). In 1995, The United Society of Shakers published *Growing Up Shaker*, Carr's autobiography up to the day she signed the covenant.

CELIBACY/MARRIAGE. Along with practices such as **united interest**, **confession of sin,** and **separation from the world**, celibacy, too, is a primary principle of **Shakerism**. Although to be a **Shaker** a person does not have to be a sexual virgin, he/she does have to abstain forthwith from all sexual activity upon becoming a member of the sect (or even a **novitiate** or a guest of a community). The Shakers' charge against sexual intercourse stems from a vision of **Ann Lee** (while she was in prison in England) in which Adam and Eve copulate for pleasure. Their indulgence in carnal gratification was the first sin on earth and the sin that has been the source of humankind's untold evil and misery: "Lust destroyed pure, heaven-born Love, and the whole creation groaneth and travaileth together in sin, passion and despair. War, brutality and crime resulted" (White and Taylor, *Shakerism* 281).

In Shaker thought (as in that of a good deal of the rest of humanity), sexual intercourse among married people is a "given," one a concomitant of the other, the two regarded as being inextricably bounded together; therefore, Shakers also do not participate in the state of marriage (often alluding to the unmarried status of Jesus and citing, for example, Matthew 22:30 and Mark 12:25, of the King James Bible, as support for their position). They have not denounced marriage as an institution, however: "Marriage is honorable, but not Christian" (*Shaker* 1, no. 2 [1871]:15). On the other hand, they also have not applauded it as the highest possible state of existence. In the words of Mother Ann,

> those who choose to live after the flesh, can do so; but I know, by the revelation of God, that those who live in the gratification of their lusts will suffer in proportion as they have violated the law of God in nature. . . . Do not go away and report that we forbid to marry; for, unless you are able to take up a full cross, and part with every gratification of the flesh, for the kingdom of God, I would counsel you, and all such, to take wives in a lawful manner, and cleave to them only, and raise up a lawful posterity, and be perpetual servants to your families; for of all lustful gratifications, that is the least sin. (Quoted in Green and Wells, *Testimonies* 233)

Thus, although marriage (and sexual intercourse) is the foundation (the essence, some people might argue) of the human generative order of things and is, of course, "legitimate" (natural), to the Shakers the pinnacle of Christian living is the pursuit of the perfection of the spirit:

> When we speak of spiritual regeneration . . . we mean, not merely a restoration to the state of innocence in which man was first created, but a renovation of the whole soul and life of the man, in such a manner as to raise him, not only from the state into which he has fallen, but into a life of righteousness and true holiness, far superior to his primitive [natural] state, even into a state of eternal life, from which he can never fall. (Green and Wells, *Summary View* 271)

Such change cannot occur when body and mind are subject in various ways to other people and, hence, other responsibilities (as might be incurred, for example, because of a woman's devotion to the welfare of her spouse and children).

The Shakers' position on celibacy/marriage has been rigorously attacked and defended. Probably the greatest concern of non-Shakers has been "what would become of the world if all should become Shakers." Little thought is necessary to figure the answer, but no cause for alarm over extinction exists, according to the Shakers, because, for one thing, "the greater part" of the world's population "are not on the plane to hear the call of the spirit" anyway (White and Taylor, *Shakerism* 281). Furthermore, even if all were to become Shakers, "we fail to see that the bringing to an end of this wicked world would be a great wrong" (Pelham *Shaker's Answer* 2). That is, if an end of the natural, generative order results in spiritual perfection and eternal life, what is the loss? In their words, "If the Shakers, by abstaining from marriage 'are running the world out,' let it run; we think Christianity a preferable institution" (*Shaker* 1, no. 2 [1871]: 15).

CENTRAL MINISTRY. *See* LEAD MINISTRY.

CHAPMAN, EUNICE (17?–?). "Eunice Chapman's three-year campaign to dissolve her marriage and gain custody of her children was a *cause celebre* in the second decade of the nineteenth century. Her husband, James, who had abandoned his family and then joined the **Shakers** at **Watervliet**, New York, in October 1812, later, without consent of Eunice, committed the care of his children to the Shakers. Eunice, who tried the Shaker faith but found it not right for her, tried to recover custody of her children after she had left the Society (Richmond, *Shaker Literature* I 62). Although the New York legislature granted her a unique divorce, she did not receive custody of the children because the law provided at the time that fathers had exclusive custody of minor offspring. The case was particularly notable because, among other matters, it involved the Shakers' practices regarding the relationships between members and their spouses and children. Neither they nor James Chapman was judged to have done anything illegal.

CHILDREN'S ORDER. Generally, regardless of the circumstances of a child's entrance into the **Society**, he/she is separated from all adults other than his/her Shaker caretakers; thus, this distinct class of **Shakerism** has been set off for minority members. At various times, some communities had large populations of young people. For example, **South Union**, Kentucky, had a school **family** numbering 150 in 1813:

> They had a schoolhouse of four rooms, containing a school of seventy-five boys and fifty-six girls. Eldress Molly Goodrich writes in 1813 that there were one hundred and fifty under the age of fourteen and thirty under five years of age, of whom a number were less than one year old. Sixteen adult members had the Children's Order in charge. (White and Taylor, *Shakerism* 123)

Usually, the Children's Order was the direct responsibility of a particular family. *See also* EDUCATION.

CHOSEN GROUND. *See* FEAST GROUND.

CHOSEN LAND. *See* SABBATHDAY LAKE.

CHOSEN VALE. *See* ENFIELD, NEW HAMPSHIRE.

CHRIST SPIRIT. As do other sects of Christianity, so do the **Shakers** adhere to messianism and call the manifestation of God by the name of "Christ." "Many times and in different races the Christ Spirit rested upon, entered into and manifested itself through human beings—special witnesses" (White and Taylor, *Shakerism* 260). In Shaker doctrine, two such manifestations (both foretold) have been especially notable. The first occurred in the form of Jesus of Nazareth, and then, "when the time was fully come, according to the appointment of God, Christ was again revealed, . . . but in the person of a female . . . , Ann Lee" (Green and Wells, *Testimonies* 1–2). Thus, Mother Ann, like Jesus, became a visible and "chosen vessel, occupied as an instrument . . . by the Spirit of Christ" (Green and Wells, *Testimonies* 265).

However, unlike some other Christians, the Shakers insist upon the distinction between the Christ Spirit and the "earthly tabernacle" (the carnal human form) it has inhabited. For example, Jesus the person (and, by extrapolation, Ann) was an actual human being: "Christ (not Jesus) is the manifestation of Deity" (White and Taylor, *Shakerism* 260); "it was *Christ,* NOT *Jesus*, who should make a *Second Appearance*" (Green and Wells, *Testimonies* 2); and "the second coming of Christ [is] not the appearance of the same personal Being, but a manifestation of the same Spirit" (Green and Wells, *Summary View* 2, 245).

> The Shakers accept *Jesus* after he was baptized with the Christ, as the first born son of God, the *elder brother* of a large family of sons and daughters of God, constituting the Christian Church of the New Spiritual Creation of God; they do not believe that Jesus was a God, but is

our guide and life exempl[a]r; believe him to be *the Saviour* of men par excellence; but only the Elder of a large class of "Saviours." (*Shaker* 1, no. 1 [1871]: 2)

With the advent of the Christ Spirit in **Ann Lee**, according to the Shakers, the promised **Millennium** (or Parousia, the Second Coming) was no longer to be a future event but actually was begun.

Ann Lee was ordinary in that she was just one in a long line of women (such as the biblical Miriam and Deborah) who did work for God:

> In past ages, there were females, as well as males, raised up and qualified to do the will of God and to accomplish his work . . . which evidently shows that women, as well as men, were not only designed to enjoy the special favor of God; but also that they were originally designed to have a correspondent share in teaching and guiding the human race. (Green and Wells, *Summary View* 258–259)

She was unique among women, however, in that she was also the "earthly tabernacle" of the so-called Second Appearing of the Christ Spirit. That the Second Appearing was in a female logically emanates from the Shakers' master metaphor: the dual-gendered **Father/Mother Deity**.

> Ann Lee was the distinguished female who was chosen [to do the work of regeneration]. . . . And having received the spirit of Christ, by the operation of which her soul was purified from the fallen nature of the flesh [as was that of Jesus by baptism], she rose superior to it, and by her example and testimony, she actually led the way out of that nature and all its works, and was prepared to stand in a proper order to manifest the Spirit of Christ in the female line. Hence the image and likeness of the Eternal Mother was formed in her, as the first born Daughter, as really as the image and likeness of the Eternal Father was formed in the Lord Jesus, the first born Son. Thus was she constituted the second heir in the covenant of promise, and was placed in a correspondent connection with Jesus Christ, as the second pillar of the church of God in the new creation. (Green and Wells, *Summary View* 265)

CHRISTIAN COMMUNISM. *See* UNITED INTEREST.

CHURCH. The title of the entity constituted by and delineated in the **Church Covenant**. Members who sign this covenant sometimes are referred to as the "**Church Family**" or simply "The Church" (or "**Believers**" or "**True Believers**"). The Shaker Church is Christian, but some of its doctrines and principles—such as **celibacy** and denial of the divinity of Jesus—clearly distinguish it from other Christian sects, such as Methodism.

CHURCH COVENANT. Both (1) the delineation of the principles constituting the nature of the **Church** and (2) the agreement or contract among **Shakers** to uphold those principles. After attaining "lawful age" (21 years) and spending enough time within the Shaker system—"a few years, and sometimes [only] . . . a few months"—"to confirm their faith by experimental obedience," persons desiring to be full-fledged members of the United Society of Believers in Christ's Second Appearing (or the **Church Family**), being then "able to make a deliberate and conscientious choice for themselves," can consecrate their lives and material possessions "to the service of God" by signing the **Church Covenant** (Green and Wells, *Summary View* 61–63). The first covenant—the model for all others—consisted of a set of principles communicated only orally. Drafted by **Joseph Meacham**, it was not written until 1795, when it was signed by 43 members. By 1796, the Church Family of each of the 11 communities had signed it.

All the people living in Shaker communities at any given time are not covenanted members—not bona fide Shakers—simply because individuals are at different stages of spiritual progress. Also, because each branch (community) of the Church has its own particular circumstances of management, each one has its own relative covenant; nevertheless, regarding the "principles of united interest," among other items, each of these covenants "is essentially the same as that of the Church" (Green and Wells, *Summary View* 64).

Although no person ever has been coerced overtly to sign the document, until recently no person could become a bona fide Shaker unless he/she did so. When the **Lead Ministry** at **Canterbury**, New Hampshire, closed the **Church Covenant** in 1965, a difference of opinion and practice developed between the Shakers at Canterbury and those at **Sabbathday Lake**, Maine, the only other extant community. Since this closing of the Covenant, the Sabbathday Lake community has added several members—both male and female.

Among other matters, a covenant deals with the power and duties of the ministry; requisites for membership in the Church; duties of **elders**, **deacons**, and **trustees**; management of community property; and obligations of members. Perhaps, no better exposition of Shaker logic and management of communal religious and secular matters exists than that contained in the **Society's** covenant. (For an example, see appendix B, The Covenant or Constitution of the Church at Hancock.)

The concept of a covenant apparently evolved (partly, at least) from deductive logic: if the early Shakers, scattered throughout New England, remained in their respective "natural" families and were, thus, encumbered by all the responsibilities of such a condition (e.g., a woman's spending virtually all her time bearing and then rearing children, not to mention paying the requisite connubial attention to her spouse, who himself might very well have had to labor daily from first light to last light to provide food for the family), then they would be hard-pressed to devote themselves to developing their spiritual character—to taking up a **cross** against the flesh and sin effectively. Furthermore, "all who had honestly confessed and forsaken their sins, and faithfully continued to take up their crosses . . . [and] had gained a sufficient degree of mortification of the fallen nature of the flesh" required a means for "further increase of gospel order." Therefore, "it was necessary that they should be brought into nearer connection together, and thereby be enabled to serve God in a more united capacity, as members of the body of Christ in a church relation" (Green and Wells, *Summary View* 58).

CHURCH FAMILY. *A.k.a.: Believers, Church Order, First Order, Senior Order, True Believers.* The covenanted members of a community.

> To enter fully into this order is considered a matter of the utmost importance to the parties concerned, and therefore requires the most mature and deliberate consideration; for, after having made such a dedication, according to the laws of justice and equity, there can be no ground for retraction . . . Yet should any afterwards withdraw from the Society, the trustees have discretionary power to give them what may be thought reasonable. No person who withdraws peaceably is ever sent away empty. (Evans et al., *Compendium* 50)

The Church Family's significance in the community is manifested commonly by, for example, the geographical relationship of its **dwelling house** to that of other **families**. To illustrate, at **Pleasant Hill**, Kentucky, the Centre Family's (i.e., Church Family's) dwelling was flanked by those of the West Family and the East Family. *See also* CHURCH COVENANT; UNITED INTEREST.

CHURCH OF CHRIST'S SECOND APPEARING. *See* SHAKERISM.

CHURCH MEETING. Worship services of the **Church Family**.

CHURCH ORDER. *See* CHURCH FAMILY.

CITY OF LOVE. *See* TYRINGHAM, MASSACHUSETTS.

CITY OF PEACE. *See* HANCOCK, MASSACHUSETTS.

CITY OF UNION. *See* ENFIELD, CONNECTICUT.

CLARION. A newsletter published quarterly by **Friends of the Shakers**. Among other entries, it contains "Home Notes," a feature article on Shaker current events, now usually written by Sister **Frances A. Carr** of **Sabbathday Lake**, Maine.

CLOUGH, HENRY (17?–?). A **New Light** preacher before he was a Shaker, Brother Henry functioned as one of the Society's itinerant ministers during the early days of its establishment as an institution. "In 1788, Henry Clough was called to Mount Lebanon to live as Father Joseph's assistant. Elder Clough was often sent to bear Father Joseph's gift to the societies" (White and Taylor, *Shakerism* 102). He was associated with the early development of the **Harvard**, **Hancock**, and **Shirley** communities in Massachusetts, as well as that of **Canterbury**, New Hampshire. Despite Elder Clough's being seemingly second in command, so to speak, to **Joseph Meacham**, **Lucy Wright** was elevated to the position of the Society's **lead** upon Meacham's death in 1796.

COMMUNITY OF PROPERTY. *See* UNITED INTEREST.

COMMUNITY OF SHAKERS. *See* SHAKERISM.

CONFESSION OF SIN. Along with principles such as **celibacy**, **united interest**, and **separation from the world**, confession is another primary element of **Shakerism**: "A radical and most important principle in the Shaker, or second Christian Church, is the *oral confession of sins to God* in the presence of one or two witnesses" (Evans et al., *Compendium* 114). "The doctrine of confessing every secret sin, one by one, to the witnesses of God, was continually taught by Mother Ann Lee and the Elders, from the beginning of their ministry" (Green and Wells, *Testimonies* 192–193).

Shaker logic for both the necessity of confession and the manner of confessing is expressed in various ways in several of their compositions. For example,

> As man, in his fallen state, is in the kingdom of darkness, and under the government of the prince of this world, who is a prince of darkness; so his introduction into the Kingdom of Christ, which is a kingdom of light, must depend upon his coming to the light, and renouncing all the works of darkness. And as all sin, and all manner of wickedness, are the works of deeds of darkness; so the first step towards walking in the light, is to bring these deeds to the light [John 3:19–21]. And the only manner in which these evil deeds can be brought to the light and truly made manifest, is by confession.
>
> The open confession of sin to the witnesses of Christ, was practiced in the primitive church, and was considered as the first necessary step

for the admission of the sinner to the privileges of the gospel, and the only door of entrance into the church of Christ. (Green and Wells, *Summary View* 339–340)

In other Shaker documents, that confession be "open" or "oral" is explained thusly:

This rests upon the premises that the natural man never has seen, and never will see, God personally, either in this or any other world. Therefore, the judgement, as well as the mercy and goodness, of God, must necessarily be administered to souls through agencies [**elders/eldresses**] appointed by a Divine revelation from God, for that express purpose. (Evans et al., *Compendium* 114)

[Early Shakers] felt that secret confession was inadequate, and that public confession led to emotionalism. They accepted confession before a witness of the same sex who had already given his life to Christ as his way. Confession, although a disconcerting and disillusioning experience, was also a very certain way to deliverance from the false self with which most of us live. (Frost, "Prose and Poetry" 68)

Mother Ann, who is quoted as saying that "the first step of obedience that any soul can take is, to confess all sins to God, before His witnesses," is quoted also as stating her contention about the benefit of confession:

Those who honestly confess all their sins, with a full determination to forsake them forever, will find strength of God to forsake them; and in taking up their cross against every known sin, and following Christ in the regeneration, in that life of obedience, they will be clothed with the righteousness of Christ, and become the sons and daughters of God, being heirs of God, and joint heirs with Jesus Christ. (Quoted in Green and Wells, *Testimonies* 194)

The death of Brother **Delmar Wilson** in 1961 at the **Sabbathday Lake** community created a "technical" problem. Because he was the last **Church Family** male, subsequent male applicants for membership in the Society had no male "agency" to which they could make oral confession of their sins. The practice of males confessing to males and females to females is a long-established one.

However, strict adherence to the practice has not always occurred. For example, records of females confessing to males do exist, as in the following entries in a **South Union**, Kentucky, record: "June 8 [1808]: Confession—Mary Shaw to John Dunlavy . . . Tuesday, [June] 9: Confession—Nancy Boyles to Malcham Worley . . . Wednesday, [June] 10: Confession—Nancy Gill to Malcham [Worley]" (MacLean, *Shakers of Ohio* 278).

COOLEY, EBENEZER (17?–?). A Baptist elder when he met **Ann Lee**, upon his conversion, he became one of the earliest itinerate Shaker preachers and was much involved in helping to develop several of the New England communities and was somewhat involved in spreading the Shaker gospel in their southwest region. In 1799 or 1800, he was appointed by **Lucy Wright** to be the first **elder** of the new North Family (or Gathering Order) of the **New Lebanon**, New York, community, which was established "for the purpose of receiving and instructing new comers, or as such have ever since been called, 'Young Believers' [or **novitiates**]" (White and Taylor, *Shakerism* 110).

COTTON, JOHN (1761–?). A Freewill Baptist and **New Lighter**, Cotton was an early Shaker convert who served as one of the first **elders** of the **Alfred**, Maine, community. Of interest is the alleged manner by which his conversion occurred via the "involuntary exercise" of his body:

> The power of God came upon me, filling my soul and controlling my whole being. It raised me from my chair and under its influence I turned around, swiftly, for the space of half an hour. The door of the house was open. I was whirled through the door-way into the yard among the stones and stumps, down to the shore of the Mascoma Lake [**Enfield**, New Hampshire], some rods distant. On reaching the shore of the lake that same power that led me to the water whirled me back again in like manner, and I found myself in the same chair that I had been taken from. (Quoted in Sawyer, "Alfred" 11–12)

COVENANT. *See* CHURCH COVENANT.

CROSS. Although probably stemming from the intense suffering and difficulty endured by Jesus while bearing his burden to Calvary, the cross of the **Shakers** is a metaphorical one. To take up a cross, as in "to take a full and final cross against all evil" (Green and Wells, *Summary View* 3), is to make an effort to eliminate imperfection. In the everyday life of an individual **Believer**, this could mean a **brother's** struggling to subdue romantic thoughts about a **sister**, say, or quashing a spiteful attitude toward, a "bossy" **elder**, say. From the Shaker perspective, imperfection is sin. To assume the burden, no matter how painful, of eradicating it, plus eliminating any possible interference with the person's **travel** in the gospel toward spiritual perfection, is "to carry a cross."

Throughout most of Shaker history, intercourse between Shakers and their natural families was discouraged in the interests of the individual's development of his/her spiritual perfection. However, around the beginning of the twentieth century, the necessity for such a "cross" was greatly modified:

> The absolute crucifixion of all natural ties and affections is no longer deemed necessary. . . . [S]uch complete absolution from all the bonds of natural kinship as was one inculcated is no longer demanded. The duty of a child to an aged or feeble parent is recognized . . . [and] association and communication with relatives and friends, providing that it does not tend to distract the mind and divert the purpose from the spiritual calling upon which one has entered, [is approved]. (White and Taylor, *Shakerism* 281)

CUMINGS, HENRY (18?–?). According to the first modern scholar who attempted a somewhat comprehensive account of the Shaker "adventure," Cumings, who served as an **elder** of the **Enfield**, New Hampshire, community, was one of the many (but lesser-known) Shaker writers of the nineteenth century. His "careful descriptions of various phases of Shaker life as related in newspaper articles have made them vivid to us today" (Melcher, *Shaker Adventure* 211). Cumings apostatized in 1881 and then married.

-D-

DANCES/MARCHES. For as long as they were performed (from the beginning of the Shaker movement and throughout the nineteenth century), Shaker dances/marches constituted a major part of **Meeting** (and a main attraction to visitors). Regarding those of the late 1770s and early 1780s, according to a modern account,

> One bafflement that quickly divided onlookers [of **the world**] into two camps, entrancing some and repelling others, was the dancing. The Shaker dance looked to non-believers like an orgiastic frenzy completely foreign to any religious exercise they had ever known. Yet for those who had shaken off the Congregationalist and Baptist decorum through the fire of revival, the Shaker dance may have been a main attraction of the sect. (Burns, *Shaker Cities* 16–17)

To the Shakers, the values of dancing—one of what they called their "**exercises**"—far exceed mere pleasure of motion or mere manifestation of happiness; regarding shaking and dancing:

> Although Shakers find abundant scriptural defense of these customs [e.g., Exodus 15:20; I Samuel 18:6; Jeremiah 31:4], they did not derive

them from the Scriptures but were so often led into them by the direct operation of the Spirit that they concluded both to be acceptable to the Divine Will as modes of worship, while they found the spiritual effect of both upon themselves very desirable: the one, in throwing off the sense of evil and the desire for indulgence in sin; the other, in quickening spiritual powers and imparting strength, joy and victory to the soul. (White and Taylor, *Shakerism* 329–330)

Despite the fact that dancing during the earliest period might have had the semblance of "orgiastic frenzy," it became quite formalized during the late eighteenth and early nineteenth centuries. Impulsiveness was replaced by "official" structured compositions that were perfected with practice. "Between 1787 and 1797 the Shakers devised some seven forms of sacred dance. Two of these—the Holy Order and the Regular Step—remained their chief laboring manners for the next twenty years." Once settled and secure in their communities in the nineteenth century, Shakers began developing various new dances and marches for their worship services. Among them were "the Round, Hollow Square, and Square Step dances and the Circular, Square, and Compound marches" (Patterson, *Shaker Spiritual* 245).

Today, at **Sabbathday Lake**, Maine, neither dancing nor marching occurs. As noted by a twentieth-century **Shakeress** (*see* SHAKER/ SHAKERESS), "At last, when about a hundred years had passed, it was decided to lay aside the custom, but members still contributed to the service by speaking as each might choose, or in selecting a hymn" (Frost, "Prose and Poetry" 75).

DARK DAY. "The first publick testimony of the gospel in America, was delivered by Father James [Whittaker], at **Watervliet** on the well known dark day: May 19, 1780" (Green, "Biographical Account" 26). (Why this day was very darkened is not known for certain. Smoke from large wood fires has been surmised. Brother **Issachar Bates**, then a fifer in the revolutionary army, recorded the following comments on this dark day all over New England:

This baffled all human skill—for it was given up by great & small, that there was neither clouds nor smoke in the atmosphere—Yet the sun did not appear all that day.—And that day was as dark as night—no work could be done in any house, without a candle! and the night following was as dark accordingly, altho there was a well grown Moon. . . . [P]eople were out wringing their hands, and howling, "the day of judgement is come!" . . . And what next!—right on the back of this—On came the Shakers! and that made it darker yet—for they came forth to fulfill the VII chapt[er] of Ezekiel. . . . Now such confusion of body & mind, I had never witnessed before.—On the part of the Shakers, it was sing-ing, dancing, shouting, shaking, speaking with tongues, turning, preach-ing, prophesying, & warning the world to confess their sins & turn to God; for his wrath was coming upon them.

All this was right in the neighborhood, where I lived; and on the other part it was cursing, blaspheming, mocking, railing, lying, threat-ening, stoning, beating with clubs & sticks, & firing pistols. (Bates, "Sketch" 113–114)

Whatever the cause of the darkness, its conjunction with the Shakers' first public profession of their religion probably was arresting to **the world**— and even to the Shakers.

DARROW, DAVID (1750–1825). *A.k.a.: Father David.* One of the earli-est of the American Shakers, Darrow had been a soldier in the Revolu-tionary War (ironically arrested as a British spy after he joined the Shak-ers). Along with others, he dedicated his property to the **New Lebanon**, New York, community, at which, beginning in 1788, he served as **elder** of the **Church Order**.

Brother David's most significant contribution to the advancement of the Shaker gospel was his work in the sect's southwest communities, for which he was much praised by his fellow members. In 1806, **Lucy Wright** released him from his eldership duties at New Lebanon and ap-pointed him to be first elder and protector of those communities. Oper-ating out of the community that eventually was named **Union Village** in Ohio,

Father David and his sturdy associates went back and forth through Ohio and Kentucky, preaching in the woods from stumps and logs, sleeping in log cabins or beneath the forest trees, sharing the wild, rough life of the frontiersman, welcoming alike Indian, pioneer or planter, ignorant [N]egro or learned Presbyterian divine. (White and Taylor, *Shakerism* 117)

Regarding Shaker politics, so to speak, associated with Darrow are the issues of the sovereignty of the southwest communities, the significance of the individual in the Shaker scheme, and the employment of the hon-orific appellation "father." After the unusually great adulation of Father Darrow following his death, apparently intending to remind the south-west colonies of the necessity of their **union** with those of the East and of the fact that the death of any one person does not alter the plan of the whole, the **Lead Ministry** in New Lebanon, New York, abolished the continued use of both "**father**" and "**mother**"; thus, in theory at least, extreme devotion to any local person was thereafter prevented.

DEACON/DEACONESS. Members—usually two of each gender—entrusted with management of the domestic business of their respective **families**, such as farming and food preparation (both for local consumption and for the markets of **the world**). Their authority did not extend beyond their own department (the kitchen, for example) and family (the West Family, for example). That is, they had no power to operate on behalf of the community as a whole. Such power was the province of other managers, such as **trustees**. *See also* CHURCH COVENANT.

DOOLITTLE, MARY ANTOINETTE (1810–1886). Born in New Lebanon, New York, Sister Mary "united with the Shakers, of her own choice and determination, at the age of fourteen" and spent the rest of her life with them—serving 50 years as **eldress** of the large North or Gathering Family of the **New Lebanon** community (White and Taylor, *Shakerism* 164).

Sister Mary is especially distinguished for her advocacy of reforms in the Shaker system during the last several decades of the nineteenth century. An observer noted in 1878

> that important changes have taken place in the internal character of Shakerism; that its leaders are more liberal and more tolerant than they were a quarter of a century ago; and that they are more ready to see good in other systems, and less prompt to condemn what does not accord with their own. It is also obvious that there is a growing party of progressives among the Shakers—men and women who, while firmly adhering to all that is deemed essential in the system, think it desirable that all non-essentials that stand in the way of genuine progress and culture should be modified or abolished. (Hinds, *American Communities* 100–101)

Along with other "progressives" of the time, such as Elder **Frederick W. Evans,** her co-leader of the North Family, Eldress Mary fostered, among other changes, not strict adherence to traditional **separation from the world** but more active missionary work in it; not narrow and unchangeable doctrine but tolerance and acceptance of alternative principles; not business as usual but financial and business affairs of **brothers** and **sisters** managed by each separately—thus giving sisters full control of their own business matters. Besides speaking on behalf of "new" **Shakerism**, she occupied the potentially highly influential position of co-editor (with Elder Evans) of the *Shaker and Shakeress* (1873–

1875), the Shaker journal that was issued to all the societies. In the estimate of two Shaker chroniclers,

> The Labors and influence of these two leaders cannot be bounded by any one family or society. The whole connection, north, south, east and west, felt and feel still the impress of the wise counsels, magnetic inspiration, strong personality and devoted consecration of Elder Frederick W. Evans and Eldress Mary Antoinette Doolittle. (White and Taylor, *Shakerism* 165)

Eldress Mary also had a penchant for speaking in and interpreting "tongues" as well as a **gift** for healing, and she engaged in **spiritualism**. One of the many visitors from **the world** to the New Lebanon community recalled

> that she talks with spirits more freely and confidingly than she does with me; yet I cannot see that Antoinette is crazy on any other point, and she certainly makes neat and sensible speeches. This room . . . which seems to me empty and still, is to her full of seraphim and cherubim, who keep on singing the livelong day. (Dixon, *New America* 332)

DUNLAVY, JOHN (17?–1826). A former Presbyterian minister and **New Light** revivalist, **Brother** John, a very significant figure in the **Kentucky Revival**, was among the first people in the southwestern region to assume the Shaker way, converting in 1805, shortly after the arrival in Ohio of the Shaker "propaganda" from **New Lebanon**, New York—**Issachar Bates Sr., John Meacham,** and **Benjamin S. Youngs.** Along with other recent converts from Presbyterianism, such as **Richard McNemar, Malcolm Worley,** and **Matthew Houston,** Dunlavy began serving immediately as an itinerate minister in parts of Ohio and Kentucky. He became "for many years an eminent leader among western Shakers" (White and Taylor, *Shakerism* 322). Among his leadership services to the Society was that of **lead** of the North Lot or Gathering Order at **Pleasant Hill**, Kentucky.

Perhaps as significant as any of his contributions to developing the Shaker gospel—but not only in the southwest—was his "contribution to the early theological work of the Shakers." Ten years after the publication of Brother Benjamin Youngs's *The Testimony of Christ's Second Appearing*, Dunlavy issued his *Manifesto; Or, A Declaration of the Doctrines and Practices of the Church of Christ* from Pleasant Hill in 1818. "Very doctrinal in tone . . . clear and forceful," Brother John's volume dwelt at length upon, among other items, cardinal Shaker principles, such as the concept of **united interest**, a major element of the Christian communism practiced by the **Shakers** (Melcher, *Shaker Adventure* 209).

John Dunlavy was among the many people who suffered from their connection to the ill-fated **West Union**, Indiana, community. He died from the malaria he had contracted there.

DURGIN, DOROTHY A. (18?–1898). An **eldress** of the **Canterbury**, New Hampshire, community, Sister Dorothy, herself "one of the sweetest singers of Israel," participated in the "musical evolution at Canterbury" by supervising the collection of hymns begun in 1875 (White and Taylor, *Shakerism* 338, 345). Also, she is credited with designing the so-called Shaker cloak, a floor-length garment for females, popular in **the world** and, hence, a much-needed moneymaker for the failing Shaker **economy** of the late nineteenth century.

DWELLING HOUSE. *A.k.a.: dwelling, dwelling place.* The building that is the "home" of a **family**. The **Pleasant Hill**, Kentucky, **village**, for example, has an East Family Dwelling House, a West Family Dwelling House, a West Lot Family Dwelling House, and a North Lot Family Dwelling House—all so named because of their geographical relationship to the Centre Family Dwelling House, home of the **Church Family**.

In some communities, the Church Family dwelling is a very remarkable construct. Again, for example, at Pleasant Hill, "dominating the village landscape, the Centre Family Dwelling is of the finest examples of Shaker construction, incorporating the best tradition of American architecture with Shaker principles of honesty and excellence in workmanship" (Clarke and Ham, *The Gift of Pleasant Hill* 89). "The size of it is 60 by 55 feet, two Story high, with a Kitchen joining it, 85 feet by 34 feet" (in Thomas and Thomas, *The Simple Spirit* 82). The building is made of blocks of Kentucky limestone and has 40 rooms (those on the left or west side occupied by **sisters**), a cellar, and a third-floor storage attic. It was constructed between 1824 and 1834. Besides retiring rooms for common members, the dwelling has, for example, a family **Meeting room**, a separate dining room for the Ministry, and an infirmary. Currently, this dwelling house is kept as the primary exhibition building in the restored village administered by Shakertown at Pleasant Hill, Kentucky, Inc., of Harrodsburg, Kentucky.

DYER, MARY MARSHALL (17?–18?). In a case similar to that of **Eunice Chapman**, Dyer left the **Enfield**, New Hampshire, community about a year after reluctantly joining it with her husband, Joseph, and five children. Prevented by various alleged machinations of her husband and **elders** from even seeing her children before she left around 1818, Marshall spent the next 30 years publishing attacks on Shaker policies, hoping to bring legal action against the Society. In 1849, the state of New Hampshire decided that the **Shakers** were able and legitimate guardians of children.

-E-

EADS, HARVEY L. (1807–1892). "A life parallel with that of Elder [Frederick W.] Evans in time as in force of character, power of leadership and influence on the thought of his people, is Hervey L. Eads" (White and Taylor, *Shakerism* 165). A southwest **Shaker**, Brother Harvey "joined" the Society at **South Union**, Kentucky, with his mother when he was a few months old. In 1836, he "was appointed assistant, associate, and helper to Elder Benjamin S. Youngs. This was a great honor for Eades [*sic*], then aged thirty-nine" (Coombs, "Shaker Colony" 166). In 1844, he was sent to **Union Village**, Ohio, as a common **brother**. In 1862, he was returned to the **ministry** at South Union. From there, in 1863, he successfully petitioned President Lincoln to exempt Shakers from military conscription. (*See also* PACIFISM.)

Judged an "eloquent preacher and writer" (Melcher, *Shaker Adventure* 268), Elder Eads was a major Shaker theologian during the latter decades of the nineteenth century. Unlike the so-called liberals and progressives in the East, who, among other things, fancied that they could do **the world** some good by mingling with it and sharing the Shaker gospel, Eads was a "conservative" who "advocated a stricter separation from the World and a return to traditional, ascetic Christian standards" (Brewer, *Shaker Communities* 190). His was among the "dissenting voices . . . raised here and there against what was considered the over-liberality of Elder Frederick [Evans and his] too venturesome ideas" (Melcher, *Shaker Adventure* 209). "Differing in many points of polity and theology from his equally original and forceful brother of the east [Evans], the battles of wit and wisdom in argument between the two were many and fierce (White and Taylor, *Shakerism* 166). Among other points, Elder Eads adamantly insisted that the world could be better served if Shakers only set an example of "pure and righteous living," rather than functioning as its reformers and becoming inevitably involved with—and contaminated by—its politics and culture (Andrews, *People Called Shakers* 234).

An invaluable service for posterity was performed by Elder Eads starting in 1804. He "transcribed all the journals and diaries pertaining to the founding and growth of the colony [South Union] down to September, 1836, collected in one large volume of 640 pages, which he designated 'Shaker Record A'" (Coombs, "Shaker Colony" 157).

ECONOMY. Located in rural areas, Shaker communistic communities always primarily have been self-sustaining agricultural entities. However, despite the Shaker principle of **separation from the world**, during the nineteenth century especially they engaged heavily in and depended greatly on capitalism—and paid the price for it, some might say, when their "cottage **industries**" for various reasons could not match the faster, vaster, and cheaper production of the factories of **the world** following the Civil War; they therefore became hard-pressed for monies to pay, for example, taxes on their properties for which they did not have sufficient membership to operate and generate capital. Even today, at **Sabbathday Lake**, Maine (a living museum, so to speak), the **Shakers** sell **fancy goods** and sundry items to visitors (customers) while maintaining a very small-scale agrarian system (supervised by "**deacon**" Brother **Wayne Smith**).

EDUCATION. The necessity for an educational program became obvious with the influx of children during the rapid increase of membership in the Society as its communal **villages** developed during the late eighteenth and early nineteenth centuries. The children, too young to join the **Shakers** themselves, were mostly the offspring of members, orphans, and **indentures** (and, of course, were a plentiful source of possible future membership). They were enrolled in the **Children's Order** (thus separating adults, even parents, from children) and given some education. Generally, boys attended school in the winter, when outside work, such as farming, was minimal. The girls attended at other times since separation of males and females was enforced in classrooms, too. Brother **Seth Youngs Wells**, who "was appointed General Superintendent of Believers' Literature . . . [and] Schools" in 1821 (White and Taylor, *Shakerism* 133), fostered the monitorial method of instruction developed by Joseph Lancaster, a young Quaker of Southwark, England, who invented the system as a way to instruct many (mostly the indigent) with the help of few.

In the statement by a Shaker that "the 'pure in heart . . . shall see God,' not the highly educated" (Eads, *Discourses* 12), the significance of "highly" cannot be slighted, for the Shakers have put limitations on the amount of time devoted to education and on the matter that composes it. "Although at first the gospel was felt to be sufficient book knowledge, it was not long before other books and subjects were studied, for which schools were created" (Barnes, "Shaker Education" 68).

Regarding "schoolhouse" (or formal) education, the main principle in the Shaker world of the nineteenth century was the acquisition of practical, functional knowledge—the kind most beneficial to **Believers** in, for example, their day-to-day activities to create and sustain what are called "creature comforts." This principle is evident in the descriptions in many works of various kinds on **Shakerism** not only by non-Shakers but also by Shakers themselves. For example, the following is an excerpt from a letter written in 1832 by an alleged worldling visitor to the Society:

> [The children] are instructed . . . in all the branches of education necessary to fit them for the useful and active duties of life. . . . This the Society considers sufficient, as it will avail nothing for children to spend their time in acquiring a knowledge of the higher branches of literature, and especially of what is called classical learning, unless they can apply their knowledge to some useful purpose. (Bates, *Peculiarities*, "Letter VII")

After touring several of the New England Shaker villages in 1837, another observer made the following remarks:

> Great tyranny is practiced over the young people by their superiors. They are discouraged from conversing with persons out of the limit of the society; books are discountenanced; no such thing is dreamed of as the pursuit of science, literature, or art. These noble intellectual occupations are regarded as toys with which the holy should have nothing to do. (*Penny Magazine* 43)

A visitor to each of the Shaker communities of the 1870s noted that "the Shakers still, with good sense, teach each boy and girl a trade, so as to fit them for earning a living" (Nordhoff, *Communistic Societies* 211). Also, two of the several twentieth-century chroniclers of Shakerism state the following about the Shaker principle of pragmatic education:

> Since the majority of their time was spent out of school, Shaker children concentrated on learning agriculture and crafts skills that would contribute to their Family's welfare and prepare them for a productive adult life. (Brewer, *Shaker Communities* 77)

> The Shakers for the most part mistrusted a too great development
> of the intellect. Mother Ann had said "hands to work and hearts to God";
> she made no mention of the mind. The teaching of the Shaker children
> was thus turned mainly into two channels: religious training and the
> learning of a trade. (Melcher, *Shaker Adventure* 160–161)

In various works, Shakers themselves express their commitment to the
acquisition of pragmatic knowledge—what today might be called "vocational training." For example, Seth Youngs Wells—"chiefly responsible
for the philosophy and content of Shaker education" (Andrews, *People
Called Shakers* 328)—notes that "there are a variety of branches of manufacture carried on in our Society" and that an indenture is trained—educated—in the branch "best adapted to his genius and capacity" (Wells
"A Plain Statement" 5). Wells also says that "there are books enough to
be found which contain useful information in many branches of business,
which not only afford much useful instruction to believers, but might be
the means of keeping out those of a pernicious nature, [such as novels]"
(Wells "Remarks on Learning" 6).

However, in another Shaker tract, a peculiar little book (with a typical Shaker very long title) issued by the Society in 1843, "education"
means more than just vocational training for temporal well-being. Also
necessary to a Believer is an understanding—an education—of what is
useful to the proper development of his/her spiritual life:

> All [children] should have hours of study allowed them. . . . They should
> be supplied with the New Testament, and the words of the sacred songs,
> which might be their duty to read on the Sabbath. . . . There is sufficient
> assortment of books for the little ones of my flock to peruse, without
> fables, news-prints, novels, picture-books, primers, and such like, which
> are injurious studies for Mother's little ones. (*The Gospel Monitor* 20)

The spirit is nourished—educated—by the New Testament and sacred
songs. Reading and singing are neither discouraged nor regarded as necessarily detrimental, but what a Shaker reads is significant in his/her
education to develop the **Christ Spirit**. (Unfortunately, exactly how
novels, for example, are "injurious" is not delineated explicitly in this
tract.) Mother Ann, the spirit speaker of this passage, probably took for
granted that her Shaker audience—"those who are entrusted with the care
of those in the order of children, in her house on earth"—were aware of
the context of her statements, understood the way a novel is damaging,
especially to a child. Probably, the children's caretakers educated them
according to the Society's principle that enjoyment and knowledge gained
from writings such as fables and novels, for example, are unworthy of

serious attention if they have no utilitarian value to the community's daily business and no value to the individual's necessary constant **labor** to quell desires for carnal indulgence.)

Shaker **Harvey L. Eads** is emphatic about the "right" education for Shakers:

> Education is of two kinds, subjective and objective. By the subjective we are educated into the child condition, which alone, according to the text [Matthew 18, 2–3], enables us to enter God's kingdom. This education is given of God by the operation of the spirit within the mind; while the objective is obtained from without by means of the five senses. . . . The latter is intellectual, the former spiritual. . . . The girl in her teens, without book education, who looks within instead of prying into the "mysteries of life" . . . knows more about God and the spirit world than any books or lecture-room can impart, or more than any persons with all the learning can have who fail to clothe themselves with the child-spirit recommended by Christ and look within instead of without. (Eads, *Discourses* 20)

Thus, to the Shakers of the nineteenth century, "classical learning" and "scholastic education"—what today might be called a "liberal arts education"—were fitted neither for the business of daily living nor for spiritual development. Their attitude toward "useless" education has been regarded as lamentable:

> It is much to be wished that the Shakers could admit the pursuit of knowledge in other departments besides agriculture, horticulture, and domestic economy. The world might derive a valuable lesson from witnessing what might be done in science, literature, and art by a body so relieved from worldly cares, so possessed, through their principle of community property, with wealth and leisure. They have not nearly enough to do; there is not one of them that could not devote some hours of every day to a new pursuit if the means were open to him. . . . It is scarcely necessary to say that this sect has never had to boast of any great men or women. No persons of mental power would join a society whose principle is to crush human nature; to extinguish the intellect. ("Shakers," *Penny Magazine* 445–448)

Of course, other and far different assessments of and perspectives on the Shakers' educational practices exist. For example, **Anna White** and **Leila S. Taylor**, familiar with Shakers in the latter part of the nineteenth century, say that

> while the Shaker societies have a fair proportion of the university trained and college bred, the common school has been the university of most of the members; but all prove discriminating readers, careful thinkers

and, what is more, the decision of the mind means, soon or late, the action of conscience, will and faculty. (*Shakerism* 326)

These same Shaker chroniclers note, too, that in 1891 the young **sisters** (*see* BROTHER/SISTER) at Mount Lebanon organized a

> self-improvement society . . . "[to] establish [among other things] a radical improvement in habits and manner, address and conversation and the cultivation of the mind in substantial, beautiful and interesting things." . . . The rules . . . "encouraged the use of grammatical language and correct pronunciation."
>
> Literary, scientific and philosophical study took their attention, and original work of a superior stamp resulted from this earnest effort at self-education. (*Shakerism* 212)

Sister **Frances A. Carr**, a graduate of the "common school" and certainly a "careful" thinker, relates in her *Growing Up Shaker* (1995) that during her own schooling in the 1930s and 1940s at the **Sabbathday Lake**, Maine, community, books "for enrichment and entertainment" were available to the girls. "These books helped to broaden our understanding of what life was like outside the shelter of a Shaker Community" (29). Also, she relates that Sister **Mildred Barker** organized the so-named "Improvement Club" for young women, "which continued our education by a special emphasis on literary work, study, and concentration. We were assigned subjects on which to write, wrote and learned poetry, and had musical presentations" (105).

Furthermore, assessments of Shaker education by learned members of **the world** are no less laudatory than those by Shakers themselves. For example,

> To label the Shakers narrow is not so helpful as seeing why the Shakers distrusted intellectual pride. The fear of useless learning derived from the fact that the Shakers had an integrated communal life in which religious faith was not merely a subject but a total world-view within which vocation, education, and all communal activities lived and moved and possessed their significance. Life had a purpose. Each moment was precious. The school subjects served higher moral and religious purposes beyond themselves. Thus, knowledge of grammar was valued as a means of keeping correct accounts of divine manifestations. (Barnes, "Shaker Education" 74)

A more general and a very complimentary assessment of the Shakers' educational program is the following one:

> The Shaker schools were flexible and innovative. Many Shaker students were exposed to what we now label as team teaching, flexible schedul-

ing, the all-year school, student published texts, activity periods during the day, infant education, oral reports, and interdisciplinary studies. . . . The Shaker schools were far ahead of their public school counterparts in many activities. In the 1840s, for example, although the Shakers did not vote, they were using the state laws and state government publications as a text. . . . The public school movement was still struggling to become a viable reality when the Shakers had schools in all eighteen of their communities. (Taylor, *Analysis* 288–289)

ELDER/ELDRESS. In their usage of this appellation, the **Shakers** are consonant with one of the traditional meanings of this word: an elder is a spiritual leader. However, in their system, generally a three-level hierarchy of spiritual leadership exists. At the top are the elders of the ministry of the "general community"—the **"lead"** or **"lead ministry"** as it is usually called. Next in line are the elders of individual communities. Depending on local situations, the same elders might comprise the ministry for a **bishopric**—two or more communities under their care. Finally, individual **families** historically have had lead elders, sometimes called **"elder sister"** or **"elder brother."**

ELDER BROTHER/ELDER SISTER. The appellation granted to the **lead brother/lead sister** at the **family** level of government, as in, "The Church Family . . . was presided over by an Elder Brother, an Elder Sister, and an assisting elder and eldress" (Burns, *Shaker Cities* 34).

ELECT LADY. A appellation usually applied derisively to **Ann Lee** by her detractors—the British, among others.

ELKINS, HERVEY (18?–18?). Perhaps the most erudite and intellectually sophisticated **Shaker** ever to leave the Society, Elkins says that he, unlike vindictive **apostates** such as **Valentine Wightman Rathbun,** "peaceably withdrew" from the **Enfield,** New Hampshire, community because of an unspecified "malady of the mind." His *Fifteen Years in the Senior Order of Shakers,* published in 1853, is an account of his experiences in the community that he knew intimately from the age of 14 to 29. It is cited very often by historians and scholars, which might be a testimony to their faith in Elkins's sincerity and accuracy.

Dissimilar to many other autobiographies of ex-Shakers, Elkins's work is at the very least an attempt to present a balanced account. After dwelling "upon the bright side of the leaf" of **Shakerism** for over 100 pages, he then presents its dark side: "it is no less my duty, to truthfully state the disadvantages of so stringent a rule of faith and conduct [as

Shakerism]." One of the disadvantages that he discusses is the absolute triumph of Shaker piety over "natural" love: "Love, in the sense employed by poets; love, in all its raptures and in all its sighs . . . is there denied, and is there made forlorn" (a charge that approaches ubiquity in narrative fictions of non-Shakers featuring Shakers).

To illustrate the truth of this allegation, Elkins recounts a "real occurrence," the history of the love relationship between a **brother** and a **sister** whom he knew personally. Unfortunately, he compromises the credibility of historiography when his passion to delineate the "truth" apparently forces him to cross the line separating history and historical fiction. The tale of the Shaker lovers is indisputably a piece of narrative fiction (very likely the only one ever written by a Shaker about Shakers).

ENFIELD, CONNECTICUT (1790–1917). *Spiritual name: City of Union.* The only Shaker settlement in the state, Enfield was situated in Hartford County, about five miles east of the Connecticut River, about 18 miles northwest of Hartford, and about 12 miles from Springfield, Massachusetts. (The town of Enfield was the birthplace of Father **Joseph Meacham**, the founder of institutional **Shakerism**.) In 1792, it had 48 adult members. As late as 1858, it had about 200 members and 5 **families**. However, by 1875, decline was well under way: "There are in the four families one hundred and fifteen persons" (Nordhoff, *Communistic Societies* 190).

A farming community, also, with about 3,300 acres, Enfield (along with **New Lebanon**, New York, and **Union Village**, Ohio) claimed "the honor of originating the seed business, which was a leading industry throughout Shakerdom for many years and netted many thousands of dollars annually to the different societies" (White and Taylor, *Shakerism* 315). Nevertheless, the community suffered not only from the loss of its seed trade with the South after the Civil War but also from uncollectible debts, which virtually annihilated the community's savings (Nordhoff, *Communistic Societies* 190). Moreover, as did most of the other Shaker communities, Enfield suffered very destructive fires. For example, "In January, 1897, . . . [it] lost by flames a large barn with several other buildings, hay, grain and valuable implements. Twenty thousand dollars would not have made good the loss" (White and Taylor, *Shakerism* 211).

Regarding everyday life at Enfield during the first half of the nineteenth century, a twentieth-century historiographer surmises that it

would have been rich and stimulating. Among his [Brother Calvin Ely's] activities were framing, sawing timber for chair rungs, turning chair rungs and whip handles, making cider brandy, piling wood, painting, . . . plowing, . . . planting potatoes, haying, . . . husking corn, killing hogs, threshing rye, mending brass kettles. . . . Ely's life was happy and content, balanced between vigorous work, hearty companionship, and the regular inspiration of the Sunday meetings. (Burns, *Shaker Cities* 66)

In 1917, Enfield (following **Tyringham**, Massachusetts) became the second **village** in the Second Bishopric to close (only **Harvard**, Massachusetts, remained). Apparently, among other matters, the community suffered from great discord between old and new members, ineffectual leadership, and unacceptable labor from non-Shakers.

On November 20, 1914, the real estate was sold for $100,000. . . . [T]he buyer paid $5000 for all of the horses, the farming tools, and the grain. . . . The remaining Shakers were allowed to live in the 1791 meeting house. . . . Between 1915 [and] 1917 the remaining Shakers moved . . . to the Hancock [Massachusetts], Watervliet [New York], and Mt. Lebanon [New York] church families. (Burns, *Shaker Cities* 185–186)

ENFIELD, NEW HAMPSHIRE (1793–1923). *Spiritual name: Chosen Vale.* Located on the shore of Mascoma Lake in Grafton County, about 12 miles southeast of Dartmouth College, Enfield was started with only one **family**, but it added another one in 1800 and one more in 1812— the North Family, an **order** of **Novitiates**. by the 1850s, Enfield had about 300 members, but by 1875, the 3 families had been reduced to 145 members, females outnumbering males by nearly 3 to 1.

As were many of the Shaker communities, Enfield was developed in a magnificent natural setting that was only improved by the orderly and creative **Shakers**. Perhaps no better account of the site has been rendered than that of the man who was the most intellectually brilliant Shaker ever to become an **apostate**. **Hervey Elkins** recounts his first approach to the Enfield community:

Rich pastures now begin to cover the hillside, and for three fourths of a mile, a continually increasing indication of feasible land and agriculture improvement welcome the eye . . . ; when lo! . . . a scene, unrivalled for novelty and rural beauty anywhere in New England, is rapidly disclosed. Level, fertile fields of great extent, with marginal trees; gardens of six, eight and ten acres' surface laid out along the shores and containing every variety of esculent herbage that the soil and climate will permit; avenues long and splendid, of sugar maple and butternut, reaching across the plain and extending far up the mountain side; orchards of ingrafted fruit; innumerable trellises supporting vines; fences with granite posts; barns which, from their rich exterior and size resemble more the market houses of our cities; beautiful edifices of capacious dimensions for houses, some of stone, others of brick, others yet of thoroughly wood and roofed with slate of Wales;—every thing . . . apprise the visitor that he has entered an arena of singular charm and occult signification. The lake itself clean, sweet, crystallike and noble in its outlines, heightens immeasurably the fascination of the spot. (Elkins, *Fifteen Years* 11–12)

The **dwelling house** of this community, like others detailed throughout this text (see, e.g., Dwelling House for a description of the **Church Family** Dwelling at **Pleasant Hill**), is a remarkable structure, one built to last "forever." Among its features are that it is composed of granite blocks, is 100 feet long and reported to be between 56 and 60 feet wide, and it has 4 full stories, 2 storage attics, about 200 windows, and a 40-by-24-foot kitchen.

From about 1838 to 1863, the Enfield Shakers "were at the height of their prosperity and success. . . . [T]heir influence was great enough to enable them to change the industrial development of the town by dictating the route the railroad should take . . . in 1847" (Melcher, *Shaker Adventure* 163).

As of 1875, Enfield owned about 3,000 acres and was quite busy with numerous **industries**, such as selling seeds; making buckets, tubs, and brooms; manufacturing herbal medicines, maple sugar, applesauce, flannel shirts, drawers, and socks; and preparing breads and pies for the local market. To accomplish all its production, the community hired about 20 to 30 non-Shaker laborers.

That the members had some leisure time during this era can be surmised from the following report:

They have a library of about two hundred volumes in each family, exclusive of strictly religious books; and almost all the younger people can read music, one of the members being a thorough teacher and good musical drill-master. . . . Once or twice a week they hold reading meetings, at which some one reads either from a book of history or biography, or extracts from newspapers. (Nordhoff, *Communistic Societies* 189)

Although Enfield officially closed in 1923 with the sale of the property to the Roman Catholic Brotherhood of La Salette for a meager $25,000 (with the proviso that it maintain the property in the Shaker way), the seven remaining Shakers, of whom only one was a **brother**, moved to the **Canterbury** community. As recently as 1997, the Enfield Historical

Society has endeavored to purchase and restore some of the community's buildings, most especially the "Great Stone Dwelling," which has been in the hands of restaurant people.

ERA OF MANIFESTATIONS. *See* MOTHER ANN'S SECOND COMING.

EVANS, FREDERICK W. (1808–1893). Argued to be "the best-known and most broad-minded of the later Shaker leaders," Elder Frederick was an English social reformer who emigrated to America in 1820 with his brother George. "Together they edited radical newspapers calling for [among other changes] land reform, women's rights, and the end of wage slavery" (Morse, *Story of the Shakers* 53). He had the good fortune, so to speak, of having an "early life . . . quite different from the usual Shaker's":

> Instead of spending his youth among God-fearing farmers in rural America, either in the children's quarters of some Shaker village or more likely exposed to bleak poverty as part of an unfortunate family, he had been born to well-off parents in England. And instead of moving to Shakerism after being disappointed in more conventional religious doctrines, he had been a convinced atheist during his early childhood. (Faber, *Perfect Life* 141)

Evans had similarities to the much-lauded **Joseph Meacham**, of the previous century. Among other commonalities, both were greatly sclf-educated; both became Shaker converts after they went to study the Society for themselves, and both had unquestioned leadership talent (although Evans never received the honorific title "Father" that was bestowed upon Meacham).

However much they were alike, nevertheless, their role in **Shakerism** was not quite the same. Whereas Meacham was most eminent for constructing the foundations of and molding the sect that Evans entered in 1830, Elder Frederick himself was most notable for his exposition of Shakerism and his involvement in various reforms in the Society during the middle and latter decades of the nineteenth century.

Being a **lead elder** of the **New Lebanon**, New York, community, the center of Shakerdom, Evans was in a powerful position from which to speak and to effect changes. His opportunity to promulgate his ideas was further increased by his being co-editor (with Eldress **Mary Antoinette Doolittle**) of the Shaker-produced monthly journal the *Shaker and Shakeress* (1873-1875). In the estimate of a visitor who conversed with Evans,

> The active power of the Society . . . lies with Elder Frederick, the official preacher and expositor of Shaker doctrine. If the Shaker communities should undergo any change, in our day, through the coming in of other lights, I fancy that the change will have to be brought about through him. Frederick is a man of ideas, and men of ideas are dangerous persons in a Society which affects to have adopted its final form. (Dixon, *New America* 336)

Confronted with a radical decline in membership after 1840 (from about 6,500 to about 2,500 in the 1870s), especially after the Civil War, the United Society of Believers in Christ's Second Appearing found itself in a crisis that it could address in one of two ways: accept the apparent moribundity of the Society or challenge it. Even though Elder Frederick himself remarked in an interview, "Of course we like to keep up our numbers, but of course we do not sacrifice our principles" (in Nordhoff, *Communistic Societies* 158–159), he was, nevertheless, the major factor in the Society's efforts to arrest the decline. Concurrent with his functioning as a Shaker missionary of sorts by promulgating the Society's principles via lectures, newspaper articles, books, correspondence with members of **the world** (such as the notable Russian literary figure and ex-aristocrat turned social reformer Lev Tolstoy), and journeys to his native England were his efforts within the Shaker community to move it out of, among other things, its "traditional isolationist thinking and into the national movement for social reform" (Morse, *Story of the Shakers* 53). Central to Elder Frederick's thoughts about reform in the Shakers' relation to the world is the concept that "the Shaker Order is the source and medium of spiritual religious light to the world; the seed-bed of radical truths; the fountain of progressive ideas" (Evans, *Autobiography* x). Thus, to him, apparently, Shakerism was not a fixed system but one that at least ought to be forever in the process of redefinition. This concept became a major source of contention among Evans and other elders, such as **Harvey L. Eads** of **South Union**, Kentucky, who preferred traditional Shaker values, such as continued and stricter **separation from the world**, to risking contamination by it while trying to improve it.

Besides commentaries on religious matters, Evans "produced a great many articles urging limitation of land ownership, woman suffrage, improvement of health through diet [especially vegetarianism] and regular hours, better housing and working conditions for the laboring classes, pacifism, etc." (Melcher, *Shaker Adventure* 278). That Elder Frederick was far from being singular in his efforts to effect various reforms is testified to by an auditor of the Society who collected data from virtually all of the Shaker communities:

> I heard some of the sisters [of **Union Village**, Ohio] say that one mat-
> ter which had occupied their thoughts was the too great monotony of
> their own lives—they desired greater variety, and thought women might
> do some other things besides cooking. One thought it would be an im-
> provement to abolish caps, and let the hair have its natural growth and
> appearance—but I am afraid she might be called a radical. (Nordhoff,
> *Communistic Societies* 204)

The final words of a passage on Evans expressed by two **Shakeress** historians reflect the reverence later members came to hold for him: "He
stood always on a mountain top, calling aloud to his people—Come up
Higher!" (White and Taylor, *Shakerism* 164).

EXERCISE(S). Operations or actions that occur during **Meeting** (worship), such as shaking, dancing, marching, singing, shouting, and walking—all of which are entailed in the Shaker concept of **labor**. After
"about a hundred years had passed," physically vigorous activities were
discontinued, "but members still . . . [contribute] to the service by speaking as each might choose, or in selecting a hymn," as is the current practice at **Sabbathday Lake**, Maine, the last viable **Shaker** village (Frost,
"Prose and Poetry" 75). *See also* DANCES/MARCHES.

-F-

FAMILY. Although the **Shakers** use this word in the literal sense in that
it designates all members of a household under the same roof, they use
it additionally and primarily in the metaphorical sense in that it designates a unit composed of a "**father**" (**elder**), a "**mother**" (**eldress**), and
their "offspring" (sons and daughters), **brothers** and **sisters**:

> The different communities, or *families*, in each society number from 30
> to 150 members, of both sexes, who generally occupy one large unitary
> dwelling-house, in which the brethren and sisters live together in a spiri-
> tual order and social relation, which is the most perfectly represented
> by a house or family where the parents have numerous sons and daugh-
> ters. (Evans et al., *Compendium* 38)

That they use metaphorically these terms of the traditional social unit,
which are undoubtedly familiar to the members, virtually all of whom
having been formerly of "**the world**," suggests to some of their auditors
that the Society's leaders not only have been well aware of the fundamental importance of literal family to human beings but also that they
have been convinced (or are very hopeful, at the least) that a surrogate

for it—a spiritual, gospel family—if administered carefully, could persuade members to strive for **union** with it. In a sense, all Shakers are, of course, just one large family having all things in common and working for the good of the whole while striving for individual spiritual perfection.

The number of members in the various families, the number of families throughout Shakerdom, and the amount of their material wealth all have been much documented. For example, one observer of the Shaker communities in 1874 recorded that

> the Shakers have eighteen societies, scattered over seven states, but each of these societies contains several families; and as each "family" is practically, and for all pecuniary and property ends, a distinct commune, there are in fact fifty-eight Shaker communities, which I have found to be in a more or less prosperous condition. These fifty-eight families contain an aggregate population of 2415 souls, and own real estate amounting to about one hundred thousand acres, of which nearly fifty thousand are in their own farms. (Nordhoff, *Communistic Societies* 117)

Four years later, another observer noted that the number of families was "fifty-seven . . . or fifty-eight if we include the Family of twenty colored persons in Philadelphia." Furthermore,

> these Societies had at one time a population of more than double their present number, reaching an aggregate of between five and six thousand souls. The largest Society is Mount [New] Lebanon [New York], with a membership of about 375. Watervliet, N[ew] Y[ork], Union Village, Ohio, and Pleasant Hill and South Union, K[entuck]y, have each between two and three hundred members. Watervliet, O[hio], Groveland, N[ew] Y[ork], and Shirley, Mass[achusetts], are the smallest, having only about fifty members each. (Hinds, *American Communities* 81)

Records kept by the Shakers themselves at Pleasant Hill, for example, in conjunction with the numbers of the latter quotation above, suggest that the community maintained a consistent number of members for several decades. Under an entry titled "Census of the Society, January 1st, 1850," the West Family, for instance, is said to have 13 brothers, 39 sisters, 6 boys, and 3 girls, and the population of the community is stated as 234 affiliated with the **Church Family**, plus 98 people in the Gathering Order (Harris, *Journal*).

Within each family, divisions of employment exist; for example, "for males, agriculture, horticulture and mechanical pursuits. The raising and preparation of [products] . . . for market." Also, they have been involved much with **inventions** and sundry labor-saving devices. Females, although certainly not exempted from these latter pursuits, perform all household duties of the kitchen and laundry; do most of the tailoring for males and make dresses for females. They carry on some branches of sale business, and aid in gathering, preparing and preserving of fruits and vegetables for market; do a large portion of preparing medicines for market, etc. (Avery, *Sketches* 5, 7)

Lest any "persons hold the erroneous idea that a religious life must necessarily be a sober, serious one, devoid of the amusements and pleasures of ordinary human existence," at least one **Shakeress** (of the **Canterbury**, New Hampshire, community), who "entered the Shaker Society in early youth, . . . found ample outlet for a fun-loving nature." She tells of making popcorn balls and candy, playing music and singing, taking sleigh rides, and playing simple games one evening a week. "Thus, whether engaged in the necessary industries of the home, or in simple recreations, the life of a Shaker was one of contentment, peace, and genuine happiness" (Phelps, "Reminiscences" 55–57).

FANCY GOODS. In Shaker parlance, this term describes:

the small items the sisters made in great numbers from about the time of the Civil War to World War I and beyond. These were largely personal and household accessories, including penwipes . . . and sewing accoutrements; boxes to hold gloves, handkerchiefs, and other items; bureau cushions (decorative cushions to hold hatpins); and fans. Most were made for sale to the "world's people." (Gordon, "Shaker Fancy Goods" 90)

FARRINGTON, RUTH (17?–1821). *A.k.a.: Mother Ruth.* Sister Ruth had been one of the earliest American **Shakers**, and in 1788, she was appointed by Father **Joseph Meacham** to serve as the very first **eldress** of the **Church Order** at **New Lebanon**, New York. Following the **Kentucky Revival**, she was included among a contingent of eastern Shakers sent in the first several decades of the nineteenth century to administrate the colonies of the Shaker southwest. Eldress Ruth arrived at **Union Village**, Ohio, from New Lebanon in 1806 "to assume the arduous duties of First Eldress in the Ministry at the west" (White and Taylor, *Shakerism* 116).

Regarding the application to her of the honorific appellation "Mother," the following comment was made by Elder **Harvey L. Eads**, transcriber of **South Union**, Kentucky, documents:

It is worthy of remark that the title of Father and Mother is the highest conferred on any Believer. Mother Ann being the first, and then on those who came with her [to America]—and Joseph Meacham and Lucy

Wright. After these there seems to be an interregnum, until about the last of the Year 1812 or the first of the present year (1813), [when] this title was conferred on David Darrow and Ruth Farrington. Since which time it is conferred on no others. (Eads, *Shaker Record A* 142)

FATHER DAVID. *See* DAVID DARROW.

FATHER JAMES. *See* JAMES WHITTAKER.

FATHER JOSEPH. *See* JOSEPH MEACHAM.

FATHER WILLIAM. *See* WILLIAM LEE.

FATHER/MOTHER. Bound to the master metaphor of the **Father/Mother Deity**, the Shaker concept of a dual-gendered God, these are the most honorific appellations for the **lead elder** and **lead eldress** of the entire Shaker society:

> It is worthy of remark that the title of Father and Mother is the highest conferred on any Believer. Mother Ann being the first, and then on those who came with her [Father William Lee and Father James Whittaker]— and Joseph Meacham and Lucy Wright. After these there seems to be an interregnum, until about the last of the Year 1812 or the first of the present year (1813), [when] this title was conferred on David Darrow and Ruth Farrington. Since which time it is conferred on no others and the present Ministry of New Lebanon [New York] have decided not to accept it tho urged upon them from various quarters. This decision was made as early as the year 1808. So I learn. (Eads, *Shaker Record A* 142)

Regarding usage of these titles, a visitor to New Lebanon in 1867 made the following comment (possibly after having discussed the matter with Elder **Frederick W. Evans**):

> When her [Mother Lucy Wright's] time had also come [in 1821], she named her successor; for who, unless the chosen, have the right to choose? But she had named an Eldress, not a Mother; and since her day the title of Mother has been abandoned, no female saint having sprung up among them worthy to bear so august a name. (Dixon, *New America* 335)

In her journal of 1847, **Sister Prudence Morrell** alludes to both Father David and Mother Ruth (of **Union Village**, Ohio). Also, she refers to "good Father Issachar [Bates Sr.?]" ("Account" 49). The title "Mother" is not used for Sister **Frances A. Carr**, who as of early 2000 leads the United Society of Shakers.

FATHER/MOTHER DEITY. "Shakers believe in One God—not three male beings in one, but Father and Mother" (White and Taylor, *Shakerism*

255). Apparently rejecting common contemporary thought of God as Father and Son and Holy Ghost/Spirit ("three male beings in one"—the so-called Trinity), the **Shakers** have founded/justified their version of the Christian religion via logic. According to one such "defense," their religion is derived from their interpretation and extrapolation of two verses in Genesis 1 (King James Bible):

26: And God said, Let us make man in our image, after our likeness. . . .
27: So God created man in his *own* image, in the image of God created he him; male and female created he them.

To whom God is speaking (the "us" here)—for example, to the Christ or to the Son or to the "wife" or to Himself, as if musing, or to some other entity—has been no small matter in Christian theology. Among other places, the Shakers' explication of these verses is expressed in the first extensive exposition (and publication) of their religion:

Was it to the Son, the Father spoke, as the divines have long taught? How then came man to be created male and female? *Father* and *Son* are not male and female; but *father* and *mother* are male and female, as likewise are *son* and *daughter*. . . .
    And without this relationship there can exist no order in creation! Without a father and a mother we can have no existence. (Youngs, *Testimony of Christ's Second Appearing* 503–504)

A later nineteenth-century rationalization for a dual-gendered deity might be described as a deduction based on scientific observation:

In the things that are made, or the universe, from inanimate matter up to man, we see the manifestation of two great and fundamental principles, *viz: male and female.* As God is the cause, of which the universe is the effect, and as every effect is like its cause, and the effect is positively male and female, it logically follows that the cause *must* be male and female. Thus it is equally true whether we say that God is male and female, or that an infinite perfection of the male and female principles is God. (Sears, Shakers: *Duality* 3)

From the concept of a male/female deity emanates a primary religious principle of **Shakerism**, one that perhaps most distinguishes it from other Christian sects: not only that in/through the person of **Ann Lee** was the promised second appearance (Parousia) of the **Christ Spirit**, but also that she was (logically and in the interests of gender parity) the female counterpart of Jesus, the male in whom the Christ made Its first appearance—Christ Jesus, Christ Ann: Son and Daughter of Father/Mother God.

    Although the concept of a dual-gendered deity (and, of course, its concomitant **father/mother**, son/daughter, and **brother/sister** units) is not unique to the Shakers, it pervades their thought at every level and is manifested throughout every department of their organization. For example, unless made impossible by uncontrollable local conditions, males and females have shared the responsibilities of governing in every Shaker community (*see* GOVERNMENT/ADMINISTRATION). That is, from the existence of a dual-gendered deity comes logically the alleged equality of the sexes. This parity in social and political condition is manifested ubiquitously in Shaker practices and attitudes:

> To Ann Lee may all reformers among women look as the one who taught and through her followers teaches still perfect freedom, equality and opportunity to woman. The daughters of Ann Lee, alone among women, rejoice in true freedom, not alone from the bondage of man's domination, but freed also from the curse of that desire "to her husband" by which, through the ages, he has ruled over her. (White and Taylor, *Shakerism* 256)

According to Shaker belief, the attributes of "power" and "truth" belong to the masculine gender of God, and "love" and "wisdom" belong to the feminine gender (White and Taylor, *Shakerism* 255), but despite the seeming parity, to the Shakers, the father/male/husband entity apparently is superior to the mother/female/wife entity. For example, before **Joseph Meacham** was sufficiently satisfied with Shakerism to become a member of the sect in 1780, he required that several questions about the Shakers' religion be answered. One of them concerned the right by which a woman governed the sect, "which thing was so diametrically contrary to the doctrine of St. Paul, who even forbid women to teach in the church" (Green, "Biographical Account" 26). *See also* HOLY MOTHER WISDOM.

> Mother Ann responded to the inquiry in the following manner: "Tell him [Meacham] that in the natural state, the man is first in the government of the family; but when the man is absent the government belongs to the woman." By this wise answer, Father Joseph easily caught the beautiful idea, that Christ Jesus in his first appearance, being present, in the body verry [*sic*] properly took the **lead**, but now Jesus being absent from the earth and the real life of Christ exemplified as his second appearance in a woman; it was her right to lead and govern the family, or children of the new creation, which constitutes the true Church of God on earth. He was fully satisfied that Mother Ann was the Bride, *the lambs* [*sic*] *wife*. (Green, "Biographical Account" 26)

FEAST GROUND. *A.k.a.: holy ground, holy hill, chosen ground, sacred ground.* A site for special outdoor religious services (sometimes called "mountain meetings") held once in the spring and once in the fall. Such places were constructed in each community during the period known as **Mother Ann's Second Coming** (1837–1847). For example,

> At Mount Lebanon [New York], by special revelation, instruction was received to establish on the highest peak of the mountain east of the village, a spot called Holy Mount, as a place of worship. . . . The procession to Holy Mount was continued till 1854, when, by spirit direction it was given up. (White and Taylor, *Shakerism* 230, 233)

A **Shaker** traveler to **Union Village**, Ohio, gives the following description of that community's feast ground:

> a beautiful square yard, ten rods each way and shaded with forest trees, ash, oak, & hickory. The fountain . . . [is] in the centre of the yard, just eighteen feet square and over the gate is as follows:
> "Purity, Holiness, and Eternal Truth, I do require of all who enter here to worship Me. Saith the Lord."
> This place is situated about half a mile northeast of the meeting house, a very level and pleasant walk. The name of the place is Jehovah's Chosen Square. (Morrell, "Account" 42–43)

The author of this description also records the kinds of metaphorical and spiritual activities that occurred at the feast ground of Union Village:

> After an anthem was sung we danced a number of quick songs and gathered love from the holy angels. We commenced our march to the chosen square. When we reached the sacred ground, we were informed that there were two pools of living water wherein we might bathe and be clean. After we had bathed, the gate was opened, and the people entered in. We placed ourselves on the south side of the pool. Elder John [Roton] spake a few words exhorting all to be free to labor for the gifts and power of god [*sic*], which will adorn the soul with beauty. We then went forth in the dances of those that make merry, and shook off all pride, lust, self-will, and everything that goes to hinder a free circulation of the pure spirit of Mother. (Morrell, "Account" 56)

FIRST ORDER. *See* CHURCH FAMILY; SENIOR CLASS/ORDER.

FITCH, SAMUEL (17?–?). Among the earliest American **Shakers**, Brother Samuel was one of the **Believers** who accompanied Mother Ann on her missionary tour of Massachusetts and Connecticut that began in May 1781.

FRASER, DANIEL (1812–??). In 1834, this young Scotsman, "endowed with a vigorous, inquiring mind, a deeply religious nature, and of a prompt, practical, mechanical bent . . . [and] an impetus toward reform of social conditions," came to America with the intent of founding his own model community (White and Taylor, *Shakerism* 166–167). Hearing of the **Shakers**, he sought them out and lived the rest of his life in the **New Lebanon**, New York, community, serving as **elder** for a while.

A contemporary of Elder **Frederick W. Evans,** Brother Daniel, was another of the outspoken and much-spoken-of members of the Society, who, during the middle and latter decades of the nineteenth century argued vehemently not only for changes within Shakerdom but also for changes in the society of **the world**, such as prohibition of land monopolies.

FRIENDS OF THE SHAKERS. A benevolent alliance of people of **the world** dedicated to the welfare of the members of the extant **Sabbathday Lake**, Maine, community and to the preservation and restoration of their **village.** The group also is focused on an appreciation of **Shakerism's** contributions to the cultural heritage of the United States. Its activities are delineated in the *Clarion*, its quarterly newsletter.

FROST, MARGUERITE (1892–1971). A latter-day expositor and apologist of the Shaker pilgrimage, **Sister** Marguerite, of the **Canterbury**, New Hampshire, community, rendered more answers to some old questions. For example, she answered "What would happen if all the world became Shakers?" by actually ignoring the question, in effect, by dismissing even the possibility of such an occurrence, for "few will make the effort" to find the "inner Christ." To become a **True Believer**, a **Church Family Shaker**, "one must become a spiritual specialist" (Frost, "Prose and Poetry" 82).

Among other matters, Sister Marguerite also dismissed the idea that the Shakers merely have been "seeking to develop a Utopia" for social betterment. "Something far more important" has been their aim: "to bring about a climate in which souls could become fully developed spiritually." Furthermore, she argued that the principle of **celibacy** was not "the one important factor" in "the diminution of the Shakers"; rather, considering that the Society grew from the original 9 to 6,000 without the assistance of its own practice of sexual intercourse posits that obviously other factors, such as the effects of the Civil War on the communities, were the cause (Frost, "Prose and Poetry" 82).

-G-

GARB. The dress of Society members usually has been "out of fashion"— the fashion of **the world**, that is—but "you may be sure a Shaker will never change his dress for the sake of conforming to fashion; if he changes at all it will be because he has fully satisfied himself that the change will be an improvement" (Hinds, *American Communities* 99–100). Whether an improvement or not, changes in clothing have occurred for whatever reasons. Today, for example, the blue jeans and T-shirt of Brother **Wayne Smith** and the shortened print dress of Sister **June Carpenter**, both of **Sabbathday Lake**, Maine (and both, by the way, with short hair and without head cover), differ remarkably from the attires and appearances of, say, the young Shaker male and female characters in Nathaniel Hawthorne's "The Canterbury Pilgrims," a tale published in 1833:

> They wore a strange, old-fashioned garb. One . . . walked beneath the canopy of a broad-brimmed gray hat; he seemed to have inherited his great-grandsire's square-skirted coat, and a waistcoat that extended its immense flaps to his knees; his brown locks, also, hung down behind, in a mode unknown to our times. By his side was a sweet young damsel, her fair features sheltered by a prim little bonnet, within which appeared the vestal muslin of a cap; her close, long-waisted gown, and indeed her whole attire, might have been worn by a rustic beauty who had faded half a century before. (In *The Snow Image* 145–146)

According to an ex-Shaker who lived at the **Enfield**, Connecticut, village for 15 years, the attire "of all classes" of **Shakers** in the 1840s was standardized (not to mention seeming somewhat elegant):

> Hats drab, crown four and a half inches high, rim from four to five inches in width according to the wearer's breadth of shoulders—the best are of beaver, but fur of the Russia rabbit is mostly used. All woolen garments for winter use, with the exception of pantaloons, shall be of a brownish drab; pantaloons of a reddish brown or claret. Summer vests of light blue; pantaloons, striped blue and white. Females' winter dress, wine colored alapacca, druggett or worsted; capuchins drab; riding cloaks deep blue; caps white muslin, and bordered with lace, not crimpled but smooth and starched stiff; vandyke of the same material; scarf white muslin, or white silk; palm bonnets, of a cylindrical ungula shape, lined with white silk, and furnished with a veil of white lace; shoes, high heeled, similar to those worn by females half a century ago. Summer dress white muslin or very light striped. (Elkins, *Fifteen Years* 29–30)

One piece of shaker attire that has persisted for about two hundred years is the V-shaped piece of material that extends from the shoulders nearly to the waist of a female's dress, thus covering her breasts with another layer of material—therefore, at least speculatively, disguising (from the males, of course) a prominent feature of a woman's procreative nature, not to mention a potential source of sensuality.

GATES, BENJAMIN (18?–?). Elder Benjamin served as **trustee** at the **New Lebanon,** New York, community. Among his greater services to the Society generally was his successful petition, along with **Frederick W. Evans,** to the U.S. government for exemption of the **Shakers** from conscription during the Civil War, making Shakers as a group "conscientious objectors."

Brother Benjamin also served the Society when he was chosen in 1894 by the ministry to head a delegation charged with developing a community "in the more salubrious climate" of **Narcoossee,** Florida (Anderson, "Shaker Community" 31). Shakers were able to make the more than 7,000 acres into an economic success, but they did not attract enough converts to keep the community viable, although it lasted until 1911. Some internal politics of the Society also involved the southern venture. Among other things, it was questioned as being a proper undertaking at a time when resources might have been used to support failing communities. *See also* PACIFISM.

GATHERING/IN-GATHERING. In Shaker usage, this term—no matter what its grammatical form—means, refers to, or designates new members or **novitiates,** as in, for example, "the Society had a large in-gathering in conjunction with the Kentucky Revival" and "People interested in joining the Society first became members of the Gathering Order" (the latter an alternate term for "**Novitiate Order**").

GATHERING ORDER. *See* NOVITIATE.

GENDER PARITY. The Shaker sect always has been composed of both genders. Indeed, its foremost belief, with far-reaching ramifications for **Shakerism** in general, is that God is both male and female—**Heavenly Father** and **Holy Mother Wisdom.** Shaker theologians have employed this duality repeatedly to explain or justify their belief that the **Christ Spirit** logically made Its second appearance in/through a female, having first come in/through a male (Jesus), thus positing that the genders are equally significant.

Regarding the roles of the sexes in the practice of Shakerism, the **Church Covenant** provides for an equal distribution of **government/administration** duties among males and females. As such, two of each gender are to serve as the **Lead Ministry** when such personnel are available, and all levels of duties are to be so composed (except **trustee**).

However, the severe and rapid decline in the number of male **Shakers** after the Civil War pressed more and more **Shakeresses** into duties without male counterparts. Hence, from the late nineteenth century throughout most of the twentieth century, Shaker leadership has been primarily the province of females. The last Lead Ministry, for example, located at **Canterbury**, New Hampshire, was composed solely of **sisters** (*see* BROTHER/SISTER). Today, if Sister **Frances A. Carr** is not the sole **lead** of the community at **Sabbathday Lake**, Maine, she at least shares the position.

In the daily routine of a **village**, work generally is portioned somewhat equally between the sexes, but no one has ever been required to attempt tasks that he/she is incapable of completing, either physically or mentally. This has generated some so-called men's work and women's work—although jobs have been alleged to rotate when available personnel allow the practice. Generally, males do the "heavy" work, such as that involved in much of the farming, and the females do the "light" jobs, often done indoors, such as cooking, ironing, and weaving.

Although Ann Lee was succeeded successively by three males, **Joseph Meacham**, the third of them, appointed **Lucy Wright** to share leadership with him—to be "the first leading character in the female line." To her especially is attributed the development not only of the character of Shaker sisters but also of much of the gender parity they experience in their daily lives. Since she alone led the Society for 25 years after the death of Meacham, she held male parity at the top level of administration in abeyance.

Today, study of the female's role in the Shaker system overshadows study of the male's. Among the major works on this topic are those by D'Ann Campbell, Lawrence Foster, Louis Kern, Marjorie Procter-Smith, Jean Humez, Beverly Gordon, and Karen and Pamela Nickless.

GIFT. A talent, aptitude, or endowment bestowed upon **Shakers** by their divine parents, the **Heavenly Father** and **Holy Mother Wisdom**. Although Shakers use the word "gift" often in their writings, the following quotation is a rare instance of their delineation of its proper employment in Shaker contexts:

> It may be well to explain an expression that often recurs in Shaker history, "receiving a gift." New thoughts or suggestions, new plans or exercises are recognized as coming from the Heavenly, Spiritual Church. From the Church in the Heavens come the blessings, the guidance, the love, the help needed in the Church on earth. Love sends its blessings through a thousands hands, but to the beloved children, working out by

patient efforts their redemption, all comes through the Order of Anointed Leaders and the pretty, grateful, expressive term, "a gift," holds in its very sound acknowledgement and gratitude for whatever the Divine Father-Mother may appoint. (White and Taylor, *Shakerism* 110)

Complementing the above general definition is this more specific example of a Shaker's actual employment of the term:

Elder Ashbel had just returned from a visit to Union Village, heard of his [fellow Shakers] illness, went in to see him, and when he saw how he was, his mouth and extremities cold, . . . spoke to him and said, "Pomeroy! Live!" "I will live!" said Pomeroy. ["]There is no gift for you to die,["] said Elder Ashbel. . . . Pomeroy *did* live, and is alive yet, soul and body. . . . This was more than forty years ago, from the time this was written, 1870. . . . Here was a remarkable case of a healing gift, in the exercise of the "will power" combined with that of faith in God, in the cure of physical disease. (Prescott, *History of North Union* 32)

Although the Shakers have experienced such gifts throughout their history, during the era known as **Mother Ann's Second Coming** (1837 to about 1847), they received a singular plethora and variety of them. Besides having visions of "the beautiful treasures of the spirit land" and learning "several beautiful forms of exercise . . . [such as the] Winding March, Lively Line, Changeable Dance, Double Square, [and] Mother's Star." Shakers at **Canterbury**, New Hampshire, for example, beginning in 1839, were the recipients of various other forms of inspiration:

It now became the privilege of the visionists and no less of the impressionists, to dispense . . . simple gifts to others in the family. It was, indeed, a pleasant manifestation, and in some respects, a very childish affair. . . . Among these simple presentations for spiritual benefit, were pens and ink, and paper; baskets of fruit, knives, forks and spoons . . . a precious gem, or a jewel, or a gold chain, [the latter of which, fortunately,] belonged to the spiritual kingdom, as no well-disciplined Shaker, would for a moment adorn himself with either gems or jewels. . . . In 1840, another phase of inspiration was brought forward . . . the mediums began to write messages, as dictated by some spirit, through whom they were in harmony. . . . Some of the mediums not only wrote messages, but also wrote books of several hundred pages, which have been valuable for instruction, for reproof, for exhortation. (Blinn, *Manifestation of Spiritualism* 31–33, 35)

In Shaker terminology, gifts are manifested by some manner of "outward operations"—that is, for example, by shaking and dancing and singing, often carried on with great zeal and vigor. According to a Shaker **apostate** (who alleges—despite his obvious sarcasm—that he is telling the truth, of course), the so-called whirling gift, for example, was part of the ritual of the Shaker **Meeting** during the period of Mother Ann's Second Coming. It took the following form when he observed it:

> The young sisters continue their turning so swiftly, that the air gathering under their garments, raises them so as to expose their red petticoats, and other under clothes, and even the fastening of their hose, and sometimes when their clothes happen to brush against a sister near them, it exposes their persons even more. But they must not be checked in their gifts, for it is by inspiration of God, that all these things are done. They often fall prostrate upon the floor, and all animation seems lost for a season. (Lamson, *Two Years' Experience* 87)

"The term 'gift,' so common in Shaker usage . . . had its origin in the scriptures. 'There are diversities of gifts,' wrote Paul to the Corinthians—miracles, prophecy, discerning of spirits, unknown tongues, 'diversities of operations'—but 'the same spirit . . . the same God which worketh all in all.'" (Andrews, *Gift to Be Simple* 8). *See also* BATES, PAULINA; STEWART, PHILEMON.

GOODRICH, DANIEL (17?–18?). Among the first American **Shakers,** Elder Daniel, son of a Baptist deacon, converted to **Shakerism** in 1779, about five years after **Ann Lee** had arrived in New York. The **Hancock,** Massachusetts, **village** was founded on the farm that Goodrich had consecrated to the Society. As part of his service to the community, he designed and helped build the unique and very efficient round stone barn of the **Church Family**, a notable departure in architecture from the straight lines and 90-degree angles of typical Shaker structures.

Also, among other services to the Society, Brother Daniel accompanied Elder **Calvin Green** and other **Believers** in 1809 "on a tour of ministration through the eastern societies . . . teaching **Believers** the manner of communicating to the world . . . truths from God" (White and Taylor, *Shakerism* 112).

GORHAM, MAINE (1808–1819). Located between **Alfred**, to the south, and **Sabbathday Lake**, to the north, Gorham was one of the shortest-lived communities in New England and the first one of them to close. One **family** constituted the initial **gathering**. Apparently, it was composed of the members of North House (or the Gathering Order) of the Alfred community, which "did all it could to sustain this small but earnest band of Believers" (Barker, "History of 'Holy Land'" 32). "Although very prosperous and in a beautiful situation, after some years it was removed to Poland Hill [Maine] and became the Gathering Order for New

Gloucester" (White and Taylor, *Shakerism* 95). Indeed, when the community was closed, the members were moved to New Gloucester, now named Sabbathday Lake.

GOSPEL ORDER. *See* ORDER.

GOVERNMENT/ADMINISTRATION. Because the leaders of the United Society of Shakers have alleged from the very beginning of the sect to govern by divine sanction, **Shakerism** is a theocratic institution.

> The order, form and manner of government established in this community, originated *in*, and was first instituted *by*, the founders of the society. Those who first declared the faith and principles of the Society, were readily received and acknowledged by all who believed and embraced the testimony, as the agents of a government which had emanated from Divine Wisdom. These, therefore, agreeable to the examples recorded in the scriptures concerning the government of Israel, and the primitive Church, appointed their successors, subject to the confirmation, support and general approbation of the Society. And this has been the manner of supplying and supporting the government of the Society, in a regular line of succession, to this day. (Green and Wells, *Summary View* 8–9)

With the advent of institutional Shakerism, a pattern developed for governing the **villages.** a ministry, usually composed of two members of each gender, was appointed by the **Lead Ministry**, also composed of two members of each gender. (For most of Shaker history, the Lead Ministry was located at **New Lebanon**, New York.) Each village itself then was divided into **family** units. Each such unit was virtually self-controlled and virtually self-sufficient. Each family was governed also, whenever possible, at every level (except **trustee)** by an equal number of males and females. At the head of each family were the spiritual and temporal **leads**, composed of **elders** and **eldresses** who were appointed to their positions by the leads of the community. Two members of each gender were appointed to these primary positions whenever such personnel were available. In turn, lead elders and eldresses appointed **brothers** and **sisters** to manage the various domestic activities of the family, such as the farm. These people were designated as **deacons** and **deaconesses**, and, again, whenever the personnel were available, two of each gender were usually appointed. Today, at **Sabbathday Lake**, the only viable community remaining, governance of the community of seven members seems to be less formal, but divisions of labor certainly exist. Brother **Wayne Smith**, for example, minds the farm animals. Moreover, since a Lead Ministry no longer exists to make appointments, how exactly the acknowledged leaders of the community, Sister **Frances A. Carr** and Brother **Arnold Hadd**, achieved their position is a matter of surmise. Regardless, none of the other members seems to gainsay the roles of Carr and Hadd.

Perceptions of the Shaker governmental system have differed, of course. For example, Shaker **apostate Hervey Elkins** makes the following analogy about the management of the **Enfield**, New Hampshire, community that he knew personally:

> The Shaker government [composed of the ministry, elders, trustees, and deacons], in many points, resembles that of the military. All shall look for counsel and guidance to those immediately before them, and shall receive nothing from, nor make application for any thing to those but their immediate advisers. For instance: No elder in either of the subordinate bishoprics can make application for any amendment, any innovation, any introduction of a new system, of however trivial a nature, to the ministry of the first bishopric; but he may desire and ask of his own ministry, and, if his proposal meet with concurrence, they will seek its sanction of those next higher. (Elkins, *Fifteen Years* 21)

Thus, from the top down—beginning with the **Heavenly Father**—leaders, the ministers of God, choose leaders; common **Shakers** are obliged only to consent to choices made for them and to exercise the utmost **obedience** to leaders.

In general, the charge of the government is for it to address itself "to man's moral and affectional nature" (refer to appendix B, The Covenant or Constitution of the Church at Hancock):

> All power and authority under it grow out of the mutual faith, love, and confidence of all its members. . . . The Ministry, who are the central executive of the whole order, consists of two brethren and two sisters, and every regularly organized community or family in a society has two *elder* brethren and two *elder* sisters, who have the charge of the *spiritual* affairs; also, two deacons and two deaconesses, who have the care of the *temporalities*. All other positions of care and trust are filled after the same *dual* order [except that of **trustee**]. (Evans et al., *Compendium* 44, 54)

GREEN, CALVIN (1780–1869). One of the very few "cradle" **Shakers**, so to speak, for his mother was converted to **Shakerism** by Mother Ann several months before his birth, Elder Calvin (named after early American Shaker **Calvin Harlow**) lived his entire long life among the **Believers** and became "one of the most important figures in the development of Believers' life and thought during the first half of the nineteenth century" (in Green, "Biographical Account" 20). Among his contributions to the Society were his preaching, his missionary work, and his help in founding the **Savoy**, Massachusetts, and **Sodus Bay**, New York, communities.

Perhaps Green's greatest contribution was his writing. For one thing, he was (along with **Seth Youngs Wells**) a major expositor of Shaker **theology**, as manifested by, for example, *A Summary View of the Millennial Church* (1823), "offered to the public" in an effort to reconcile "various and contradictory accounts," to correct "false and erroneous statements concerning the principles of the [Shakers]," and "to afford the candid and unprejudiced of all classes a fair opportunity of examining for themselves, and obtaining a correct knowledge of, the truth from the proper source" (iii). After a slight history of Christianity, Green begins his exposition of Shakerism with the following statement: "About the year 1770 . . . by a special manifestation of Divine light, the present testimony of salvation and eternal life was fully revealed to *Ann Lee*, . . . the distinguished personage to whom Christ revealed himself in his true character, in this day of his second coming" (11). (Note that the author does not say that Lee *is* the Christ—that any Shaker ever did allege such to be the case is one of those "false and erroneous statements" addressed in the work.)

Another genre of writing that Green left for the edification of posterity was his histories/biographies. Even a cursory examination of histories of the Society by non-Shakers reveals, via quotations, that Elder Green has been a very significant source of information. Besides his own "Biographic Memoir" (still in manuscript form only), his biographies of significant Shakers he knew personally, such as **Joseph Meacham** and **Lucy Wright**, are virtually invaluable.

GREEN, MINNIE (1910–?). One of the three extant (as of 1999) **Shakeresses** (*see* SHAKER/SHAKERESS)—along with **Frances A. Carr** and **Marie Burgess**—to have signed the **Church Covenant** before it was closed in 1965 by the **Lead Ministry** at **Canterbury**, New Hampshire, Sister Minnie, of the community at **Sabbathday Lake** in New Gloucester, Maine, resides in a nursing home.

GROVELAND, New York (1836–1895). *Spiritual name: Union Branch.* A continuation of the **Sodus Bay**, New York, community, sold to the Sodus Canal Company, Groveland (situated in an area sometimes called "Sonyea") was located in Livingston County, about 4 miles south of

Mount Morris and 37 miles from Rochester. "The number of members including children, averaged about 125 from 1837 to 1858, dropped below 100 in 1860" (Wisbey, *Sodus* 25). In 1875, it had "two families, with fifty-seven members in all. . . . Of the adults, thirty [were] . . . females and eighteen males" (Nordhoff, *Communistic Societies* 198).

> In Groveland, as in Sodus, the economic basis of the community was agriculture. The seed routes were maintained and expanded as a significant source of income. The Shakers' grist mill and saw mill were important to the economic support of the community. (Wisbey, *Sodus* 25)

> They own a home farm of two thousand acres, and [an] out-lying farm of two hundred and eighty acres, mostly good land, and very well placed, a canal and two railroads running through their home farm. . . . The women make fancy articles for sale. They also keep fine cattle, and sell a good deal of high-priced stock. . . . They employ eight hired laborers.

> [Although] one of the families is in debt, through an imprudent purchase of land made by a trustee . . . and have suffered severely from fires and by a flood . . . the society seems now [1875] to be prosperous; its buildings are in excellent order. (Nordhoff, *Communistic Societies* 198–199)

In 1894, the property was sold to the state of New York, which has used it for various state institutions—a prison, for example. All the remaining members of the last successfully established community relocated to **Watervliet**, New York, the Society's first community in America. As of 1982, "Two brick buildings, a few frame buildings, and the old burying ground are the only tangible evidence of the Shaker occupation" (Wisbey, *Sodus* 27).

-H-

HADD, ARNOLD (1957–). Along with Brother **Wayne Smith**, Brother Arnold is among the extant male **Shakers** residing in the community at **Sabbathday Lake**, New Gloucester, Maine. Both brothers were admitted to membership in the community after the closing of the membership rolls in 1965 by the **Lead Ministry**, located at **Canterbury**, New Hampshire. Among them, Brother Arnold was the first admitted.

Having made himself a scholar, writer, and public speaker of things Shaker, Brother Arnold continually has assumed, apparently with the approval and encouragement of the current "boss" of the community (and, hence, of Shakerism), Sister/Eldress **Frances A. Carr**, a larger role as spokesperson and apologist for the Society, a position not occupied "officially" by a male since the death of **Theodore E. Johnson** (the first "new" **brother**) in 1986.

HANCOCK, MASSACHUSETTS (1790–1960). *Spiritual name: City of Peace.* The third longest-lived Shaker community, Hancock was in the county of Berkshire and was located about three miles southeast of **New Lebanon**, New York, and about five miles west of Pittsfield, Massachusetts. In 1790, along with the society at **Enfield**, Connecticut (and **Tyringham** in 1792), it was gathered by Father **Joseph Meacham** "into the Second Bishopric (the First, or Mother's, Bishopric consisting of Watervliet and New Lebanon [both in New York]" (Burns, *Shaker Cities* 35). In the estimate of one auditor, it had between 200 and 300 members in the 1850s (Evans et al., *Compendium* 36). In the surprisingly terse estimate of another auditor, otherwise rather talkative, Hancock in 1875 was "small, and [had] . . . no noticeable features" (which was all this author had to say about the **village**) (Nordhoff, *Communistic Societies* 195).

"As the nineteenth century swept like a torrent into the twentieth, the Shaker communities had to struggle to stay afloat" (Burns, *Shaker Cities* 169). Apparently, Hancock, too, among other problems, paid the price of owning more land than it could properly manage: "in the East, small communities of a dozen or so Shakers, mostly women, paid hefty on vast properties and either watched the farms slide into neglect or paid hired laborers to maintain them" (Burns, *Shaker Cities* 168).

According to Marguerite Fellows Melcher, who produced the first scholarly attempt by a non-Shaker to render a comprehensive view of the Shaker pilgrimage in America, Hancock, one of the four villages still viable in 1940, had a gift shop "where small Shaker-made articles such as pincushions, sewing-boxes, baskets, etc. [i.e., "**fancy work**"] . . . [were] sold, as well as maple sugar and candy. Some of its farm lands . . . [were] still being cultivated, but with the [then-ubiquitous] hired labor" (Melcher, *Shaker Adventure* 262–263).

Fortunately for posterity, non-Shaker citizens were successful in their attempt to preserve a significant part of the heritage of the United States, for on June 29, 1960, the **Shakers** agreed to sell the Hancock property to the nonprofit Hancock Shaker Village Steering Committee, dedicated to creating a museum of the village, which it indeed did. The 170-year history of the Shakers at Hancock ended on October 14, 1960.

HARLOW, CALVIN (1753–1795). A New England **New Light** and associate of **Joseph Meacham,** Harlow was among the first American **Shakers.** Impressed by **Ann Lee** when he visited her at Niskayuna, New York, Brother Calvin joined the Society in 1780 (as did Meacham). He was regarded as an excellent itinerate preacher and attended Mother Ann on her missionary tour eastward during 1781–1783 (and received his share of physical abuse by persecutors).

When Mother Ann died in September 1784, Harlow was among the **elders** who acknowledged **James Whittaker** as her successor. After the death of Whittaker in 1787, which left Harlow, **David Meacham,** and Joseph Meacham as the main leaders of the Society, Elders Calvin and David both supported Joseph Meacham as the new **lead,** thus making him the first in the long line of Americans to lead the **Believers.**

In 1790, Father Joseph appointed Elder Calvin to be First Elder (synonymous with "Lead Elder") in the **Hancock,** Massachusetts, Ministry. He was to assist the **in-gathering** for the Hancock and **Tyringham,** Massachusetts, and **Enfield,** Connecticut, communities, which were combined into a **bishopric.** His death at the age of 42 and the resultant loss of his leadership were not borne easily by the organization, especially because it had lost several principal members in the previous decade through death. It also was to lose the architect of institutional **Shakerism,** Joseph Meacham, in the same way in 1796.

HARVARD, MASSACHUSETTS (1791–1918). *Spiritual Name: Lovely Vineyard.* In 1823, Harvard, located in the county of Worcester, about 30 miles northwest of Boston, had about 200 members. According to an auditor in 1875,

> It now has four families, containing in all ninety persons, of whom sixteen are children and youth under twenty-one—four boys and twelve girls. Of the seventy-four adults members . . . fifty-seven [are] women. The Church Family has fifty members, of whom forty-one are women and girls. . . . It is usual among the Shakers to find more women than men in a society or family, but at Harvard the disproportion of the sexes is uncommonly great. (Nordhoff, *Communistic Societies* 191–192)

In the estimate of a twentieth-century historian,

> The Harvard Shakers occupy a place unique in the development of the Order—not that the village was the place of origin . . . nor the first organized, but because it was the community which was first in Mother Ann's heart, and where she probably spent more time [during 1781–1783] than at any other place (with the possible exception of her own

home). It was the spot where she and her followers endured more violence than at any other community. (Horgan, *Shaker Holyland* xvii)

The Harvard **Shakers** (as well as all other Shakers, of course) were constantly harassed because of "their consistent refusal to uphold war." In 1840, the community (along with the one at **Shirley**) was "the apparent target of some secret persecutor, who, under the cover of a Petition to the Legislature [of Massachusetts], aimed to overthrow by legal compulsion" the Shakers' refusal to support war in any way. "The Petition called for legislative action requiring all citizens to pay an equal proportion of military tax, either in service or money." In presenting their case to the state legislature in Boston, Shakers issued an article stating that all of them in the state who were entitled to a Revolutionary War pension made no claim to the money—calculated to be about $97,000. Legislators were overwhelmingly impressed by the Shakers' "detestation of the war spirit . . . [and principle] 'that neither the honor, fame, gold nor silver that is to gained by shedding human blood has ever stained Christ's holy banner of peace on earth, good will to men' " (White and Taylor, *Shakerism* 175–177). The petition of the clandestine persecutor was denied.

In 1918—10 years after the closing of its sister community, Shirley—Harvard suffered the seemingly inevitable fate of Shaker communities. "Daily life among Shakers . . . during the period of retrenchment and decline . . . was far from grim," but the 12 women remaining in the community were unable to keep it viable and, thus, were forced to relocate when the deed to transfer the 600 acres and the buildings was signed by the Central Ministry on April 15, 1918. After 136 years, the "Shaker Holy Land [Harvard and Shirley] was bereft of members: all that remained were buildings, fields, woodland, and graves" (Horgan, *Shaker Holyland* 138, 153).

HASKELL, RUSSELL (18?–18?). Identified mainly with Shaker music, Brother Russell, of **Enfield**, Connecticut, along with Brother **Isaac N. Youngs**, of **New Lebanon**, New York, "developed and perfected the [Shaker] system of letter notation" of music based on the letters A through G (White and Taylor, *Shakerism* 337). His *Musical Expositor* (1847) details the system.

HASKETT, WILLIAM J. (17??–18??). Among the several **apostates** who chronicled their experiences with the **Shakers**, along with their estimates of the Society, Brother William, once a covenanted member of the **New Lebanon**, New York, community, and obviously very knowledgeable about **Shakerism,** contributed significantly to the edification of posterity by publishing 300 pages of material in 1828 that "unmasks" Shakerism. For example, during his exposition of the **Backsliding Order**, Haskett insinuates that **elders** he knew actually were devious because they exposed newcomers only to "the exterior beauty of the Society and the apparent harmony of its members" while withholding "the severity of its discipline from them" (Haskett, *Shakerism Unmasked* 152, 153).

HEALTH. The general good physical constitution of the **Shakers**, at least as measured by their longevity, has been much noticed by **the world**, as in the following remarks made in 1867 and 1878, respectively: "The Shakers, who have no doctors among them, . . . smile at our Gentile ailments—headaches, fevers, colds, and what not" (Dixon, *New America* 308); "the Shakers are especially long-lived even for Communists. Their eightieth year is often reached, and some live far past the ninetieth" (Hinds, *American Communities* 104).

Shakers themselves have been well aware and mindful (not to mention proud) of their health, as illustrated by the following excerpts:

> A mortality rate study made by Brother Micajah Burnett in 1846, confirmed that rigorous daily chores were not detrimental to . . . health. He assumed the village's average yearly census to be conservatively 300, and then calculated that only 1.4% died annually and their life expectancy was 71, almost twice the national average. (Thomas and Thomas, *Simple Spirit* 12)
>
> The food, though it is very good of its kind, and very well cooked, is simple; being wholly, or almost wholly, produce of the earth; tomatoes, roast apples, peaches, potatoes, squash, hominy, boiled corn, and the like. The grapes are excellent . . . and the eggs, hard eggs, boiled eggs, scrambled eggs, are delicious. The drink is water, milk, and tea. Then we have pies, tarts, candies, dried fruits and syrups. . . . "Good food and sweet air," says [Elder] Frederick [Evans], "are our only medicines. . . . Is it not strange," says he, "that you wise people of the world [non-Shakers] keep a set of men [doctors], who lie in wait for you until by some mistake of habit you fall sick, and who then come in, and poison you with drugs?" How can I [author W. Hepworth Dixon] reply to him, except by a laugh? (Dixon, *New America* 312)

Since the Shakers developed a thriving commercial herbal medicine business, perhaps Elder Evans was not reporting the whole truth here. Besides rigorous exercise, nutritious food, and unpolluted air, **celibacy** has been considered an additional factor in the good health of Shakers: "As to celibacy, he [Elder **Frederick W. Evans**] asserted in the most positive manner that it is healthful, and tends to prolong life; 'as we are constantly proving'" (Nordhoff, *Communistic Societies* 159–160).

HEAVENLY FATHER. This is the appellation for the male attribute of the dual-gendered deity of the **Shakers**. Consonant with the Judeo-Christian tradition, the Shakers' God is the Almighty—omnipotent and omniscient. In Shaker **theology**, although God has a feminine attribute, which is in **union** with the male, the male is ultimately dominant. He is the "husband" of the feminine attribute, which is Itself His helper in creating but, unlike Him, is identified with wisdom rather than power. The Heavenly Father is also the "father" of the **Christ Spirit**, incarnated in both Jesus and **Ann Lee**. *See also* FATHER/MOTHER DEITY; HOLY MOTHER WISDOM.

HOCKNELL, JOHN (1723–1799). Designated in **Frederick W. Evans** et al.'s *Compendium* as one of the six founders of the Shaker Society— along with **Ann Lee**, **William Lee**, **James Whittaker**, **Joseph Meacham**, and **Lucy Wright**—Brother John was the principal benefactor of Ann Lee's small group, the "moneyed man of the Society" (Webber, *Escape to Utopia* 46). In England, as a member of the religious society of **James** and **Jane Wardley**, he gave economic support to the poor members. Regarding America, Brother John not only was one of the original **Shakers** to immigrate in 1774, but he also financed the voyage from England and the tract of land called "Niskayuna," in New York, where the Shakers first gathered into a community in September 1776. Besides monetary support, "Elder Hocknell was remarkable for meekness of disposition and for special gifts in vision and the power of healing" (White and Taylor, *Shakerism* 71).

HOCKNELL, RICHARD (17?–?). Son of **John Hocknell** and one of the original **Shakers** who immigrated to America in 1774, Brother Richard seceded from the Society when **James Whittaker** assumed leadership of it following the death of **Ann Lee** in September 1784 (Filley, *Recapturing Wisdom's Valley* 13). He has been alleged to have married **Nancy Lee**, another of Mother Ann's original companions from England (Garrett, *Spiritual Possession* 218).

HOLLISTER, ALONZO GILES (1831–1911). Besides being a pharmacist and involved in the Shaker medicine venture at **New Lebanon**, Brother Alonzo was a prolific writer and editor of, among other things, materials supporting Shaker traditions—during the time and at the place where changes in the Society were vigorously advocated by Elder

Frederick W. Evans, for example. Hollister's greatest contribution to **Shakerism** and posterity is most likely his "preservation of many priceless heirlooms of the old time Shakers" (White and Taylor, *Shakerism* 337). He was "keenly aware of the changes and the decline that had taken place in the Society during his lifetime. Under these circumstances he seem to have felt the need to preserve records of the Society as it had been in its prime" (Sasson, *Shaker Spiritual Narrative* 86–87).

HOLY GROUND. *See* CANTERBURY, NEW HAMPSHIRE; FEAST GROUND.

HOLY LAND. *See* ALFRED, MAINE.

HOLY MOTHER WISDOM. A spiritual personage who began to appear to the **Shakers** via **instruments** (or mediums) during the period called "**Mother Ann's Second Coming**," beginning in 1837 and lasting until about 1847. Holy Mother Wisdom—not to be confused with **Ann Lee**, Her "daughter"—is the female side of the Shakers' concept of a dual-gendered deity: "The ancient language of Scripture distinguishes God when power or truth are emphasized as masculine; when love or wisdom is the important attribute, the masculine name has the feminine complement (White and Taylor, *Shakerism* 255).

An early expression of the feminine attribute is contained in Hymn 1, "The Testimony of eternal Truth," in *Millennial Praises* (Wells, 1812), the first published collection of Shaker gospel hymns:

> Long ere this fleeting world began
> Or dust was fashion'd into man,
> There *Power* and *Wisdom* we can view,
> Names of the *Everlasting Two*.

> The Father's high eternal throne
> Was never filled by one alone:
> There Wisdom holds the Mother's seat
> And is the Father's helper-meet.
> This vast creation was not made
> Without the fruitful Mother's aid.

That the Father is mentioned first, that the throne is the Father's, and that the Mother is the Father's "helper" seem to imply that She is subordinate to Him, which, if true, conflicts somewhat with the Shakers' claim of fostering gender parity—"that equality of the sexes [is] a cardinal principle" (Frost, "Prose and Poetry" 75). *See also* FATHER/MOTHER DEITY; HEAVENLY FATHER.

HOLY MOUNT. *See* NEW LEBANON, NEW YORK.

HOLY SINAI PLAIN. *See* PLEASANT HILL, KENTUCKY.

HOUSTON, MATTHEW (1764–1848). Brother Matthew was among the Presbyterian ministers who became **New Lights** and who were instrumental in starting the so-called **Kentucky Revival** around about 1800. He came under the influence of Shaker missionaries **Issachar Bates Sr**, **John Meacham**, and **Benjamin S. Youngs** and converted to **Shakerism** in 1806 at Paint Lick, Kentucky, where he was holding his congregation. Along with **Richard McNemar**, **John Dunlavy**, and **John Rankin Sr.**, other notable New Lights who converted to Shakerism, Houston became an itinerate preacher of the Shaker gospel. He helped in **gathering** the **Pleasant Hill** and **South Union**, Kentucky, societies in particular.

A man with a classical education, Houston had, in the estimate of two Shaker historians, "superior mental endowments" and was a "great and good man" (White and Taylor, *Shakerism* 125), although he had been a slaveholder prior to his conversion to Shakerism.

HUDSON, ETHEL (1896–1992). The last **Shaker** to occupy the **Canterbury**, New Hampshire, **village**, **Sister** Ethel died on September 7.

-I-

INDENTURE. "Ever since the Society was established," the **Shakers** have considered it "a matter of the first importance that children . . . should be trained . . . in the principles of virtue and morality, and be formed to habits of industry and good conduct while young"; hence, they have had "from time to time, many children . . . urged upon . . .[them] by poor parents [and guardians] who are not of . . . [the Shaker] community, as well as those who are." The general plea of these adults has been "that they believe their children will be better taken care of, and more morally brought up among . . . [Shakers] than any where else" (Wells, "Plain Statement" 1–2).

Motivated always by benevolence regarding children, the Shakers thus have signed contracts—indentures—with adults that bind children in their charge to the care of the Shakers. In the agreement, although "the name of one of the **Deacons** or **Trustees** of the Society is usually inserted in the Indentures and is the person to whom . . . [the child] is indented" and because such administrators have the care of temporal matters, among which is the duty "to see that the Indentures are justly and equitably fulfilled," the actual governing and teaching and disciplining of children are assigned to other adults (Wells, "Plain Statement" 3).

INDUSTRIES. Despite its withdrawal into somewhat isolated and self-sustaining communities, the United Society of Believers in Christ's Second Appearing ironically has not been adverse to commerce with **the world** (which has contributed much to the eventual economic difficulties of the Society, for, among other matters, it lost much of the membership capable of carrying on successful capitalistic ventures). For example, during much of the nineteenth century, "for their major source of income, most Shaker societies specialized in just one or a few garden products to grow in large quantities"; they turned surplus into cash crops, thus generating money to buy what they could not supply for themselves (Buchanan, *Shaker Herb and Garden Book* 16). Even today, the **Sabbathday Lake**, Maine, community still maintains a gift shop open to the public and a mail-order business for sundry items, such as candies, books, and posters. The community also conducts an annual Shaker Christmas Fair—offering items such as Shaker herbs, Shaker-related books, candies, breads, cakes, Shaker-made pickles, cider, and crafts products (primarily not Shaker made).

Not surprisingly, the Society's greatest participation in capitalistic economy occurred prior to the Civil War, when its talented membership, workforce, and economic creativity were at their apex. Among the many business ventures of the **Shakers** have been broom making (especially the flat broom, invented by a Shaker), dried corn (with a kiln invented by a Shaker), the hugely successful seed manufacture (started around 1800 and prospering "until in all parts of the country the Shaker Seed wagon and the shrewd, honest, sedate but kindly Shaker Brother, who sold the seeds, were familiar as the springtime"), botanical medicines (such as a wintergreen throat medication), cloth manufacture (e.g., wool and silk), clothing (notably the woman's wrap called the "Shaker cloak"), wooden products (such as chairs, tables, buckets, and the ever-famous oval boxes), maple sugar products, milk products, exportation of livestock, and sundry produce (White and Taylor, *Shakerism* 314–318).

IN-GATHERING. *See* GATHERING.

INSPIRATIONAL DRAWING. *A.k.a.: gift drawing; spirit drawing.* Despite an injunction by Shaker leaders against owning, creating, and displaying pictorial and decorative objects, graphic and usually rather abstract representations of signs, figures, and objects alleged to be those of the spirit world were one of various types of **gifts** received by **Shakers** most prolifically during the decade known as "**Mother Ann's Second Coming**" (approximately 1837–1847). As recorded by a Shaker,

> Another feature of this nearness of the Other World was the receiving of spiritual drawings. These were pen and ink drawings largely of scrolls with symbolic trees, birds, musical instruments, altars and stars, with intricate borders that look like some ancient language—perhaps Sanskrit. When a sensitive felt the Spirit call him or her, he withdrew to where he could be alone, lived on a meager diet, and kept in the spirit of prayer that he might be a channel of the spirit. (Frost, "Prose and Poetry" 79)

The following generalization about these drawings is just one of several written by non-Shakers:

> They were full of forbidden, worldly, and probably longed-for ornaments, quaint symbols, and small cramped verses and blessings in neat spidery script.
>
> Drawn with joyful flourishes, though not abandon, were wings of freedom, swords of power, trumpets of wisdom, crowns of glory, doves of love, birds of paradise, tempered by cups of humility. Colors like red, ordinarily considered immodest, were used. (Morse, *Story of the Shakers* 41)

Another general but quite different description of these inspired drawings is as follows:

> These inspirational drawings are primitive in the sense given the word today [1962]. They tend to be linear in execution and resolved in flat pattern, simple color combinations, and frequently incorporate supporting text in the design. The technique is explained by the fact that they were not done by artists, as such, but by highly skilled penmen who had an intense respect for order in all things and who had a brand new vision with no artistic precedent. (Sellin, "Shaker Inspirational Drawings" 93)

One of the most published inspired drawings is *The Tree of Life* (said by Flo Morse, among others, to be a symbol of **Shakerism**). It was created between July 3 and October 1, 1854, by Sister Hannah Cohoon of the **Hancock**, Massachusetts, community. It has been described in the following impressionistic manner:

> The bright red and green spheres [14 of them]—the fruit—vibrate as the viewer glances from one to another while the movement of the branches and the fluttering of the checked leaves refuse to allow the eye to rest.

Cohoon has successfully created "the illusion that her tree rustles with a living spirit." (Stein, *Shaker Experience* 192)

Today, *The Tree of Life* serves as the logo of Shakertown at Pleasant Hill, Inc., in Harrodsburg, Kentucky.

INSTRUMENT. Communications and associations with the spirit world via intercessors "'have ever been the inheritance of the Christian Church; to this, the Shaker branch has not been an exception.' . . . **Ann Lee's** child life, [for example,] was full of vision and spirit teaching" (White and Taylor, *Shakerism* 219–221).

Regarding this phenomenon of **Shakers** functioning as intermediaries, chroniclers often dwell particularly upon a singular period: for about 10 years beginning in 1837—the period dubbed variously as "**Mother Ann's Second Coming**," "Mother Ann's Work," and "Mother's Work"— spirit communications were remarkably profuse. Although some auditors of the Society's history might question why such workings have existed at all and especially in superabundance during this era, Shakers themselves have testified to their validity and described the "outward operations," which are the apparent manifestations of their existence.

> I have, myself, seen males, but more frequently females, in a superinduced condition, apparently unconscious of earthly things and declaring in the name of departed spirits, important, and convincing revelations. . . . I have the most unequivocal evidences . . . that the declarations of those inspired beings were true—astoundingly true and superhuman. (Elkins, *Fifteen Years* 34–35)
>
> In 1838, the media began to speak in unknown languages, sometimes the loss of speech altogether is recorded. . . . Some could be sent into a trance at a moment's notice. The visionist would be sent on an errand to Mother Ann saying that the Elders wanted advice or counsel, perhaps, though without specifying for what. Immediately, the answer would come through the lips of the entranced, always to the point and what was needed. In one society, forty members were at one time thus ready for service at a moment's warning. (White and Taylor, *Shakerism* 227)

This remarkable era came to a close in 1847, when the "spirits took their departure" from the Shakers to "go out into the world. They would visit every city and hamlet, every palace and cottage in the land, and then they would return . . . to the . . . [Shakers]" (White and Taylor, *Shakerism* 238, 237). *See also* TRANCE-GOER; VISIONIST.

INVENTIONS. "One of the greatest paradoxes of Shakerism was that, not only was it a deep and intensely spiritual movement, but that its driving force was to appear to such a vigorous degree in the application of the practical" (Williams, *Consecrated Ingenuity* 1). That **Shakerism** is a total lifestyle rather than merely a portion of one (and that **the world** is richer for it) is manifested clearly by the results of the Shakers' principle that the "consecrated brain can work out an easier method" of performing labor. "A heart at peace, a conscience clear and [a] sense bright with the joy of holy living," along with "Shaker wit and wisdom," have produced a very long list of labor-saving inventions—not to mention improvements to existing devices—that have been incorporated into the world's way of doing things. Furthermore, "Nearly all of their valuable inventions have been unpatented. To the Shaker, patent money savors of monopoly. . . . Whatever he invents is for the use of the whole world" (White and Taylor, *Shakerism* 310).

The following list suggests the range of items produced through the "consecrated ingenuity" of the **Shakers**: a screw propeller, a soft metal called "Babbitt metal," a window sash balance, a governor for an overshot waterwheel, a board planer, a board tongue-and-groove machine, the circular saw, cut nails, a fertilizing machine, an "industrial" washing machine, the one-horse wagon, an apple parer, the metal writing pen (nib), the clothespin, the flat broom, and a lathe for turning broom handles (White and Taylor, *Shakerism* 311–314). Some of their inventions have been patented, among them a truss for hernias; a harvesting machine; a folding stereoscope; a tipping device for chairs; machines for stripping seed from broomcorn and for dumping wagons; the churn; a pea sheller; a wind wheel; and improvements to the washing machine, the fly-trap, the waterwheel, the mop-heads, and the land-leveller (Richmond, *Shaker Literature* I, 168–170).

IRELAND, SHADRACH (17?–?). Only incidentally related to the Shaker pilgrimage, Ireland was a New England **New Light** who fancied himself immortal and resurrectional. His residence—the so-called **Square House** in Harvard, Massachusetts—served as the headquarters of **Ann Lee** during much of her missionary trip in 1781–1783. As has been the case several times in Shaker history, many of the people of the Harvard area, too, who had been followers of mortal Ireland were left without spiritual leadership. Thus, Mother Ann had a vulnerable audience to which to minister the Shaker gospel. The **Harvard village** was established in 1791.

-J-

JACKSON, REBECCA COX (1795–1871). Although the **Shakers,** as a matter of principle, historically did not participate in the politics of **the world**, at least not directly, they were abolitionists and, thus, not adverse to receiving as members non-Anglos with political problems, such as runaway slaves. Also, of course, they admitted to the Society so-called free Negroes. Of these, Rebecca, a black free woman much given to spiritualism, visions, and dreams, was unquestionably the most notable, if for no other reasons than that she became a Shaker **eldress** (*see* ELDER/ELDRESS) and founded a community for people of her race in Philadelphia, Pennsylvania.

While a member of a small religious group called "Perfectionists," located in the Albany, New York, area, she became acquainted with the **Watervliet** Shakers in 1842–1843 and "was among the sixteen Perfectionists . . . who ultimately became Shakers." Rebecca became attracted to the Shakers because, among other things, "Believers struck her as the living embodiment of Christian perfection . . . which she herself had been pursuing since the early 1830s" (Humez, *Gifts of Power* 25, 26). She began residence at Watervliet in 1847. However, apparently at odds with elders about the validity and importance of fulfilling her own private sacred mission to take the Shaker gospel to "her own people," she left the **village** in 1851 to begin developing a community for African-American Shaker converts in Philadelphia, an endeavor about which she had had a vision but a mission, nevertheless, that was unauthorized by the Shaker leadership, possibly because, among other reasons, Rebecca's venture would be difficult for them to supervise and also probably would require her frequent contact with the world—something not permitted to members, except for business matters deemed necessary, since the founding of institutional **Shakerism** in 1787.

Following her pursuit of her own **gift** for several years, Rebecca returned to Watervliet in 1857. After her **confession of sin** and her acceptance of both **obedience** to the elders and the cardinal principles of Shakerism, her missionary work in Philadelphia was approved and supported by the Shaker leadership:

> "Now, Rebecca, you may go to your people and do them all the good you can. Now you can go in the gift of God, and the gift of the Ministry and Elders. Now you are endowed with power and authority. Now the Lord hath sent you. You have waited for the Lord, and you go un-

der a blessing. All that you bless, we bless—and whoever sets out to you, and honestly confesses sins, we own and bless, and receive into our Society—and we will withhold no good thing from you or your people" (Eldress Paulina Bates, quoted by Rebecca).

So I [Rebecca] left my peaceful home in Wisdom's Valley [Watervliet], Friday, October 8, 1858, and returned to Philadelphia . . . Saturday evening, April 30, 1859. I held my first solemn meeting. We went forth and worshiped God in the dance. . . . And we were noticed by our Heavenly Parents. (Quoted in Humez, *Gifts of Power* 277, 280)

JASPER VALLEY. *See* SOUTH UNION, KENTUCKY.

JOHNSON, MOSES (1752–1842). Brother Moses, who entered the Society in 1782 at **Enfield**, New Hampshire, but disappeared from Shaker records around 1795, is most notable for his design and construction of Shaker buildings, most especially **Meeting houses**. "As the first Shaker builder whose work can be documented, Johnson may be said to have formed the style of Shaker architecture" (Peladeau, "Shaker Meeting Houses" 594).

Between 1785 (when he began building the Meeting house at **New Lebanon**, New York) and 1794 (when he finished building the Meeting houses at **Sabbathday Lake** and **Alfred**, Maine), Brother Moses created 10 such houses in the New England communities. "They were all about the same size [approximately 44 × 32 feet] and style, with [English-style] gambrel roofs, dormer windows, two entrance doors in front for the brethren [left door] and sisters, and end doors leading to the ministry's 'apartments' on the second floor" (Andrews, *A Shaker Meeting House* 3). The Meeting House at Sabbathday Lake, built with boards, cut nails, and bricks fashioned by the **Shakers** themselves, remains largely in its original condition and is a testimony to Brother Johnson's skill. Its clapboard siding painted white, large single shutters, and blue interior trim are typical of such structures. The Shakers still use it regularly for **Meeting**, the public often being invited.

JOHNSON, THEODORE E. (1931–1986). Johnson will be identified perhaps forever with the political rift between the **Shakers** of **Canterbury**, New Hampshire, and those of **Sabbathday Lake**, Maine. With the death in 1961 of Brother **Delmar Wilson**, the last covenanted Shaker male, and the closing of the membership rolls of the Society in 1965 by the Canterbury **Lead Ministry**, no non-Shaker male had an "official" means by which to become a bona fide member of the organization, for a would-be male Shaker now could not partake in the traditional **confession of sin** to a male; therefore, he could not formally join the Society. However, at Sabbathday Lake, "Brother" Ted began to evolve, so to speak, much to the aggravation of Shakers who supported the Lead Ministry's decision. Since his apparent inclusion in the Sabbathday Lake membership, two other males have been added to that community: **Arnold Hadd** and **Wayne Smith.**

Apart from his role in the controversy among the Shakers, Brother Ted was a well-educated scholar, writer, and public speaker. To say that he was a latter-day apologist for **Shakerism**, along with his contemporaries Sisters **Mildred Barker** and **Frances A. Carr**, would not be an error, as evidenced by his publications and lectures regarding it. Johnson also served the Society as director of the valuable Shaker Library and as editor of and contributor to the *Shaker Quarterly*, begun in 1961—the first Shaker-produced journal since 1899, when the *Manifesto* ceased (*see* LITERATURE).

JOINT INTEREST. *See* UNITED INTEREST.

JUNIOR CLASS/ORDER. Unlike the class/order of **novitiate** members in Shaker communities, this class consists of people unencumbered by natural family and any other conditions that would prohibit their coming into **union** with a community **family.** However, although Junior Class members may choose to allow their Shaker family to use their property for the "mutual benefit of the family to which they belong, . . . [they] may retain the lawful ownership of all their own property" and resume its possession at any time—without claiming any interest for its having been used, that is (Evans et al., *Compendium* 48–49).

-K-

KENDAL, HANNAH (17??–??). One of the early American **Believers** and one of **Ann Lee's** companions on part of her missionary trip eastward from 1781 to 1783, Eldress Hannah was among the first **sisters** (*see* BROTHER/SISTER) to be appointed a position in the male/female dual leadership system initiated by Father **Joseph Meacham** when he named **Lucy Wright** first in the female line to co-lead the Society. In 1791, Sister Hannah was also among the first **Shakers** sent by the Ministry of **New Lebanon**, New York (in what was very likely a means of securing control of the various newly forming societies), to help the **in-gathering** (*see* GATHERING/IN-GATHERING) at **Harvard** and **Shirley**, Massachusetts. Furthermore, she was the first female in the ministry of the Harvard/Shirley **bishopric**.

KENTUCKY REVIVAL (BOOK). *See* LITERATURE.

KENTUCKY REVIVAL (EVENT). "One of the most remarkable religious revivals ever recorded" occurred in Ohio, Kentucky, and Tennessee during the late eighteenth and early nineteenth centuries (Melcher, *Shaker Adventure* 57). It was even more serendipitous to the Shaker cause than was the earlier revival in the east from which the Society garnered the great **Joseph Meacham**, among others.

Without question, the history of the event and the most graphic accounts of its revival meetings (at which as many as 20,000 people attended) have been rendered by **Richard McNemar**, a former Presbyterian preacher turned **New Light** revivalist at the time, a participant at and "the principal mover" of the events, and, eventually, a **Shaker**, along with many of his congregation (MacLean, *Sketch* 15). The following is an example of the kind of activity that **Brother** Richard recorded:

> No circumstance at . . . [the] meeting appeared more striking, than the great numbers that fell on the third night; and to prevent their being trodden under foot by the multitude, they were collected together and laid out in order, on two squares of the meeting-house; which, like so many dead corpses, covered a considerable part of the floor. (McNemar, *Kentucky Revival* 24)

Regarding the Shakers themselves, who "received repeated intelligence of this work through the public papers" (Evans et al., *Compendium* 30), their direct connection to the event occurred when

> there arrived at Turtle Creek [Ohio, later the cite of the **Union Village** community, on], May 22, 1805, three men. . . . They came from Mt. Lebanon, N[ew] Y[ork], having traversed on foot a distance of 1233 miles. They were Issachar Bates, Benjamin S. Youngs and John Meacham. Their mission was to establish Shakerism in the West. (MacLean, *Sketches* 21)

Starting with the conversion of **Malcolm Worley**, who had been much involved in the revival and to whose house the three Shaker emissaries "were spiritually led" (Evans et al., *Compendium* 31), the men were so successful in spreading the Shaker gospel that their efforts eventually resulted in the establishment of seven Shaker communities—four in Ohio, two in Kentucky, and one in Indiana, three of which remained viable into the twentieth century. One Shaker chronicle of 1859 alleges that the combined population of the six new *villages* (omitting **West Union**, defunct by 1827) was between 1,700 and 1,900 (Evans et al., *Compendium* 32–33).

KING, EMMA B. (18?–19?). To the author of the most recent attempt by a non-Shaker to render a comprehensive description of the Shaker pilgrimage and to state his estimate of it, Eldress Emma was "the most significant member of the central ministry in this [the twentieth] century" because she "made a number of critical decisions that shaped the subsequent fortunes of the society" (Stein, *Shaker Experience* 365).

An **eldress** (*see* ELDER/ELDRESS) at **Canterbury**, New Hampshire, since 1913, Sister Emma was selected to serve in the Central **Lead Ministry** in 1946. At this time, only the **New Lebanon**, New York, community (the traditional site of this ministry) and those at Canterbury, **Hancock** (Massachusetts), and **Sabbathday Lake** (New Gloucester, Maine) were viable. Regarding highly significant decisions, King participated in the one to close New Lebanon in 1947 (thus ending its position as the traditional center of Shakerdom). In 1959, having risen to the **lead** of the ministry (now located at Hancock), King established the **Shaker Central Trust Fund** for, among other things, the future care of the remaining few and aging **Believers.** In 1965, Eldress Emma, along with Eldress **Gertrude Soule**—contrary to nearly 200 years of Shaker tradition of "open enrollment" for people who accepted the Shaker gospel—ended acceptance of new members into the Society. In effect, its institutional life would end with the death of the last member.

However, despite the orders of the Canterbury Lead Ministry, the Sabbathday Lake community has never ceased admitting new Believers. The rift between the two remaining communities ended with the death of the remaining Canterbury **Shakers.** Now, since only Sabbathday Lake Shakers exist, they can do as they please. *See also* CONFESSION OF SIN; THEODORE E. JOHNSON.

-L-

LABOR/LABORING. This term, whatever its grammatical form, denotes specific Shaker actions. To "labor down," for example, is to engage in "peculiar movements" and **exercises**, taught through revelation to Father **Joseph Meacham**, "which he gave to the people" (White and Taylor,

Shakerism 101). Through physical actions such as shaking, whirling, clapping, dancing, and marching, common **Shakers** as well as **elders** seek "spiritual assistance"; thus, they "labor," for example, for **gifts** they can share—a new song or a personal improvement, such as acquiring humility: " 'Labor to become little, and put away the great *I* and little *you*' " (Quoted in Sears, *Gleanings* 198).

Becoming quite formalized in the nineteenth century (and much commented on by **the world**, which attended public **Meetings**), the marching and dancing exercises, for example, were not merely frivolous entertainment for the visitors: "The march step indicated going on in the Way of God, the dances expressed joy in the Lord and the self discipline needed to perform the steps acceptably" (Frost, "Prose and Poetry" 75). *See also* OPERATIONS.

LAMSON, DAVID RICH (1806–1886). Much interested in social reform, Lamson, along with his wife and their two children, took up residence among the **Shakers** in 1843 at the **Hancock**, Massachusetts, community, after "having heard much of the Shakers, both good and bad, and hoping the good was true, and bad false" (Lamson, *Two Years' Experience* 21). With **Mother Ann's Second Coming** at its height, Lamson encountered, among other things, what to him were so many absurdities of behavior regarding so-called **gifts** and deceit by **elders** that he left the community after two years and in 1848 published at his own expense his exposition and estimate of the Society, ostensibly so that other people of **the world** interested in the Shakers as he once had been would not have to endure the "costly and vexatious way of obtaining knowledge of Shakerism" that he had suffered (Lamson, *Two Years' Experience* 5). Despite inaccuracies in his text (such as omission of **Richard Hocknell** from the group who came to America with **Ann Lee**), Lamson's *Two Years' Experience among the Shakers* has provided posterity with a perspective on the Shakers by an obviously intelligent person who lived among them during one of their more fantastic eras.

LEAD. Both the singular and collective noun form for the administrators or ministry of each Shaker community. Each **bishopric**, such as **Harvard/Shirley**, had a lead composed of two **elders** and two **eldresses**. The lead of leads is identified as the **Lead Ministry**.

LEAD MINISTRY. This is the supreme spiritual and temporal governing unit of the entire Shaker organization. It usually is composed of two **elders** and two **eldresses**. From the beginning of the formal organization of communities in 1787, **New Lebanon**, New York, was the seat of the

Lead Ministry until that **village** closed in 1947. The Lead Ministry then was moved to **Hancock**, Massachusetts, and when that community as well became defunct in 1960, the Lead Ministry was relocated to **Canterbury**, New Hampshire. Today, no traditional Lead Ministry exists because only one community exists, thus negating the need for a collective governing body. **Sabbathday Lake** is therefore guided primarily by one person, Sister **Frances A. Carr**; she is not addressed as "Eldress" but she functions as one. In the last several years, Brother **Arnold Hadd** has assumed an increasing number of leadership responsibilities and activities. For example, he often travels with Sister Frances as her cospokesperson for things Shaker.

LEE, ANN (1736–1784). *Alt. sp.: Lees. A.k.a.: Mother Ann.* The founder of **Shakerism** in America. Virtually the whole early history of the sect is contained in her biography, which has been constructed by many **Shaker** and non-Shaker historians (e.g., Green and Wells, *Testimonies*; Stein, *Shaker Experience*). Most scholarship and information directly from Shakers concur that Ann Lee was born on February 29, 1736. One of eight children, a daughter of an impoverished blacksmith, she grew up among the unfortunate of Manchester, one of England's manufacturing towns during the Industrial Revolution. She received no formal schooling because her lot and that of her siblings was to work in order to add to the meager income of her family. Ann Lee's lifelong illiteracy, especially her inability to create her own verbal compositions, has been damaging to historiography because it has forced posterity to rely only on other people for information about her (much as it has had to do with the life of Jesus).

Presupposing her adult role as a religious leader was that even in her childhood she is alleged to have had a plethora of religious experiences and tribulations of soul about her own iniquity, which eventually caused some family and friends to regard her as somewhat of a monomaniac on religion. As she matured in the squalid environment into which she was born, she became increasingly depressed by the great depravity of people "and of the odiousness of sin, especially the impure and indecent nature of sexual coition for mere gratification" (Evans et al., *Compendium* 122). She openly expressed her repugnance to the matrimonial alliance, but she married nevertheless—possibly because of the importunities of her family, who might have believed that marriage would end the "drifting" of Ann's mind. She and **Abraham Stanley**, also a blacksmith, generated four children, all of whom died in infancy or very early childhood.

Still convinced of her own depravity (maybe even more so as a result of the deaths of her children), she continually sought deliverance from her sins:

> I labored anights in the work of God. Sometimes I labored all night, continually crying to God for my own redemption; sometimes I went to bed and slept; but in the morning I could not feel that sense of the work of God which I had before I slept. This brought me into great tribulation. Then I cried to God and promised Him that if He would give me the same sense that I had before I slept, I would labor all night. This I did many night; and in the day time I put my hands to work and my heart to God. . . . In my travail and tribulation my sufferings were so great that my flesh consumed upon my bones, bloody sweat pressed through the pores of my skin and I became as helpless as an infant. (Quoted in White and Taylor, *Shakerism* 16–17)

During her twenty-third year, Ann became acquainted with the religious society conducted by **James Wardley**, formerly a Quaker, and his wife, **Jane**. The Wardleys, so-called spiritualists, part of the "new" religions developing throughout Europe, were regarded by their followers as having "a greater degree of divine light, and a more clear and pointed testimony against sin than had hitherto been made manifest . . . [so] Ann readily embraced their testimony" in September 1758 (Green and Wells, *Testimonies* 3). In line with the practices of the group, she made open confession to its leaders of every sin she had committed and took up a **cross** against everything she regarded as evil.

Despite her soon becoming a prominent member of the group by virtue of her confessions, tribulations, and visions, Ann's mental struggles continued; she suffered from dearth of rest and proper diet, but she did have periods during which her body gained strength and her mind filled with visions of heaven and revelations, which she communicated to the small society. She especially continued to rue her ignorance of two related and extremely important matters that had occupied her mind for years: What was the origin of mankind's depravity, and by what means could people gain redemption? She believed that without such knowledge, she could never save her soul. In the summer of 1770, she received the answers to both questions. While in prison for allegedly profaning the Sabbath with singing, dancing, and shaking (thus the appellation **"Shaking Quakers"**), practices that were not embraced by the official state church of England and apparently offensive to some of the townsfolk of Manchester and its vicinity, she had a divine vision that humankind's initial iniquity—the source of man's original sin, the cause of humanity's fall from uprightness and loss of purity—lay in its self-indulgent use of sexual union. She saw that Adam and Eve had engaged in sexual intercourse not as a natural function for the divinely directed purpose of propagation but only for carnal gratification. Therefore, they had committed the primary transgression.

From what was to become the Shaker perspective, the extent of the depravity generated by the pursuit of sensual pleasure was summarized 134 years later by **Shakeresses Anna White** and **Leila S. Taylor**, who declared that "Lust destroyed pure, heaven-born Love, and the whole creation groaneth and travaileth together in sin, passion and despair. War, brutality and crime resulted" (White and Taylor, *Shakerism* 281). For Ann and all others wishing to recover from their portion of humanity's fallen state, taking up a cross against sexual gratifications via **celibacy** was the logical means of redemption.

Convinced that God had especially enlightened Ann, the other members of the Wardley society henceforth acknowledged her as the visible leader of the church of God upon earth. Because she was regarded as the vessel of the true **Christ Spirit** by those who received her **testimony**, Parousia, also known as the Second Coming of the **Millennium**, was believed by them to have begun. She is alleged to have had such a profound effect upon those witnessing her testimony—filling them with visions of heaven and revelations and power over their own sins—that they acknowledged her as their spiritual **mother** (*see* FATHER/ MOTHER) in Christ, hence the derivation of the epithet "Mother Ann," applied to her by all subsequent followers.

In the adverse, her strong testimony against all sin, along with the so-called **operations** of the Spirit of God (e.g., "shaking") that prevailed at the meetings of her little society, attracted enough public attention and created enough malignant feelings that she had to suffer several more imprisonments and threats to her life by officials of the government, by mobs, and by individuals. Once, for example, as Shakers have alleged, she was the intended victim of a plot by prison officers to kill her by starvation. After her final imprisonment, again the result of an alleged plot to indict her and her small society for supposedly profaning the Sabbath by their unorthodox practices during worship, her opposers apparently concluded that they were not going to quell her testimony, for she and her small band of worshippers were left to enjoy their faith in peace for the remaining two years before Mother Ann and her small contingent of **Believers** took their gospel to America. In the spring of 1774, Ann Lee is said to have received a divine revelation directing her to repair to America; also that the second Christian Church would be established in America; that the Colonies would gain their independence; and that liberty of conscience would be secured to all people, whereby they would be able to worship God without hinderance or molestation. (Evans et al., *Compendium* 23)

The pilgrimage in America that came to be known as "Shakerism" had a humble commencement. On May 19, 1774, nine people embarked at Liverpool, England, on an old, leaky ship named *Mariah*. After enduring the storms and dangers of the sea in a vessel condemned as unfit for the voyage, they arrived at the harbor of New York colony on August 6. For a little over two years, Ann Lee was, as were most of the other immigrants of her group, busy securing food and lodging for herself and helping to make a home for the group at Niskayuna (later **Watervliet**), New York, about seven miles northwest of Albany. During this period, she also separated from her husband, who thereafter apparently never pursued any interest in Shakerism. Along with the other Believers, she moved to Niskayuna in September 1776, thus establishing it as the first Shaker settlement in America (not to be confused with **New Lebanon**, usually regarded as the first formally organized Shaker community, founded in 1787, three years after the death of Ann Lee). In Niskayuna,

they remained in seclusion till the spring [May 10] of 1780, when in consequence of religious awakenings in various places, particularly in the vicinity of New-Lebanon, [they held their first meeting open to the public, and] they were discovered and visited by numbers who embraced their faith and testimony. (Green and Wells, *Brief Exposition* 22)

Also during this time, as a result of the "addition to their number," they were "discovered" by colonial patriots: "opposition and persecution were excited; and, as the [R]evolutionary [W]ar was then in progress, some designing men accused them of being *unfriendly to the patriotic cause*, from the fact of their bearing a testimony against *war in general*" (Evans et al., *Compendium* 141–142). As a consequence, in July, the **elders** and leaders of the Society were imprisoned at Albany. Ann Lee was separated from the others and "was conveyed down the river, with the intention of banishing her to the British army"; however, she was jailed only at Poughkeepsie. After a six-month confinement, she and the other Believers were released by Governor Clinton in December of the same year, "without any trial" and "without any cause, except their religious faith" (Evans et al., *Compendium* 142–143). However, suspicion of the Shakers' alliance with the British continued throughout the war.

Undaunted by the imprisonment, Mother Ann persevered in her public testimony. In May 1781, she began a missionary journey through Massachusetts and Connecticut that lasted until September 4, 1783. That some Shaker chroniclers have very highly regarded the significance of the journey is evidenced, for example, by **Calvin Green** and **Seth Youngs Wells**, whose *Testimonies of the Life, Character, Revelation, and Doctrines of Mother Ann Lee* devotes nearly 100 pages to the mission. Not only did the journey add numbers to the Shaker faith, but also it became immensely valuable to posterity because the testimonies of the witnesses to it are among the most plentiful sources of information about Ann Lee and her gospel in America. Shakers first published these testimonies in 1816 and then released several revised editions throughout the nineteenth century.

Mother Ann has been reported to have left Niskayuna with **William Lee**, **James Whittaker**, **Samuel Fitch**, **Mary Partington**, and Margaret Leland. As usual, "the spirit of opposition manifested itself, more or less, wherever she went":

> Persecution, the usual engine of religious intolerance, was immediately set in motion; and no means were left untried to arrest the progress of the testimony. Every evil report and every wicked device, that falsehood and malice could dictate, were called forth to calumniate and debase the character of Mother Ann and her companions, and render them odious in the eyes of the people, with a view to excite them to acts of persecution. The charges of being enemies and traitors to the country; of having fire arms and munitions of war concealed among them; of living in drunkenness and debauchery, and practicing witchcraft and other base crimes, were continually alleged against them. . . . [Shakers] were scourged with whips, beaten with clubs, stoned, kicked and dragged about by their legs and arms, and sometimes by the hair of their heads. (Green and Wells, *Summary View* 27)

In the estimate of Shaker chroniclers, these persecutions, as did the imprisonment of the Shakers at Albany in 1780, "served only to accelerate the means of extending the testimony, which greatly increased the number of believers" (Green and Wells, *Summary View* 28). In each case, the treatment of the Believers was witnessed by people both sympathetic to them and appalled by the ironic treatment of them by colonists who were themselves struggling to realize their own civil and religious rights.

Despite the great adversity she encountered, Mother Ann, from her base at the so-named "**Square House**" in Harvard, Massachusetts, traveled extensively throughout that state and Connecticut, teaching new

Believers "how to bear their crosses, how to overcome their evil propensities, and gain a final victory over the nature of evil in their own souls" (Green and Wells, *Testimonies* 28–29). For an inexplicable reason, but maybe because her forbearance of persecution was exhausted, Mother Ann turned toward New York in July 1783 and arrived back at Watervliet at 11:00 p.m., on September 4, "beaten and bruised, black and blue" (Green and Wells, *Testimonies* 153). Then,

> after the death of her brother William the following July, Ann Lee continually grew weaker in body, without any visible appearance of bodily disease, till on the 8th of September, 1784, between twelve and one o'clock in the morning, when she breathed her last, without a struggle, or a groan. . . . A little before she expired, she said, "I see Brother William, coming in a golden chariot, to take me home." (Green and Wells, *Testimonies* 274)

Much concern and speculation about the fate of the Society attended the death of Mother Ann:

> it was generally and confidentially believed by the world around them [the Shakers], that the society would be dissolved, and the people return to their former course of life; so that (as they often expressed themselves) "the delusion would soon be at an end." (Green and Wells, *Summary View* 30)

However, through the leadership of James Whittaker, "evidently called . . . of God . . . to be Mother Ann's successor" (Green and Wells, *Testimonies* 278), as well as through the unifying efforts of elders such as **Joseph Meacham**, **Calvin Harlow**, and **John Hocknell**, the little United Society of Believers in Christ's Second Appearing not only survived the death of its founder and the subsequent initial apostasies of disheartened members, but it also began an increase in membership that continued well into the nineteenth century.

With the death of Ann Lee, the initial and very constructive phase of the Shaker pilgrimage in America ended. Although four of the original Believers remained, all three of the dynamic leaders were dead. Nevertheless, Shakerism had become known in much of New England, and it had had sufficient "increase" to warrant continuance. The work of making it an American institution fell to the Americans.

Shakers' descriptions and estimates of Mother Ann Lee's person, character, and significance are laudatory. Regarding Mother Ann's person, the Shakers have perpetuated the following description:

> In her personal appearance . . . [she] was a woman rather below the common stature of woman; thick set, but straight and otherwise well pro-

portioned and regular in form and features. Her complexion was light and fair, and her eyes were blue, but grave and solemn. Her natural constitution was sound, strong and healthy. Her manners were plain, simple and easy; yet she possessed a certain dignity of appearance that inspired confidence and commanded respect. By many of the world, who saw her without prejudice, she was called beautiful; and to her faithful children, she appeared to possess a degree of dignified beauty and heavenly love, which they had never before discovered among mortals. (Green and Wells, *Summary View* 31–32)

Furthermore, according to Shaker authors, "though our blessed Mother Ann was a woman of few words, yet her soul was filled with divine wisdom" (Green and Wells, *Testimonies* 242).

Some of Mother Ann's sayings, philosophy, advice, and the like, have achieved the status of proverb, a linguistic honor of sorts. Among the more commonly known of her utterances are the following ones:

When speaking to John Deming, Sr., distressed over his economic problems, Mother Ann said, "put you hands to work and you heart to God," and while describing to followers her own tribulations of the spirit when she was in England, she said, "I put my hands to work, and my heart to God."

To a young man seeking advice on planting peaches and plums, Mother said, "do all your work as though you had a thousand years to live, and as you would if you knew you must die tomorrow."

In replying to a colonial general who wanted Shakers to be soldiers, Mother said, "You never will kill the devil with a sword."

When Talmadge Bishop was ready to return home, he was concerned about what he should say to his neighbors about the Shakers, about whom they were alarmed. "Tell them," Mother replied, "that we are the people who turn the world up side down."

After an accusation that she was a witch, Mother Ann said, "There is no witchcraft but sin."

Mother's insistence on cleanliness is epitomized in her comment to Lucy Bishop, who was scrubbing a room: "There is no dirt in heaven." (Green and Wells, *Testimonies* 29, 36, 242–243, 247, 250, 208)

Although Ann Lee had detractors aplenty, as witnessed by continual persecutions, people other than Shakers themselves believe that this humble and unlettered woman contributed significantly and positively to the cultural heritage of the United States—and to that of humanity, many would say. No less laudatory are many of the interpretations and judgments of Ann Lee by various recounters of **the world** of her pilgrimage. For example:

> Whatever may have been the limitations in the strange personality and simple teachings of Ann Lee, it is certain that her testimony attracted . . . men and women of personality, intelligence, and virtue. . . . [I]t is difficult to believe such people could have been deluded followers of a false prophet. (Andrews, *People Called Shakers* 238–239)

LEE, NANCY (17?–?). *Alt. sp.: Lees.* The niece of **Ann Lee** who immigrated to America with her in 1774. Her role in the development of early **Shakerism** is rather obscure. In Shaker-produced chronicles, she is virtually unmentioned except for her name. She has been reported to have left the Society and married **Richard Hocknell**, a fellow Shaker immigrant (Garrett, *Spirit Possession* 18).

LEE, WILLIAM (1740–1784). *Alt. sp.: Lees. A.k.a.: Father William.* Although given little attention by some non-Shaker chroniclers, William is designated by other Shaker historians as one of the six founders of the sect, along with **Ann Lee, James Whittaker, John Hocknell, Joseph Meacham**, and **Lucy Wright**. He was the biological younger brother of Mother Ann and was one of the original **Shakers** who immigrated to America with her in 1774. By trade, he was a blacksmith. Unlike his sister Ann, he was not inclined to religion as a child or young adult. Rather, "he was a proud, haughty young man, fond of gayety, and was able to dress himself in silks" (Green and Wells, *Testimonies* 261). Perhaps because of his acquaintance with Ann's religious convictions, William began to be troubled about the manner by which he was conducting his own life. Eventually, during a conversation with her about himself, she severely castigated him, as was her wont in matters of sin. He "immediately threw off his ruffles and silks, and put his hands to work and his heart to God" (Green and Wells, *Testimonies* 261) and forever became to his sister a devoted follower and "an invaluable assistant and protector; the scars from wounds he received in her defence he carried to his grave" (Evans et al., *Compendium* 157).

In America, William's reputed great strength of body and spirit was much tested during the persecutions of the Shakers while they were engaged in their missionary work in Massachusetts and Connecticut in 1781–1783. Undaunted by threats and brute force, he remained ever faithful to the Shaker gospel. Although some Shaker historians record that he did not seem to die of a natural infirmity "but seemed to give up his life in suffering" (Green and Wells, *Testimonies* 266), the beatings he endured on the journey have raised questions about the cause of his death. For example, one non-Shaker historian recounts that when William's body was disinterred and reburied beside that of Ann at **Watervliet**, "it was found that his skull had been badly fractured" (Melcher, *Shaker Adventure* 41)—on the missionary trip or during a persecution in England?

Along with his mercy, kindness, and charity, among other traits William is said to have had was his **gift** to suffer—that is, to empathize with the tribulations of other **Believers**. Thus, even though he did not often preach in public, "he was eminently useful in teaching, encouraging and strengthening the believers under all their trials and difficulties" (Green and Wells, *Summary View* 47). His "violent" condemnation of all sin led him to admonish Believers as severely as Ann had rebuked him in England. For example, he once said to Shakers about to eat,

> I feel you are not so thankful as you ought to be, for the good things that God provides for you; but you will eat and drink of these precious things, and not consider from whence they come. The sin of ingratitude is a great sin; see that you are not guilty of it." (Quoted in Green and Wells, *Testimonies* 264–265)

William died on July 21 at the age of 44. His death was a great deprivation to his sister, who died just a few weeks later, also from unspecified causes. The epithets "Elder" and "Father," as well as no epithet at all, have been applied to William by Shakers themselves. Whether the use of "Elder," as in Green and Wells's *Summary View*, as opposed to the employment of "Father," as in Green and Wells's *Testimonies*, has any significance is enigmatic, for in the Shaker system, "Father" (and "Mother") is a more honorific appellation than is "Elder."

LINDSAY, BERTHA (1897[?]–1990). Eldress Bertha was the last member of the Shaker Ministry. Her death at **Canterbury**, New Hampshire, the last seat of the **Lead Ministry**, ended the existence of the office that had controlled Shakerdom for about 200 years, from the time of **Joseph Meacham**, who created the entity and served as its first lead.

LITERATURE (A BRIEF CHRONOLOGY OF SHAKER PUBLICATIONS). The **Shakers** seem to have produced virtually no writings prior to the establishment of institutional **Shakerism** in the late eighteenth century. Around that time, however, they started to become prolific writers of various kinds of documents, such as journals of daily **family** affairs, treatises on Shaker **theology**, **songs/poems**, rules for proper conduct by Shakers, **testimonies**, and personal narratives. Much of this material, especially journals kept by family scribes, is still in manuscript form, but copies of some of it can be obtained for little or no cost via, for example, interlibrary loan services.

Regarding materials published—by the Shakers themselves, by non-Shaker private enterprises solicited by them, and by news media—from 1790 until the present day, the Shakers have dwelt upon compositions regarding their history and faith. Among other things, they seem never to tire of explaining and defending themselves, as in *A Summary View of the Millennial Church* (Green and Wells, 1823) and *Shakerism, Its Meaning and Message* (White and Taylor, 1904); this is somewhat an oddity since their principle of **separation from the world** seems to preclude any interest in what **the world** thinks of them.

Another oddity about Shaker publications is what is absent from them: imaginative narrative and dramatic literature. Although the Shakers wrote thousands of songs and poems, many of them published, other than a published short story attacking vivisection, produced by Brother Frederick McKecknie, no other Shaker seems to have written a single work of fiction about either the Society or anything else. Why this is so is a matter of speculation. Perhaps it is because the leaders always have believed that fiction is, by definition, not truth; thus, it cannot minister to either the temporal or to the spiritual welfare of Shakers. Therefore, they have been discouraged, especially during the nineteenth century, not only from writing it but also from reading it (an exception being *Uncle Tom's Cabin*, undoubtedly because of the Society's antislavery position).

For the edification specifically of the membership, the Society's major literary instrument during the latter decades of the nineteenth century was its journal titled generally as the *Manifesto*. It contained articles on matters such as Shaker history and doctrine, news from the various Shaker communities, poems, death notices, tributes to the recently dead members, and editorial commentary—often concerning statements made about the Shakers by people of the world. After the publication of this journal ceased in 1899, the Shakers did not publish another one until they established the *Shaker Quarterly* in 1961. Unlike the *Manifesto*, this journal often publishes scholarly articles by non-Shakers.

1790   *A Concise Statement of the Principles of the Only True Church According to the Gospel of the Present Appearance of Christ*, a small pamphlet presumably written by **Joseph Meacham** that also contained a letter by **James Whittaker** headed "Minister of the Gospel in This Day of Christ's Second Appearing—to His Natural Relations in England. Dated October 9th, 1785"

1807	*The Kentucky Revival* (McMemar)
1808	*The Testimony of Christ's Second Appearing* (Youngs)
1812	*Millennial Praises* (Wells, Comp.)
1816	*Testimonies of the Life, Character, Revelations and Doctrines of Our Ever Blessed Mother Ann Lee* (Bishop and Wells)
1818	*The Manifesto* (book, Dunlavy)
1821	*Orders and Rules of the Church at New Lebanon*
1823	*A Summary View of the Millennial Church, or United Society of Believers (Commonly Called Shakers)* (Green and Wells)
1827	*Testimonies concerning the Character and Ministry of Mother Ann Lee and the First Witnesses of the Gospel of Christ's Second Appearing* (Wells and Green)
1830	*A Brief Exposition of the Established Principles and Regulations of the United Society called Shakers* (Wells and Green)
1845	*Millennial Laws or Gospel Statutes and Ordinances*
1858	*Shakers: Compendium of the Origin, History, Principles, Rules and Regulations, Government, and Doctrines of the United Society of Believers in Christ's Second Appearing* (Evans et al.)
1860	*Rules and Orders for the Church of Christ's Second Appearing* (revision of *Millennial Laws*, 1845)
1869	*Autobiography of a Shaker* (Evans)
1871–1899	A regular Shaker publication in journal form was published during these years under various names: *The Shaker* (1871–1872 and 1876–1877); *Shaker and Shakeress* (1873–1875); *Shaker Manifesto* (1878–1883); *Manifesto* (1884–1899)
1879	*Shaker Sermons* (Eads)
1887	*Orders for the Church of Christ's Second Appearing* (further revision of *Millennial Laws,* 1845; in effect at the present day)
1888	*Testimonies of the Life, Character, Revelations and Doctrines of Mother Ann Lee, and the Elders with Her* (Green and Wells, 2nd ed.)
1904	*Shakerism: Its Meaning and Message* (White and Taylor)

1961	*Shaker Quarterly*, journal currently published by the Sabbathday Lake, Maine, community; described as a "scholarly investigation into Shaker art, architecture, biography, history, industry, music, literature, and theology"
1995	*Growing Up Shaker* (Carr)

LOMAS, ALBERT GEORGE (1840–1889). "He was certainly destined for a leading role in the Society," but he died at age 49 (Shaver, *Watervliet Shaker Cemetery* 4). Brother Albert entered the **Watervliet**, New York, community around 1850. Among his early contributions to the Society's pilgrimage was his service as the boys' teacher. Later, "during the period covered by the sixties and seventies," he was among "leading Shakers from different societies" who participated in "several missionary tours . . . of an educational nature,—to promulgate explain and illustrate Shaker beliefs, customs and character" (White and Taylor, *Shakerism* 206). Also, Elder Albert served twice (1871–1872, 1876–1881) in the influential position of editor of the *Shaker*, a journal, according to Lomas, dedicated to, among other matters, communicating "to the world of mind our ideas of life and happiness" (*Shaker* 1, no. 1 [January 1871]: 1).

Besides his work on and in the Society's monthly, Lomas wrote other tracts supporting its beliefs and practices. Regarding his participation in Shaker politics, he was aligned with the so-called progressives, many of whom—most notably **Frederick W. Evans**—resided in the **New Lebanon**, New York, community and with some of whom he participated in the above-mentioned missionary tours.

LONELY PLAIN OF TRIBULATION. *See* WHITEWATER, OHIO.

LORD'S SUPPER. *A.k.a.: Eucharist, Last Supper.* "Of the Lord's Supper, their [Shakers'] views differ from the great majority of the Christian world" (Bates, *Peculiarities* 87).

> As baptism, or the washing with water, was [only] a figure of the true baptism of the Holy Spirit: so that institution which is commonly called, *The Lord's Supper*, was also designed as [only] a figure. . . . [A]s bread is used to nourish and strengthen the body; so the bread of life will nourish and strengthen the soul. . . . When Jesus Christ kept the Jewish passover for the last time [the so-called Last Supper] . . . the only alteration [to the traditional ceremony] that he introduced and directed his disciples to observe, with regard to this feast of the passover, was, that they should do it in remembrance of him . . . instead of doing it as they

had done, in remembrance of the deliverance from their Egyptian bondage.

[W]here can we find any evidence to show, that the apostles and primitive Christians ever pretended to a ceremonious consecration of a little bread and wine, and to make a formal distribution of it among the members of the church, and call it *the sacrament of the Lord's Supper?* This practice was first introduced into the church by Gentile philosophers . . . "to give their religion a mystic air, in order to put it upon equal footing, in point of dignity, with that of the pagans." (Green and Wells, *Summary View* 286–288)

LOT. An alternate term for "level" in the hierarchy of Shaker leadership, as in "the first lot in the Ministry" (Pelham, "Sketch" 76).

LOVELY VINEYARD. *See* HARVARD, MASSACHUSETTS.

-M-

MACE, AURELIA GAY (18?–?). Along with other female leaders during the latter part of the nineteenth century, such as **Anna White** (of **New Lebanon**), Sister Aurelia (of **Sabbathday Lake**, New Gloucester, Maine) was much involved in, among other matters, the politics of the Society's relationship to **the world** and the role of **sisters** (*see* BROTHER/SISTER) within the organization. Much of her thought appears in the book, *The Aletheia: Spirit of Truth* (1889), which consists of a series of letters to the press and other articles. In an amiable social manner, she talks about Shaker homes, lives, and principles. "One feels while reading as if in the enjoyment of a good talk with the warm-hearted, motherly author, in whose pictured face, genial and humorous, shine stability, common sense, genius and faith" (White and Taylor, *Shakerism* 325).

MANIFESTO **(JOURNAL; 1884–1889).** *See* LITERATURE.

MARRIAGE. *See* CELIBACY.

McNEMAR, RICHARD (1770–1839). *Alt. sp.: M'Nemar. A.k.a.: Eleazer Wright*, pseud. Brother Richard, along with colleagues such as **John Dunlavy**, **John Rankin Sr**, **Malcolm Worley**, and **Matthew Houston**, was among the ministers in Ohio and Kentucky who became dissatisfied with Presbyterianism and thus became "**New Lights**," much involved in the **Kentucky Revival**. Converting virtually instantly to **Shakerism**

upon the arrival of the "propaganda" troupe—**Issachar Bates Sr., John Meacham**, and **Benjamin S. Youngs**—from **New Lebanon**, New York, in the spring of 1805, McNemar and the others were very instrumental in the great success of Shakerism in the southwestern region, not only because of their own conversions but also because of those of members of their congregations. In the words of one of McNemar's most ardent biographers,

> No man has ever lived who had greater powers of swaying a multitude. . . . He was a classical scholar, and read Latin, Greek and Hebrew. . . . Any history of the Kentucky Revival must be very incomplete that does not fully identify Richard McNemar as the principle [*sic*] mover. (MacLean, *Sketch* 3, 4, 15)

Besides his participation in the Kentucky Revival, "one of the most remarkable series of events in the long history of psychological phenomena" (White and Taylor, *Shakerism* 115), McNemar's account of the event—"of which I was an eye witness" (McNemar, *Kentucky Revival* 19)—first published in 1807 at Turtle Creek, Ohio (later **Union Village**)—is "the best history of the phenomenal occurence [*sic*] yet [1905] written" (MacLean, *Sketch* 15). His graphic accounts of actions ("**operations**" in Shaker parlance), such as jerking, dancing, rolling, and barking, at the camp meetings, alleged to have been attended by as many as 20,000 souls seeking salvation, are fascinating and seem to testify that the physical phenomena of the revival were more notable than "anything that was practically effected" by them (MacLean *Sketch* 15).

McNemar served the Society variously. For one thing, he was a far-ranging itinerant preacher mainly in Ohio and Kentucky (though he also went to Busro, Indiana, with Issachar Bates). For another, he helped **David Darrow** in organizing the Union Village community. Furthermore, besides allegedly assisting Benjamin Youngs in the composition of *The Testimony of Christ's Second Appearing* (1808), this "father of Shaker literature" (MacLean, *Sketch* 43) promulgated Shaker **theology** as a writer of pamphlets, articles, and a plethora of verses (for which he had a penchant like that of Brother Issachar). Regarding the latter, McNemar "composed more hymns, anthems, and exercise songs for the early order than any other individual" (Andrews, *Gift to Be Simple* 11). In addition to all these activities, McNemar was a printer and a skilled wood craftsman.

In 1839, supposedly because of insubordination resulting from a presumed sense of overweening self-importance, Brother Richard was expelled from Union Village. However, he was reinstated after his appeal to the **Lead Ministry**. Saddened nevertheless, he returned to **North Union**, where he died in the fall of that year. A twentieth-century auditor of the Shaker adventure remarks that McNemar "was the last of the great ones of the early Believers . . . the prototype of all that was best in the Shaker Church" (Melcher, *Shaker Adventure* 151, 274).

MEACHAM, DAVID (17?–?). The natural (i.e., biological) brother of **Joseph Meacham**, Brother David was "a man of wealth and prominent social position" who joined the **Shakers** after meeting with the **elders** at **Watervliet**, New York. He "became a noted preacher . . . [and] the founder of one of the strongest and most devoted of the Shaker communities, in his own town, Enfield, Connecticut" (White and Taylor, *Shakerism* 40).

During **Ann Lee's** missionary journey east during 1781–1783, Elder David was one of her fiercest defenders against persecutors, beginning with those who appeared at his own home when she first arrived there. With the deaths of both Ann Lee and **William Lee** in 1784, David, along with Joseph Meacham, **Calvin Harlow**, and **James Whittaker**, became a prominent leader of the Society. Upon the death of Father James in 1787, both Elders David and Calvin acknowledged Joseph Meacham as the sect's **lead**, the first American to hold the position. Under Father Joseph, Elder David served as **deacon** of the **Church Family** at **New Lebanon**, New York.

MEACHAM, JOHN (1770–1854). The eldest son of **Joseph Meacham**, Elder John, along with **Issachar Bates Sr.** and **Benjamin S. Youngs**, was one of the pioneer missionaries sent by the **Lead Ministry** at **New Lebanon**, New York, southwestward to preach the **Shaker** gospel during the latter part of the **Kentucky Revival**. In 1818, after the earliest colonies were well established, Brother John was recalled to New Lebanon.

Besides his preaching, he and Eldress Lucy Smith served as the first "spiritual Parents" of the **Pleasant Hill**, Kentucky, community (though neither of their names appears among the signers of the **Church Covenant** of June 2, 1814). Although not noted as a writer, Elder John was an apparent co-author of Youngs's *Testimony of Christ's Second Appearing* (1808), the first greatly developed statement of Shaker **theology** to be published.

MEACHAM, JOSEPH (1742–1796). (Joseph's birthday has been recorded variously as February 11 and 22, and his birth year as 1740, 1741, and 1742.) *A.k.a.: Father Joseph.* Designated in the *Compendium* (Evans et al., 1859) as one of the founders of the Shaker Society—along with **Ann**

Lee, William Lee, James Whittaker, John Hocknell, and **Lucy Wright**—Elder Joseph was the first American-born **Shaker** to be the principal leader of the United Society of Believers in Christ's Second Appearing, to which position he ascended (though not without some opposition) after the death of Whittaker in July 1787. According to witnesses, Mother Ann referred to him as "the first man in America" and as her "first-born son in America" (Green and Wells, *Summary View* 42). He was born in Enfield, Connecticut, the son of a Baptist elder.

Although Joseph had little formal education, his "persevering cultivation & improvement of his intellectual faculties and mental powers" removed any deficiency on that account (Green, "Biographical Account" 23). Distraught by his inability to find for himself a convincing way to the salvation of his soul, Joseph became an active participant in the religious revival that occurred during the Revolutionary War:

> the people of America, seeing war & bloodshed prevail among the professed followers of Christ; & seeing them biting and bickering one another; & those who professed to be Brethren, & followers of the prince of peace, destroying ravaging & rending each other miserable as was in their power, many were led to believe that the very foundation of such professions was corrupt & rotten. Hence their minds were stirred up to search after something better. (Green, "Biographical Account" 23)

The revival itself did not outlast the war. However, a few despairing revivalists encountered the small band of Shakers at **Watervliet**, New York. Impressed by what they saw of the Shakers in the spring of 1780, they reported their experience to other disappointed revivalists, who, in turn, asked that Joseph Meacham and others visit Mother Ann's little society and then relate their impressions.

After being convinced that a woman (i.e., Mother Ann) had a legitimate right to govern a religion (simply because the woman—Christ in Ann Lee—second after the man, was in charge when the man—Christ in Jesus—was absent), Joseph became a Shaker himself and encouraged other despairing revivalists to visit the group of Shakers and decide for themselves. They did. In conjunction with the influx of inquirers, on May 19, 1780 (the ironically labeled "**Dark Day**"), "the first publick testimony of the gospel in America, was delivered by Father James [Whittaker], at Watervliet" (Green, "Biographical Account" 26). Thus, the first significant increase in membership in the Shaker society in America had its genesis.

Following Whittaker's death in 1787, Joseph became the Society's **lead**—but not without some anxiety on the part of Shakers about the future of their **Society** now that all three of its original English leaders were dead. Although Joseph, **David Meacham** (Joseph's brother), and **Calvin Harlow** seemed at first to lead jointly, Joseph eventually was acknowledged by the other two **elders** to be their leader. "The union of Believers in the appointment was hearty and spontaneous" (White and Taylor, *Shakerism* 72). As the lead, Joseph began immediately to fashion the Shakers into "the first great communitarian sect" (Webber, *Escape to Utopia* 40).

After an "immediate revelation of God" to do so (Green, "Biographical Account" 29) or simply after a decision by him and his co-lead, **Lucy Wright**, that "the time had come for all true Shakers to separate themselves from the world" (Andrews, *People Called Shakers* 56), Joseph started gathering **Believers** into "gospel order" (i.e., communities) in December 1787 at **New Lebanon**, New York, the scene of the first Shaker communal dinner on December 25 and the village soon replaced Watervliet, New York, as the center of Shakerdom. New Lebanon became "the spiritual Mount Zion, when the Law and Gospel went forth to Believers" (White and Taylor, *Shakerism* 77). All who gathered there

> were exhorted to put their hands to work & hearts to God, to serve God with all the faculties of body, soul & spirit, to devote themselves with all their temporal property to God, to build up the kingdom of Christ. But nothing was done by compulsion . . . nothing appeared too much to do, no sacrifice too great to make to obtain the blessing of that revelation. (Green, "Biographical Account" 30)

By the time of Joseph's death in 1796, the Shakers had established 11 communities in 5 New England states. Neither Shaker nor non-Shaker chroniclers gainsay the monumental significance of Joseph Meacham to the development of **Shakerism** after the deaths of Ann Lee, William Lee, and James Whittaker. Indeed, it became mostly what he made it (which is not to say that he had no help).

Among other of his actions in the foundation of Shakerism as the most successful communal society in U.S. history was Joseph's establishment of a visible set of "parents" for Shakers, a manifestation of their spiritual parentage; that is, Mother Lucy Wright was "to stand in a spiritual correspondence with Father Joseph, in the first joint parentage in the spiritual order of the Church of Christ in the visible order of his kingdom established on earth" (Green, "Biographical Account" 31). The appointment of Mother Lucy to the Shakers' first liturgical team made manifest the principle in Shaker **theology** that spiritual parents are no less a necessity than are natural parents. A person cannot be "born" (again) without them, for "life" (everlasting) emanates from them—the **Heavenly Father** and **Holy Mother Wisdom**, the dual-gendered deity of the Shakers.

Logically emanating from Joseph's institution of a male/female lead was the mode of leadership developed throughout all departments of the Shaker organization. Following the system instituted at New Lebanon (which originally had three **families** or **orders**), each subsequent village was composed of self-sustaining families, and the villages were organized into **bishoprics**. An equal number of **brothers** and **sisters** (at least one, sometimes two, of each) served as family elders, **deacons**, and **trustees**. "At the head of all was the Ministry, in the direct line of spiritual influx and revelation, between the Divine Parents and the visible earthly parents—Elders of the Elders" (White and Taylor, *Shakerism* 77). All offices were gained by appointment—never by election of the **Church** membership, although they "were supported by the general approbation of the people" (Green and Wells, *Summary View* 31).

Another of Joseph's very significant actions was his capitalizing on the talents of members to begin the Shaker **industries** and economic system—geared to make each community a self-sustaining entity. By the first decades of the nineteenth century, Shaker products—leather goods, furniture, clothing, and seeds, for example—were widely distributed in and much lauded by **the world** from which Shakerdom was supposedly separated but which, ironically, became instrumental in the Shaker **economy**.

Regarding social matters, Joseph also is alleged to have affected the lives of Believers by virtue of his establishing **union meetings** in 1793, during which small groups of brothers and sisters could engage "profitably" in social intercourse. Apparently, promotion of discussions of various policies and everyday matters was intended to nurture the spiritual **union** of the genders and the family atmosphere of the communities.

Much of Joseph's thinking about the best way to follow the Shaker way became some of the substance of *Millennial Laws*, first published as *Orders and Rules of the Church at New Lebanon* in 1821 but revised by the leaders when the state of the Society warranted it, as it did in 1845. (Refer to appendix A for excerpts from this document.) One of his own "laws," which was written into *Orders and Rules* in 1821, is contained in the following passage:

> Father expressly taught us to be careful in all our ways to conduct in such a manner as to act in, & show our union in all our proceedings when walking together side by side, we should keep step, with the same

foot, & when two were either walking or riding together, they should never suffer any person of world, nor an animal of any kind to pass between them, it was a sign that such were not in that union, which the gospel requires, & forbades that some loss will follow. (Green, "Biographical Account" 93)

In *Orders and Rules* itself, the following comment about this practice appears: "Father Joseph was very careful in this particular, he would while riding on the road, turn his horse to the opposite side of the way to prevent either man or beast from passing between him and his companion" (Chap. 8).

Certainly, historians might very well argue that Joseph Meacham's intelligence and his dedication to and love for the Society for 16 years make him at least as significant in the history of the Shaker pilgrimage as is Ann Lee because he not only helped to define it, but he also created a way for it to happen. The judgment of one modern historiographer is that "the authority claimed by Father Joseph extended far beyond the sphere usually conceded to a religious leader—embracing such minute points of personal behavior as proper table manners" (Faber, *Perfect Life* 66). His total involvement in both spiritual and temporal matters posits the Shaker concept that religion and daily life are not mutually exclusive experiences but are inextricably bound to each other. Perhaps, Joseph Meacham rightfully could be deemed the father of American Shakerism.

MEDIUM. *See* INSTRUMENT; TRANCE-GOER; VISIONIST.

MEETING. In Shaker parlance, members gathering together to worship is called "Meeting":

> Worship Meetings are attended by both sexes and all ages, in one hall, at the same time. The worship consists in songs of praise and thanksgiving, and those expressing sentiments prompting to Christian life and duty; exhortations, prayers and bodily exercises in marches, orderly dances in circles and ranks, and sometimes promiscuously, each sex grouped apart. (Avery, *Sketches of Shakers* 12)

Because the Sunday worship service of the **Shakers** often has been open to public scrutiny, many people of **the world** have witnessed it, and some have been fascinated. These observers have left to posterity a plethora of their accounts of and attitudes about the Shaker Meeting, such as the following one:

> Shaker worship has some peculiarities. The division of the sexes was maintained in the church with strictness. The churches usually are ob-

long, the men sitting at one end, the women at the other. The minister conducting the service would stand at one side of the building, but about midway from end to end. Time was not considered in the worship, and anyone who had a message or an exhortation was at liberty to deliver it.

A novel feature of Shaker worship was the dance. This was regarded as sacred, and as the first mode of divine worship. Its perpetuation was considered most acceptable to God and productive of blessings upon the people.

Mr. J. M. Griffith . . . furnishes . . . the following account of the Shaker service [he witnessed]:

"It was my privilege frequently during the summers of 1871 and 1872 to visit the Shakers at Union Village [Ohio]. We always tried to visit on the days they performed their dance. . . . [A]bout nine-thirty, they would begin to assemble at the church. The women and girls, clad in their usual costumes, wearing the straight straw bonnet, would arrive in two-horse wagons, driven by one of the brethren, would alight and enter the chapel at the end of the building. The men in their broad-brimmed hat and sleeveless coats would come in wagons and enter the door near their end of the house. The meeting-house was about twice as long as wide; so, when divided in two parts, it would make two rooms about square. The elders, or preachers we would call them, would have chairs at one side between the women and men. At ten o'clock the service would begin. The elders would talk or exhort quite at length, several taking turns in speaking for about an hour and a half, when they would arise and give the notice that their exercises would change. The women and girls would proceed to carry in their end of the room and stack them up so as to give as much floor space as possible. The men would do the same, leaving the room with a good clear space. The singers were then asked to take their places. There were from twelve to twenty of them, about all young men. The women and men would form for the march, two and two, each party having its own end of the room; but, if the ring encircling the singers would be too crowed in twos, they would put three in line, or more if necessary. The older women came first, and on down to the little girls seven or eight years old. The men were formed in like manner, the older ones first, down to the little boys. Thus was formed a circle, half men and half women. At a given signal the singers begin to sing, keeping time by swinging both arms and rising on their toes. Then the procession would begin to move around and around, the singers keeping the time with their hands and step with the music. . . . [It] was all done decorously and with as much religious solemnity as any other part of the worship." (Phillippi, *Shakerism* 19, 21–24)

One Shaker chronicler records material that clearly distinguishes what she calls "public meeting" from "Church meeting." When members of the world were in attendance, they sometimes got a goodly dose of preaching directed their way. For example, on June 27, 1847, at **Union Village**, Ohio, a **Shakeress** recorded the following:

> I attended public meeting. . . . After some exercise . . . [Brother] Charles Clapp came forward to speak to the world. He took his text on *Truth*. He open the matter very clear, what course a soul must take and pursue in order to obtain the truth; and also what sacrifices they must make to become worthy heirs of the kingdom of Heaven. . . . Then Brother Enoch took the floor and rather admonished the world for their indifference of feeling that was manifested. . . . [H]e said they did not manifest that anxiety to hear the truth spoken, as he would be glad to see. . . . He spoke with a good degree of power and energy of spirit, but whether one soul was aroused from the slumbers of death or not is more than I can tell. (Morrell, "Account" 48)

In contrast, on July 4, for example, the substance of the "church meeting" was of quite a different ilk, indeed:

> We had a good and precious feast of love and simplicity. The meeting began by bowing in thanks to God for the gospel and for the blessings which we daily enjoy. After some exercise we sat down on the floor to gather simplicity and I never saw a more simple acting people than they were. . . . When we arose to our feet James McNemar spake of the vast difference there is between the sense of the world and that of Believers. The world, said he, was generally employed on the 4th of July to show how big they could appear. . . but we have been striving to see who can be the least. (Morrell, "Account" 50)

Currently, at the **Sabbathday Lake**, Maine, community, Meeting usually consists of readings from the Bible followed by testimony and song, as each member might choose. To visitors—the public, the world—no lecture is delivered, and they can, after a decent interval following the Shakers' testimonies and songs, render their own testimonies and Shaker songs. Gone are the formalized **dances/marches** that for "about a hundred years" were a significant part of Shaker worship services: "It was decided to lay aside the custom" (Frost, "Prose and Poetry" 75). A highly probable reason for ending the performance of dance and march during the late nineteenth century was the demographics of Shaker membership—an aging population and a great disproportion between females (dominant) and males.

Of course, no introduction to the Shaker Meeting would be complete without a description of it in the words of a Shaker detractor—in the following case, one who witnessed an early version (1780) of the event:

> When they meet together for their worship, they fall a groaning and trembling, and every one acts alone for himself; one will fall prostrate on the floor, another on his knees and his head in his hands; another will be muttering over articulate sounds, which neither they nor any body else understand. Some will be singing, each one his own tune; some without words, in an Indian tune, some sing jig tunes, some tunes of their own making, in an unknown mutter, which they call new tongues; some will be dancing, drumming on the floor with their feet, as though a pair of drumsticks were beating a ruff on a drum-head; others will be agonizing, as though they were in great pain; others jumping up and down; others fluttering over somebody, and talking to them; others will be shooing and hissing evil spirits out of the house, till the different tunes, groaning, jumping, dancing, drumming, laughing, talking and fluttering, shooing and hissing, makes a perfect bedlam; this they call the worship of God. (Rathbun, *Account* 11–12)

Besides regular Sabbath Meetings, Shakers held some special worship services during the nineteenth century, such as the so-called mountain meetings and the **Yearly Sacrifice**.

MEETING HOUSE. This is the appellation for the building in which **Shakers** hold their worship services. The first one—the model for most of the others of the New England Shakers—was framed by **Moses Johnson** under the direction of **James Whittaker** at **New Lebanon**, New York, in 1785–1786. Some of the original Meeting houses still exist, and the Shakers at **Sabbathday Lake**, New Gloucester, Maine, still use theirs and still invite the public to worship with them.

MEETING ROOM. Some **dwelling houses** contained a Meeting room only for the activities of the resident **family**. For example, "This morning the first order [**Church Family**] assembled in the meeting room and sung a solemn song of praise by request of the Holy Angel Micalon" (Morrell, "Account" 44).

MIDNIGHT CRY. A.k.a.: *Midnight Call*. One of several rituals inaugurated during the period of **Mother Ann's Second Coming**, this one, beginning at **New Lebanon**, New York, in 1842, was performed annually until about 1850. Six **brothers** and six **sisters** functioned as **instruments** or mediums and wore upon the right wrist "a strip of scarlet flannel . . . and attached to this a written inscription as follows: 'War hath been declared by the God of Heaven, against all sin, and with the help of the saints on earth, it shall be slain.' " (Blinn, *Manifestation of Spiritualism* 49). The two leaders (one male and one female) carried lighted lamps, and the whole company visited every room in every building over a period of two weeks. On the third night, "a company of four sisters passed through all the halls, and then through all the Sisters' apartments, in the family dwelling. Their song was 'The Midnight Cry' ":

> Awake from your slumbers,
> for the Lord of Hosts is going through the land,
> He will sweep he will clean his holy sanctuary.
> Search ye your camps, yea read and understand
> For the Lord of Hosts holds the Lamps in his hand.

Brothers and sisters suddenly awakened from sleep, joined the company of singers, and then everyone assembled for an hour of worship, around 3 A.M. (Blinn, *Manifestation of Spiritualism* 50; Andrews, *People Called Shakers* 160–161).

MILLENNIAL CHURCH. *See* SHAKERISM.

MILLENNIAL LAWS. The general abbreviated title of several versions of the principal governing publication of **Shakers** released throughout the nineteenth century. As the title implies, the volume contains rules, **orders**, statutes, and standards of conduct, though all of these "laws," in the judgment of the **Lead Ministry**, apparently have been deemed necessary of revision at certain times and under certain conditions; that is, the rules and orders of **Shakerism** have been adapted to reflect the values of the Society at any particular time in its contextual history. The document is thus a good primary source of information about the communal life of the Shakers during the course of the nineteenth century.

First released in 1821, six months after the death of Mother **Lucy Wright**, under the title *Orders and Rules of the Church at New Lebanon, August 7th, 1821*, authorized revision and expansion of the principles therein produced in 1845 (during the time called "**Mother Ann's Second Coming**") an adapted title, in full: *Millennial Laws or Gospel Statutes and Ordinances by Father Joseph Meacham and Mother Lucy Wright, by the Presiding Ministry, and by Their Successors*. By revelation, it is reported, Shaker scribes received the revised rules from Father **Joseph Meacham**, the number of orders in the 1845 edition more than doubled the number in the 1821 edition. Yet another major revision to the work was issued in 1860, under the title *Rules and Orders for the Church of Christ's Second Appearing*. Expunged from it were "the more exotic features of the 1845 laws" (Johnson, "the 'Millennial Laws' of 1821" 41). Still other revisions were issued in 1878 and 1887, which have remained in effect to this day. (Refer to appendix B for excerpts from both the 1821 and 1845 texts.)

As to the actual content of the *Millennial Laws*, Shaker **elders** devised it for achieving **union** in a variety of matters, apparently cognizant that Society members are inherently imperfect by virtue of their humanity. For example:

> The life is really military, only, that the enemy is spiritual; and heaven rather than earth, and quietness, rather than tumult, are its concomitants. Not a single action of life, whether spiritual or temporal, from the initiative of confession, or cleansing the habitation of Christ, to that of dressing the right side first, stepping first with the right foot as you ascend a flight of stairs, folding the hands with the right hand thumb and fingers above those of the left, kneeling and rising again with the right leg first, and harnessing first the right hand breast, but that has a rule for its perfect and strict performance. (Elkins, *Fifteen Years* 32)

MILLENNIUM. *A.k.a.: Second Advent, Second Coming, Parousia.* In Shaker **theology**, the Millennium is not a future event but one that actually was already begun in the person of **Ann Lee**, as she was the female counterpart of the **Christ Spirit**—first manifested in the male form as Jesus. Indeed, one of the official names of the Shaker organization reflects this concept: the United Society of Believers in Christ's Second Appearing.

Another departure of the Shaker theology from that of other sects of Christianity is the concept of the nature of the commencement of the Millennium. That is to say, although various biblical passages (such as Matthew 24:30, King James Bible) have been interpreted as meaning that Christ "will suddenly appear in the most public manner, so as to be seen at once, by all mankind," the **Shakers** believe differently:

> The light of the millennial day is as gradual and various, in its commencement and progress, as the light of the natural day; and, like this, cannot possibly take place throughout the world at once, any more than the light of the sun can be seen at once over the face of the whole earth. (Green and Wells, *Summary View* 256)

Of course, to Shakers, "the light of the millennial day" commenced in Ann Lee, who, ironically, at the time was in prison in England for "profaning the Sabbath." That the progress of the Second Coming of Christ has been "gradual and various" seems to be evidenced by the somewhat slight and local influence of **Shakerism** on **the world**.

One of the many severe critics of the Shakers disputes not only their contention that the Second Coming is through the person Ann Lee but also their contention that the Millennium has already begun:

> But of one thing we are certain, and that is, that the reign of Anti-Christ is not yet come to an end, much less that the Millennium is already begun. Several prophecies remain yet to be fulfilled, before the commencement of that blessed era; such as the restoration of the Jews, the grand confederacy of the beast, the false prophet and the kings of the earth, the battle of Armageddon, and the binding of the dragon. (Brown, *Countercheck* 43)

MILLER, WILLIAM (1782–1849). Founder of the so-called Millerites, a Christian sect most prominent during the middle decades of the nineteenth century, Miller reckoned from the Bible that Christ was to come again in the year 1843—quite contrary to the Shaker belief that the Second Coming was well under way already. When the event did not occur on the assigned date, **Shakers** serendipitously held an **in-gathering** for many disheartened Millerites. This aroused hope in the Shakers that the long-awaited significant increase in their own membership was beginning, but that event did not occur either.

MINISTRY. *See* LEAD; LEAD MINISTRY.

MORRELL, PRUDENCE (1794–1855). A member of the **New Lebanon** community, **Sister** Prudence is especially notable for leaving to posterity her "Account of a Journey to the West in the Year 1847," a record of her visit to eight Shaker communities between May 18 and October 6, 1847, near the end of the era called "**Mother Ann's Second Coming.**" Among other features, her detailed accounts of public meetings and **feast grounds** at the various **villages** are edifying, and her perception of the attitude of western Shakers toward New Lebanon is insightful:

> But I think it [the expression of love and kindness] is not because it is Eliza and I that have come . . . but because it is some sisters from the east, for they love the very name of Lebanon. . . . And furthermore it is their meat and drink to be like believers in the east; they feel willing to make any sacrifice that the gospel requires, to be accepted of their blessed Mother, and are willing to do anything to have the blessing of those before them. The respect they feel towards the Church at New Lebanon cannot be so well express'd as realized. (85, 89)

MOTHER/FATHER. *See* FATHER/MOTHER.

MOTHER ANN. *See* LEE, ANN.

MOTHER ANN'S SECOND COMING (1837–1847). *A.k.a.: Mother Ann's Work, Mother's Work, Shaker Revival.* The appellation for one of the most (perhaps the most) notable decades in Shaker history. Beginning on August 16, 1837, Shaker communities were sites for innumerable liaisons between members of the **villages** and the so-called spirit world. Besides the intercourse of individuals with the world beyond natural life, communication between the two realms was manifested at the Shaker **Meeting**, as in the following account written in 1847 (which, given its context, is not to be construed as totally literal):

> In the evening we attended meeting with the family, they appeared to have a good gift and sung some beautiful songs. After some exercise [e.g., trembling, shaking] Eliza and I received a beautiful green branch full of white apples from Eldress Betsey; and from Father David [Darrow] and Mother Ruth [Farrington] we received a gold basket of precious treasures for us to distribute among the brethren and sisters. We also received from Father James [Whittaker] the love and blessing of all our heavenly parents. . . . There was a company of holy angels assembled and ministered to our necessity. We also received holy Mother's [Mother Ann's] love. (Morrell, "Account" 49, 51)

Why a period of such remarkable **spiritualism** should have occurred at all and at this time in the Shaker pilgrimage might invite speculation by non-Shakers, but **Shakers** themselves have assigned the cause:

> This evening [July 9, 1847] we attended meeting with the [Church] family. Brother Amos spoke feelingly to the young in particular, exciting their minds to a spirit of love and simplicity. He manifested a great anxiety for the prosperity of the rising generation and for their present as well as future happiness. (Morrell, "Account" 51)

This concern for the "prosperity" of young Shakers and would-be young Shakers is the nexus to this period of focus on the spirit world. Indeed, to Shakers themselves, Mother Ann's Second Coming was

> the result . . . of the prayers of aged members of the Order, her first born children of the faith, who had for years been praying that something might come to . . . the young people who had grown up under the protection of the communities, but who had not experienced the deep work of faith. They exerted a constant pressure on Elders . . . for more liberty and indulgence in their worldly tastes and selfish desires. (White and Taylor, *Shakerism* 228)

Besides unnumbered spiritual experiences, a plethora of other phenomena occurred during this era. Among them were gift songs—"between two and three thousand" of them (Frost, "Prose and Poetry" 79), **inspi-**

rational drawings, and new rituals, such as the **Midnight Cry** and **Sweeping Gift.**

MOTHER ANN'S WORK. *See* MOTHER ANN'S SECOND COMING.

MOTHER LUCY. *See* WRIGHT, LUCY.

MOTHER RUTH. *See* FARRINGTON, RUTH.

MOTHER'S WORK. *See* MOTHER ANN'S SECOND COMING.

MOUNT LEBANON. *See* NEW LEBANON.

MYRICK, ELIJAH (18?–1890). An **elder** at **Harvard**, Massachusetts, Brother Elijah was involved with Shaker academic education along with fostering the development and use of time- and labor-saving devices (which not only could earn the Society money but also could provide extra time for **Believers** to cultivate their intellects rather than just their job skills.) Along with "progressives" of the latter nineteenth century, such as **Frederick W. Evans**, of **New Lebanon**, New York, Elijah promoted reform in diet by use of, for example, whole rather than refined flour (Melcher, **Shaker Adventure** 160; Stein, **Shaker Experience** 303, 306).

-N-

NARCOOSSEE, FLORIDA (1896–1911). *Spiritual name: Olive Branch* (given although the period of **Mother Ann's Second Coming**, the period when such special appellations were assigned and had singular meaning, had long receded into the Shaker past). The first of the southern experiments taken by the Society, Narcoossee was situated in Osceola County, a few miles from Kissimmee, St. Cloud, and Lake Tohopekaliga. According to one auditor, "a small delegation" of **Shakers** in 1894 was sent from **New Lebanon**, New York, to establish—ostensibly, at least—"a group in the salubrious southern climate" (Anderson, "Shaker Community in Florida" 31). "They located at Narcoossee, and, by dint of hard work and great frugality, have succeeded [as of 1904] in establishing themselves and are engaged in raising and marketing pine apples and other southern products" (White and Taylor, *Shakerism* 213).

The success of the Shakers' business ventures in Florida is reflected in an article by a non-Shaker that appeared in the Shakers' *Manifesto*:

The writer recently inspected the place through an invitation from the business manager, Mr. [Elder] Benjamin Gates, and came away convinced it only needed the patient, intelligent industry manifested here to make farm life not only a delightful, but a remunerative occupation. In the grounds connected with the house and business office are orange, peach, apricot and persimmon trees with a large number of flowering plants. . . . An irrigating plant supplies the five acres immediately adjoining the house. For field crops they are this season growing Irish and sweet potatoes, cane, velvet beans, cow peas, beggar weed, rice and pumpkins.

The design of the community has always been to make cattle growing the great industry, and for this the place is admirably suited. . . . At present there are about nine hundred head of cattle in the portion enclosed. (26 [October 1898]: 153–154)

However, despite such temporal success, the Shakers' ability to establish a spiritual community apparently was inadequate, and the Narcoossee venture, similar to the one at **White Oak**, Georgia, was questioned as being a proper undertaking at a time when the resources expended on it might have been used more wisely to bolster faltering communities in the north. Furthermore, Shaker Brother Andrew Barrett, "who was to become the head of the colony before he went to Union Village, Ohio, in 1902," believed early in the experiment that the primary reason for its existence had been lost by those running the colony:

When I see greed of money step in and engross our whole attention I begin to think we have forgotten the primary object of our *exit* into *Florida*. . . . To me this was not intended as merely a *speculative scheme* for a quiet and comfortable home with a chance to make a few dollars to still keep the thing a running. (Quoted in Anderson, "Shaker Community in Florida" 31)

To the Society's chagrin, undoubtedly, one of the more sensational events of the Narcoossee community was the criminal charge against a Shaker **brother** and **sister** in 1911 for the "mercy killing" of a woman suffering from tuberculosis. Although the charge was dropped, how much influence the case had on the closure of the colony in the same year is debatable.

NEALE, EMMA J. (18?–19?). A **Shakeress** for over 90 years, Sister Emma was among the many females "forced" to serve the **Society** in administrative positions by themselves in the twentieth century because of the dearth of males. She was both **eldress** and **trustee** at **New Lebanon**, New York. As trustee, she created an investment portfolio that manifested the Shakers' complete immersion into the economic culture of **the world** (Andrews, *People Called Shakers* xv; Stein, *Shaker Experience* 285, 288).

NEW BIRTH. To the **Shakers**, despite mankind's degenerate nature, people can begin again—can experience a spiritual regeneration, a new birth, which is

> a renovation of the whole soul and life of the man, in such a manner as to raise him, not only from the state into which he has fallen, but into a life of righteousness and true holiness, far superior to his primitive state, even into a state of eternal life, from which he never can fall. (Green and Wells, *Summary View* 271)

NEW CREATION. The logical concomitant of **new birth**, or spiritual regeneration, will be the demise of the old, temporal, and degenerate nature of the world. It was to be superseded by the "everlasting Kingdom of Christ"—"the holy city, *New Jerusalem*"—effected through "the great principles of the gospel revived and brought to light by Mother Ann, and the succeeding Witnesses":

> This great spiritual work has now commenced. . . . Those gloomy clouds of religious intolerance, and pelting storms of persecution, which once deformed the heavenly atmosphere, and deluged the earth with blood, are now blown away; and the cheering spring of Christ's second appearance is now made manifest, and will extend from clime to clime, and from shore to shore, until "all the ends of the earth shall see the salvation of the Lord." (Green and Wells, *Summary View* 281–282)

NEW GLOUCESTER. *See* SABBATHDAY LAKE, MAINE.

NEW LEBANON, NEW YORK (1787–1947). *A.k.a. Mount Lebanon* (after 1861). *Spiritual name: Holy Mount.* On December 25, 1787, at New Lebanon, the **Shakers,** led by Father **Joseph Meacham**, ate their first communal dinner after the move to come into "gospel order." The **village** was the first formally established Shaker community and immediately became the center of Shakerdom. It was "the spiritual Mount Zion, whence the Law and the Gospel went forth to Believers" from the **Lead Ministry** (White and Taylor, *Shakerism* 77).

> [New Lebanon is] situated about 2 1/2 miles south of Lebanon Springs, in the county of Columbia . . . about 25 miles southeast from Albany, and containing, at present [1848], between 5[00] and 600 persons, including old and young, male and female. (Green and Wells, *Summary View* 76)

At this time [1875] it [New Lebanon] has three hundred and eighty-three [persons], including forty-seven children and youth under fifteen. This society is divided into seven families; and its membership has one hundred and thirty-six males and two hundred and forty-seven females, including children and youth. It owns about three thousand acres of land within . . . New York, besides some farms in other states. . . . The different families . . . raise and put up garden seeds, make brooms, dry medicinal herbs and make extracts, dry sweet corn, and make chairs and mops. The women in all the families also make mats, fans, dusters, and other fancy articles for sale. (Nordhoff, *Communistic Communities* 195)

The Society at New Lebanon owns about 6000 acres of land, a large proportion of which is devoted to fuel, timber and sheep, it being very mountainous and rocky. . . . The proportion of land is about ten acres to each individual. Other Societies do not vary much from the same ratio. (Evans et al., *Compendium* 40)

NEW LIGHT[ER]S. The metaphorical appellation of some of the defectors, especially ministers, from established sects of the Christian religion, such as Baptist, Congregational, and Presbyterian, during the late eighteenth and very early nineteenth centuries (following the so-called Great Awakening in religion during the middle of the eighteenth century). From New England to Kentucky (the "southwest," in Shaker parlance), religious revivals flourished, partly, maybe even mostly, because the established sects were failing to meet the needs of humble people seeking, among other things, the assurance and means of the soul's salvation. Among the prominent New Lighters who eventually became prominent **Shakers** (along with many from their congregations and personal families, thus making the revivals serendipitous to **Shakerism**) were **Joseph Meacham** and **Calvin Harlow** in the East and **Richard McNemar**, **John Rankin Sr.**, **John Dunlavy**, and **Malcolm Worley** in the West (Burns, *Shaker Cities* 4; MacLean, *Sketch* 15–32). *See also* KENTUCKY REVIVAL.

NISKAYUNA. *Alt. sp.: Niskeyuna, Nesquiuna, Niskenna, Niacayune. See* WATERVLIET, NEW YORK.

NORTH UNION, Ohio (1822–1889). *Spiritual name: Valley of God's Pleasure.* Located about eight miles northeast of Cleveland, "North Union was most numerous about 1840, when it contained two hundred members. It is now [1875] divided into three families, having one hundred and two persons, of whom seventeen are children and youth under twenty-one" (Nordhoff, *Communistic Societies* 204).

Like all the Shaker communities North Union was meant to be a "Colony of Heaven" where men and women lived apart from each other and from the sinful world, dedicated to their religious principles as a way of life. And the records indicate the Shakers were in many ways successful in achieving their ideals at North Union. The membership increased from 89 in the 1828–1829 period to 148 in 1841 and to 153 in 1860. (Conlin, *North Union* 3)

To one very notable chronicler of Shaker history who surmises the causes of the effects regarding this community,

the history of the North Union Society is the history of the elders. If the chief leader possessed judgement and was full of enterprise the society flourished. This is particularly true during the first twenty years of its existence. Then came the stationary period, followed by a rapid decline that ended in extinction. (MacLean, *Shakers of Ohio* 115)

The following chronology of North Union was provided by the Shaker Historical Society, Shaker Heights, Ohio:

1821	**Ralph Russell** journeyed to **Union Village**, near Lebanon, Ohio, and was converted to **Shakerism**.
1822	Russell returned to Warrensville and established a Shaker colony on his land. Many in his family converted to Shakerism. First public meeting held on March 21.
1823	Three Shaker **families** established: Center, Mill, and East.
1826	**James S. Prescott**, stonemason, came to North Union and converted to Shakerism. Served as historian (wrote a history of North Union, for example), educator, journalist, and **elder**. Ashbel Kitchell appointed head elder, replacing Ralph Russell, who left the colony.
1828	First written covenant.
1837	Doan Brook dammed up to form Lower Lake.
1840–1858	Elder Samuel Russell served as leader of North Union through period of greatest prosperity and spiritual fulfillment.
1843	Five-story gristmill constructed, the largest in northern Ohio.
1848	New **Meeting house** built on northeast corner of Lee Road and Shaker Boulevard.
1850	Peak year of North Union membership: 150 (total c. 400).
1854	Doan Brook dammed up again to form Upper Lake.

1870	Colony began to decline. Families consolidated.
1886	As part of a Fourth of July celebration, Charles Reader of Cleveland blew up the stone gristmill, which he had been operating as his own business.
1888	Death of James Prescott.
1889	North Union dissolved. Remaining Shakers moved to southern Ohio colonies. Shaker artifacts preserved from auction on October 24.
1892	1,366 acres of land sold to Shaker Heights Land Co. for $316,000.

NOVITIATE. As an adjective, the term is most often used to specify a particular Shaker body, such as a class, a **family**, or an **order**. As a noun, the term literally denotes a beginner in the Shaker system—a person who has expressed interest in joining the Society but who has not yet signed the **Church Covenant**. After the formally established communities began in 1787, the influx of potential members began to be handled in the so-called Gathering Order (or Novitiate Family), where novices generally lived as **Shakers** for a year. Originally, this class of Shakers was composed of

> those who receive faith and come into a degree of relation with the Society, but choose to live in their own families and manage their own temporal concerns. Any such who choose may live in that manner, and be owned as brethren and sisters in the Gospel, so long as they live up to its requirements. . . . They may continue thus as long as it comports with their faith, circumstances, and spiritual improvement. . . . Such persons are permitted to all the privileges of religious worship and spiritual communion in the novitiate order, and receive instruction and counsel, according to their needs, whenever they feel it necessary to apply for it; and are not debarred from any privilege of which their choice, local situation, and circumstances will admit. (Evans et al., *Compendium* 45–46)

After a period of introduction to **Shakerism**, persons of legal age wishing to become full-fledged members traditionally have been required to sign the **Church Covenant**. (This is not possible any longer, at least theoretically, since the covenant was officially closed in 1965 by the **Canterbury**, New Hampshire, **Lead Ministry**. However, the matter has become moot because the **Sabbathday Lake** Shakers are now the only ones in existence and can accept whomever they wish.)

Among other things, the thoroughness with which Shaker leaders designed and implemented the novitiate system suggests that they have been concerned greatly about the possibility of charges against them for fraud and extortion of the innocent and ignorant. If nothing else is, at least their success in court legal battles is testimony to the circumspection with which they devised their system.

-O-

OBEDIENCE. In the earliest days of **Shakerism** in America, when its membership hardly extended beyond the number who had arrived in New York in 1774, total submission to **leads** seemed not to be a crucial element of the sect's ideology. Perhaps the smallness and intimacy of the group engendered enough respect all around that **orders** were not necessary. However, after **Ann Lee** died in 1784, the Society began to increase rapidly in membership, becoming the institutional entity **the world** identifies as Shakerism. At this time, when the sect was under the leadership of Father **James Whittaker** and, shortly after him, that of Father **Joseph Meacham**, the principle that "the first duty which God requires of man and in which is comprehended all other duties, is obedience" became a cardinal factor in the Shaker system—maybe because the **elders** thought it necessary to help control members and to achieve unity among them, for they were spread far apart throughout New England.

The importance of subjection in Shakerism is aptly expressed, among other ways, in a quaint analogy devised by **Shakers** themselves in which **brothers**, **sisters**, elders, and God are likened to common soldiers, officers, and the supreme commander of an army, respectively:

> Every soldier is required to yield implicit obedience to his immediate commander, and every officer must be subject to the command of his superior officer. This order of subjection extends . . . from the common soldier to the highest officer . . . and thus the whole army is led and governed by the commander in chief. Without this subjection, the largest army would soon lose all its strength and power. (Green and Wells, *Summary View* 334, 336)

In the Shaker top-down chain of command, God (the Commander in Chief) issues revelations to Shaker leaders (the ministry), who, in turn, divulge them to the rest of the membership. Thus, to obey elders is to obey God, and to be obedient is to be in order and **union** with the **Church**—to **travel** in the gospel.

OFFICE DEACON. *See* TRUSTEE.

OFFORD, DANIEL (18?–18?). Among the so-called progressives of the North Family of **New Lebanon**, New York, Elder Daniel argued against meat, among other things, in the Shaker diet, and he promoted land reform as an aid to cure social problems (Stein, *Shaker Experience* 306, 312).

OPERATIONS. *A.k.a.: outward operations.* Physical movements, such as shaking, whirling, and clapping, performed by **Shakers** in the process of, for example, seeking spiritual help in any kind of endeavor, perhaps to become more loving. *See also* EXERCISE(S); LABOR/LABORING.

ORDER. In one sense, this term is used in conjunction with an adjective to indicate the status of members regarding their association with the **Church**. For example,

> The second class, or degree or order, is composed of those persons who, not having the charge of [personal] families, and under no embarrassments to hinder them from becoming members of a [Shaker] family, in a united capacity ch[oo]se to enjoy the benefits of such a situation. (Green and Wells, *Brief Exposition* 13)

In another adjectival usage, when the word "gospel" precedes order, the phrase refers to institutional **Shakerism**, as in "**Father Joseph** brought the Church into gospel order" (i.e., gave it a governmental structure headed by the **Lead Ministry**). Another form of the word commonly employed by the Shakers is as a noun, used as a surrogate for "rule" or "law." For example, in *Rules and Orders for the Church of Christ's Second Appearing* (1860) the following passage appears (*see also MILLENNIAL LAWS*):

> Section III: Orders Concerning the Sabbath. 1. No books, except the Bible, and Believers' publications may be read on the Sabbath, except by permission of the Elders, and Newspapers, Periodicals, Advertisements, Almanacs, Pamphlets, Literary, Scientific, Miscellaneous, unreligious or worldly books of any kind, should not be read on the Sabbath. (Johnson, "Rules and Orders" 150)

OUTSIDE SHAKER(S). In the early days of the movement particularly, members who for various reasons had not fulfilled all the requirements to be bona fide members of the Society lived apart from or outside the communes and were thus designated by this name.

OUTWARD OPERATIONS. *See* OPERATIONS.

-P-

PACIFISM. Although the **Shakers** have not adhered exactly to their principle of **separation from the world**, they have been adamant about it regarding politics. Besides not participating in the election process of the general public, for example, no Shaker has ever been an agent bearing arms for any governmental entity engaged in war.

This position of "conscientious objection" (as it has come to be called) jeopardized the Society's welfare several times during its early history. For instance, the Shakers' refusal to bear arms against the British during the colonial era, when their fellow citizens were sacrificing their lives for the very freedom that the newly arrived Shakers enjoyed, caused the incarceration of several of them and suspicion of all of them as spies for the enemy. Also, although they had established their position on not bearing arms, they still had to petition the federal government for exemption from military service during the Civil War.

A testimony to the Shakers' position on nonviolence is that even though members of the Society had served in the military during the American Revolution, they refused to accept the pensions due them. *See also* BLANCHARD, GROVE; EVANS, FREDERICK W.; GATES, BENJAMIN.

PARENT MINISTRY. *See* LEAD MINISTRY.

PAROUSIA. *See* MILLENNIUM.

PARTINGTON, JOHN (17?–18?). A member of early Shakerdom in England, Brother John, unlike his wife, **Mary Partington**, did not accompany **Ann Lee** to America; instead, he came in December 1775 with **John Hocknell**, who had returned to England for his family after the **Shakers** were in the process of making a settlement at Niskayuna, New York. When **James Whittaker** assumed the **lead** of the Society following the death of Mother Ann in September 1784, Partington, along with **James Shepherd**, "would not submit to him and lost all relation to the work of God" (White and Taylor, *Shakerism* 69)—that is, they became apostates.

PARTINGTON, MARY (1755–1833). Among the members of early Shakerdom in England, Sister Mary was one of the eight Shakers to immigrate to America with **Ann Lee** in 1774. She was the wife of **John**

Partington, who joined the Shakers in America in December 1775. She was among the **Believers** jailed in 1780 for alleged antiwar activities.

PELHAM, JOSEPH (1792–18?). Indirectly, Brother Joseph, older natural (i.e., biological) brother of Elder Richard W. Pelham, helped to give the **Shakers** more cause to make missions to the burgeoning religious revival areas of western New York, when in 1825 he requested that **New Lebanon,** New York, send to Lyons members who could instruct people in **Shakerism.** The resultant converts were plentiful enough for the Society to establish the **Sodus Bay** community in 1826.

PELHAM, RICHARD W. (1797–1873). In his autobiography, "A Sketch of the Life and Religious Experience of Richard W. Pelham," a work urged by friends—"otherwise there is no probability . . . that it would ever have been performed" (20)—Richard reveals, among other aspects of his character, his great humility and complete submission to the authority of his **elders.** Often transferred to different societies and given different tasks, he was "enabled to meet all these changes, and submit to them with cheerful obedience, . . . satisfied that all has worked for good to me" (90).

The younger natural brother of **Joseph Pelham** of the **Sodus Bay,** New York, community, Richard "was to have been heir to a large property, but abandoned all to seek a pure form of religion. A man of great intellectual ability, he mastered Greek and Hebrew . . . and translated the Bible into English" (White and Taylor, *Shakerism* 125). Elder Richard spent nearly his entire Shaker life in the western societies, principally three of the ones in Ohio—**Union Village, Watervliet,** and **North Union**—at which he served variously as "first lot in the Ministry," **trustee,** and elder. He also was a tailor, a horticulturalist, and a teacher in the Shaker schools, a task he refers to as a "very unexpected . . . and disagreeable requirement" but one to which he, typically, "cheerfully submitted" (81).

Moreover, Richard was an author and a missionary. Among his texts is the oft-cited *The Shaker's Answer* (1868), a treatise on, among other concepts, the rightness of **celibacy.** As a missionary, Richard "assisted at the foundation of the societies of North Union [Ohio], Groveland [New York] and Whitewater [Ohio]. He died at Union Village" (White and Taylor, *Shakerism* 125).

PHILADELPHIA FAMILY. *A.k.a.: Twenty-fifth Village.* African Americans were not excluded from the **United Society of Believers in Christ's Second Appearing,** for several references to them appear in Shaker journals, for example, and in accounts by observers from **the world**, such as Charles Nordhoff. Perhaps most of them, prior to the Civil War, were escaped slaves who accepted the sanctuary offered them by the antislavery **Shakers**.

Apart from the scattered numbers of African Americans in various Shaker **villages**, such as **Watervliet**, New York, the only accumulation of them into a unit approaching the Shaker **family** is the one organized in Philadelphia after the Civil War. Although it is occasionally mentioned, even by Shakers themselves, in accounts of Shaker communities, it seems not to have been fully sanctioned by the **Lead Ministry**. If it was, it was unique among Shaker settlements. For one thing, it was established and led for about 10 years by a single person, Eldress **Rebecca Cox Jackson**, who was just an authorized agent, so to speak, of the Watervliet, New York, community. For another thing, it bore little similarity to the usual Shaker village: it neither had an agrarian economy or a manufacturing enterprise, nor was it a community physically separate from the world. Perhaps, then, calling it a "branch" or an "out-family" rather than a full-fledged Shaker "village," would be a more fitting term for it.

> In 1875, an auditor of the Society reported that the group then consisted of twelve colored women, who live together in one house. . . . The members find employments as day servants in different families, going home every night. They mainly support themselves, and have never asked for help from the society, but this occasionally makes them presents, and keeps a general oversight over them. (Nordhoff, *Communistic Societies* 198)

When Jackson's successor died in 1901,

> the community continued. . . . It is not known in what form they continued, who the leadership was and how close the sect remained to Shakerism. To date [1981] the last mention of Shakerism in Philadelphia comes from a *New York Times* article in 1909[:] "Pittsfield, Mass. March 20 . . . When Elder Pick left Wednesday . . . he went from Pittsfield to Philadelphia, where there is a colored community of Shakers, small in numbers." (Williams, *Called and Chosen* 129–130)

PLEASANT GARDEN. *See* SHIRLEY, MASSACHUSETTS.

PLEASANT HILL, KENTUCKY (1806–1910). Apparently, Pleasant Hill had no spiritual name or else it has been lost. The only alternate name ever used in reference to the community is "Holy Sinai Plain," which was actually the name of its **feast ground**. The earlier organized and shorter lived of the Kentucky communities, Pleasant Hill, "the topmost bough upon the tree, the cream of Kentucky" (White and Taylor, *Shakerism* 124), was located in Mercer County, about 7 miles east of Harrodsburg and about 21 miles southwest of Lexington. It was on a high plateau, a few miles from the Kentucky River, which it used much in its commercial enterprises. In 1823, it contained between 400 and 500 members. By 1875, the community, situated in the so-called Bluegrass region of the state, owned about 4,200 acres, was composed of 5 **families**, and housed about 245 persons, males constituting about one-third of this number (Nordhoff, *Communistic Societies* 211–212).

A fellow **Shaker** visiting Pleasant Hill in 1847, during the period called "**Mother Ann's Second Coming**," made the following comments about the community she witnessed:

> [August] 20th: We are now at Pleasant Hill, feasting on good things. This we realize every time we stop anywhere among Believers, for when we are traveling among the world in this state we cannot get anything to eat but what is cooked by the colored people that look as dirty and greasy as an old saddle cloth. . . . Traveling in Kentucky to see good Believers is some like climbing a thorn tree to get honey. [August] 22nd: Sabbath morning. . . . Elder John gave out the love from Lebanon. . . . They acted some like little children at the return of their parents after a long absence. The singing here is very strong, as a mighty host of angels, or among an army in battle array against their enemies, no holding back among the young people, all appear awake & alive in the worship of God. [August] 29th: This morning we visited the little girls. . . . We then commenced our march to Holy Sinai's Plains a good half mile. Before we left the meeting house Bro[ther] James Cuney informed us that our heavenly parents and many holy angels were going with us. This place is east of the meeting house; the yard is a handsome oval round. . . . They had a very good outpouring of the Spirit and power of God. And among the many beautiful gifts we received a ball of joy and gladness. . . . [T]hey sent much love and thanks to Lebanon which I believe was genuine love. (Morrell, "Account" 85–87)

Testimony to the industriousness of the Shakers at Pleasant Hill can be found in the following words of one twentieth-century auditor of the community:

> Next to their religion, work was the main aim of their lives. . . . At Pleasant Hill the Shakers farmed some 1,500 acres. . . . They grew oats, wheat, corn, hay, potatoes and broom corn, as well as apples, peaches, pears, strawberries and raspberries. In harvesting some of the crops they employed as many as 60 hands, men and women, who were paid from 75 cents to $2 a day . . . with substantial meals thrown in. . . . [Further-

more, they] conducted a saw mill, a grist mill, a fulling mill and an oil mill. They also had a tanyard and paper mill. They spun and wove, made silk and cloth, straw hats for both sexes and manufactured all kinds of furniture. They also had a printing office. Broom-making was a specialty.

The present broad [or flat] broom was invented by the Shakers, and still retains the name, Shaker broom. (Hutton, *Old Shakertown* 27–28)

In the midst of the period of its greatest prosperity, Pleasant Hill was caught in the Civil War. "One of the greatest threats to the well-being of the Society was the possibility of Kentucky's becoming a battleground." For one thing, "The Shakers stood to lose heavily by war because the southern market for their products would be destroyed" (Clark and Ham, *Pleasant Hill* 74). For another thing, in conjunction with troop movements and battles, such as the awful battle of Perryville, only a few miles from the village, "both armies foraged upon them, taking their horses and wagons; and they served thousands of meals to hungry soldiers of both sides" (Nordhoff, *Communistic Societies* 214).

Among other adversities that eventually rendered the community defunct were failure to manage capital effectively and to develop new commercial markets; inability to attract new members and, thus, "to feed into the system youthful leadership [which] confronted the Shakers with almost insoluble problems"; and engagement in internal squabbles between the members who wished to maintain the traditions of the Society and those who wished to liberalize them, such as participating in voting on matters of **the world** relevant to Shaker interests (Clark and Ham, *Pleasant Hill* 85–87).

In September 1910, Pleasant Hill went the way 10 other Shaker villages had gone. The property remained in private hands for 50 years. However, beginning in 1961, "a group of concerned Kentuckians . . . began the arduous task of acquiring original Shaker lands, restoring their buildings, and devising programs to attract visitors to this once-prosperous site" (Thomas and Thomas, *Simple Spirit* 5). Today, "nearly 2700 acres of Shaker land have been preserved and thirty original buildings restored with meticulous care, down to faithfully duplicating the 'original blue' paint trim. . . . Pleasant Hill is a National Historic Landmark and the largest of all restored Shaker villages" (in Thomas and Thomas, *Simple Spirit* 12).

PRESCOTT, JAMES (1803–1888). Well educated and a mason by trade, Prescott responded to a call from North Union [Ohio], and assisted in laying the foundation for the Centre House. As a result of this meeting with the Shakers and of subsequent study of their history and principles, the foundation of the Gospel was laid in his soul and in 1826, he was admitted to the society. (White and Taylor, *Shakerism* 125)

Elder Prescott was probably the most notable figure in **North Union** history, for he was not only a builder and craftsman, but he was also a historian of the community, an ecologist, a naturalist, an educator, a devotee of music, a spiritualist, and an interpreter of Shaker gospel. Regarding the latter, his understanding of the principle of **confession of sin** "clearly diverged from the 1845 Millennial Laws" by, for example, Prescott's apparent repugnance to the requirement that members inform **elders** of one another's transgressions. He negated the practice by not even mentioning it.

Auditors of Prescott's character and of his value to North Union in particular and to **Shakerism** in general have been only laudatory. For instance, one historian of the colony says that

> no member of the North Union was ever better qualified to write down the thrilling story of the Herculean labors, the moral triumphs and Christ-like devotion of these simple Believers [of North Union] than was James Prescott. . . . He laid the community's foundations, reared walls, erected chimneys, made furniture for many of its rooms, taught school, planted trees and shrubbery and served as elder, deacon and trustee and was ever a devout and loyal member of the community. (Piercy, *Valley of God's Pleasure* 5)

The latest biographer of Brother James claims that "it would be more appropriate to refer to him as a Renaissance man in the world of the Shakers" (Klyver, *Brother James* 8). Beyond doubt, the most ardent assessment of Prescott is the following one:

> Rest, sweet saint, thy labors are over. The society which thou didst give thy life for its welfare and promotion, like thee, has passed away. But thy life was not a failure, and the course thou didst pursue will be admonition to the generations that must follow. (MacLean "Society of Shakers" 98)

PRIVILEGE. This concept appears often in Shaker writings, as in "privileges of religious worship," "privilege of instruction," "privilege . . . to give . . . all their property . . . for the mutual benefit of the family to which they belong" (Green and Wells, *Brief Exposition* 12, 13, 14). It is also used in the phrase "granted another privilege," applied to reinstated

apostates. As such, although "privilege" sometimes is clearly synonymous with "right," in Shaker parlance it also denotes opportunity, liberty, and choice—absolutely necessary conditions in some aspects of the Shaker scheme of things. For example, if a member of the **Junior Class** gives his/her property to the support of the Society, it "is a matter of *free choice*" (Evans et al.,*Compendium* 49), not a matter of necessity for junior membership or the right of the Society to have it. That is, the junior member has the liberty—or privilege—to give the property, or at least to offer it.

However, if a member of the Junior Class wishes to become a member of the **Senior Class** (or **Church Family**), the choice or liberty not to offer his/her property for the benefit of the Society is abrogated. In another sense, no member of the higher order has a right to withhold anything, for a requisite of membership is to "agree to devote . . . all . . . [he/she] possess[es], to the service of God" (Evans et al, *Compendium* 50). Looked at another way, the Shaker way, the opportunity to consecrate oneself totally to the service of God is a privilege—the primary privilege, an opportunity and an advantage not enjoyed by everyone because all people are neither desirous nor capable of such devotion. Thus, Church Family Shakers are rare individuals, the "chosen" few.

PUBLIC MEETING. *See* MEETING.

-R-

RAND, ELEAZER (17?–18?). Elder Eleazer, one of the first American **Shakers**, was with **Ann Lee** during some of her missionary tour of 1781–1783. He was also among the early **Believers** first appointed to high positions in the developing Shaker communal system. In 1791, Father Eleazer and Mother **Hannah Kendal** were sent to "gather" (*see* GATHERING/IN-GATHERING) members for what became the **Harvard** and **Shirley**, Massachusetts, **bishopric**, for which Rand served until 1808 (White and Taylor, *Shakerism* 86).

RANKIN, JOHN, SR. (1757–1850). Another of the several southwest **New Light** ministers who converted to **Shakerism** on October 28, 1807, following the arrival in the spring of 1805 of Shaker missionaries from **New Lebanon**, New York, Brother Rankin became an itinerate minister of the Shaker gospel and was mostly closely connected to the colony at Gasper

(Logan County, Kentucky), which had been the place of his home and congregation and which was renamed **South Union** in 1811. Among Elder John's gifts to posterity is his autobiography, which contains, among other informative material, his experience in and perception of the **Kentucky Revival** (a complement to the work on that subject written by fellow Presbyterian turned New Light turned Shaker **Richard McNemar**) (Coombs, "Shaker Colony" 156–159).

RATHBONE, REUBEN (1760–1807). *Alt. sp.: Rathbun.* One of the sons of **Valentine Wightman Rathbun Sr.**, Brother Reuben became a **Shaker** in 1780. In 1795, he was appointed **elder** of the **Church Family Elder** of the **Hancock**, Massachusetts, community. However, in 1799, as his father had, he apostatized because of, among other things, disagreements with the ministry over doctrines, such as the meaning of "**gift**" and his failure to be advanced to the ministry eldership. Rathbone, again as his father had, wrote an anti-Shaker tract. In his *Reasons Offered for Leaving the Shakers* (1800), he declares that he will avoid, "if possible, everything that may create or increase a spirit of hatred or envy against this people, for it is to be lamented there is a great deal too much already" (2). Nevertheless, the **apostate** could not avoid recounting therein a fistfight between **Ann Lee** and **William Lee**, her brother. At the time of the incident, according to Rathbone, Mother Ann appeared to be "very much overcome with strong liquor, and was under the influence and power of Satan" (27).

RATHBUN, VALENTINE WIGHTMAN, SR. (17?–18?). *Alt. sp.: Rathbone, Rathburn.* Leader of a Baptist congregation in Pittsfield, Massachusetts, Rathbun joined the **Shakers** in 1780 but left the Society after only a few months because, among other reasons, he did not receive the eldership he allegedly had been promised. Further, "he may have disagreed with the Shakers on dogma; more likely, he had difficulty subduing his strong personality" (Burns, *Shaker Cities* 16). Whatever the causes of his quick apostasy, he soon became an archenemy to the Shakers. His *Account of the Matter, Form, and Manner of a New and Strange Religion* (1781), which he says he wrote "at the request of many enquiring minds" (3), was the first of the anti-Shaker tracts published by early **apostates**.

Among his charges against the Society is that it "differs from the true religion of the gospel, regarding faith. . . . [T]he people in this new religion, do not so much talk about faith in Christ; but they place their whole knowledge in their religion, on their pretended visions, prophesies and signs" (16). Rathbun cautions his readers about "the growing evils that are prevailing in our land, especially the fatal delusion"—that is, **Shakerism**—he has just delineated (22). Rathbun's anti-Shaker activity also included persecution of the Shakers. For example, in 1783, during **Ann Lee's** missionary trip eastward, he "was the principal instigator and leader of . . . [the] mob" that harassed the Shakers in Hancock, Massachusetts (Green and Wells, *Testimonies* 126–127).

RESURRECTION. "The Resurrection is a doctrine generally believed by all who profess a belief in the Christian religion. But what constitutes the real nature and substance of the [R]esurrection, seems to be a subject of dispute among many" (Green and Wells, *Summary View* 352). As is the practice of **celibacy**, for example, so is the Shaker concept of the Resurrection another point of departure from mainstream Christianity. **Shakers** do not argue against the belief that after physical death both the just and the unjust will experience being brought back to "life"; however, whether "the natural body of man . . . will be . . . reanimated with the same living spirit" is the point of debate in Shaker thinking (Green and Wells, *Summary View* 352).

In Shaker doctrine, "the resurrection of the soul[,] the quickening of the germ of a new and spiritual life" (Evans et al., *Compendium* 56), "not the revivification of the dead physical body," is "the Christian resurrection . . . the rise from the death of sin and from the natural, carnal plane of existence into the life of regeneration" (White and Taylor, *Shakerism* 258). To argue their position, Shakers employ, among other passages, John 11:25–26 (King James Bible): "I am the resurrection and the life." The following is an example of their logic:

> If then, Christ is the resurrection and the life, it necessarily follows, that all who are in Christ, are in the resurrection of life, whether their bodies be dead or living. And also, if he that believeth in Christ, shall live, tho' his body be dead; then it must be the soul to which Christ had reference: for the dead body of a man cannot believe, any more than the dead carcass of any other animal. And again: If by the expression "Whosoever liveth, and believeth in me, shall never die," Christ alluded to the animal body, his has certainly failed: for the bodies of all Christians do die. Therefore Christ must have had particular reference to the soul, and not to the body. (Green and Wells, *Summary View* 353)

RETIRING TIME. As part of the routine of common days, after their last meal, usually at six o'clock, **Shakers** would return to their bedrooms (neither public nor exactly private abodes) for contemplation prior to attending evening meetings of various sorts, such as **union meetings** and worship services. As another manifestation of the continuous efforts of Shaker **leads** to ensure that nothing is left to suffer promiscuity, even the condition of retiring rooms and that of the persons "retiring" are under orders. In fact, an entire section (part 2, section 7) of the *Rules and Orders* of May 1860 (*see MILLENNIAL LAWS*) is devoted to "Orders concerning the Furniture of Retiring Rooms," while another section (part 2, section 2) states that "all, while sitting in retiring time, should sit erect, and in straight ranks."

RUSSELL, RALPH (1789–1864). In the fall of 1821, Russell "became interested in the Shaker religion through his friend James Darrow, whose brother [David Darrow] was an Elder in the Union Village [Ohio] community." After visiting **Union Village**, Russell planned to join the **Shakers** there, but he "was so successful in interesting other members of his family and his neighbors in becoming Shakers that the Union Village Ministry asked him to stay on his property and establish a new Shaker community" (Conlin, *North Union* 1). He did. "The first public meeting was held . . . March 31st [1822]" (Piercy, *Valley of God's Pleasure* 77). The new community became the relatively short-lived **North Union**.

Although Elder Ralph served temporarily as **lead** of the community, "the Head Church at Mt. Lebanon [i.e., **New Lebanon**] established an outside Ministry at North Union" in 1826 (Piercy, *Valley of God's Pleasure* 82). In 1829, the founder of North Union, who had not signed the **Church Covenant** of 1828, withdrew from the community and from the Society, perhaps because of his diminished significance.

-S-

SABBATHDAY LAKE (New Gloucester), Maine (1794–). *Spiritual name: Chosen Land.* Shortly after Nathan Merrill of New Gloucester (in Cumberland County and about 25 miles northwest of Portland), was converted to **Shakerism** in November 1793, "neighboring families were gathered in. Much opposition was experienced as the separating fires of truth broke up old natural ties of relationships" (White and Taylor, *Shakerism* 95). The following April, the Sabbathday Lake community was established.

Two years prior to this time timber had been cut and hauled to Poland Center to be sawed. This was used in building the Meeting House and first Central Dwelling. The Meeting House was raised June 14, 1794. It was patterned after the old Dutch style then in vogue in New York. It was wholly finished and ready to use on Christmas Day of that year. . . . The interior of the Meeting House was and is, something of a marvel. The meeting room, simple and unpretentious is unadorned except for the beautiful blue paint which is seemingly impossible to duplicate. It is still in its original state of beauty, never having been retouched since the house was built. (Barker, *Sabbathday Lake Shakers* 8–9)

According to Shaker chroniclers, the community had 3 **families** and about 150 members as of 1823. In 1875, it had about 70 members and 2 families. A visitor to the community during this latter time notes that it

has two thousand acres of land, and owns a saw-mill, gristmill, and a very complete machine shop. The people raise garden seeds, make brooms, dry measures, wire sieves, and the old-fashioned spinning-wheel. . . . But its most profitable industry is the manufacture of oak staves for molasses hogsheads, which are exported to the West Indies. . . . This society is less prosperous than most of the others. It has met with several severe losses by unfaithful and imprudent trustees. (Nordhoff, *Communistic Societies* 82–83)

Not exempt from the general decline in Shakerism, the Sabbathday Lake community has struggled throughout the twentieth century, but it was bolstered a bit in 1931 when it received the members from the defunct **Alfred**, Maine, community. In 1981, in an action similar to that taken in 1969 by the **Canterbury**, New Hampshire, community, Sabbathday Lake "turned over its property to a self-perpetuating, nonprofit corporation [The United Society of Shakers, Inc.] set up to continue the life of the community as an educational institution and museum. . . . the [nine] sisters continuing to live in their former home rent free." (Horgan, *Shaker Holyland* xxi).

With the death in 1992 of Sister **Ethel Hudson** of Canterbury, Sabbathday Lake became unique among Shaker communities: it is the only Shaker **village** occupied by Shakers—Sisters **Frances A. Carr**, **Minnie Green**, **Marie Burgess**, and **June Carpenter** and Brothers **Arnold Hadd** and **Wayne Smith**. They are very hospitable to an ever-increasing number of people from **the world** interested in them and in Shakerism. In effect, their village is operated as a "living" museum and a small business enterprise. In addition, some of them—most notably, Sister Frances and Brother Arnold—are very active in public service and travel extensively to answer requests for information about Shakerism. Sabbathday Lake also houses the Shaker Library, a very significant source of primary and secondary materials concerning the Shakers, and a small museum of Shaker artifacts. Both operations are in the care of hired non-Shakers.

Despite the rift with the Canterbury Shakers for several decades over the **Lead Ministry**'s closure of the **Church Covenant**, the Sabbathday Lake Shakers have continued to add members to their community: two **sisters** (one of whom apostatized in 1994) and two **brothers**, both younger than any of the current female members.

SAVOY, MASSACHUSETTS (1817–1825). Except for the **White Oak**, Georgia, **village**, Savoy was the shortest-lived Shaker community. It was situated in the northwestern part of the state, a few miles from Vermont, in the Green Mountain range. Its founding was largely the result of a revival, too—one that netted the **Shakers** about 80 members by the time the village closed. The revival allegedly was brought to the attention of the Shakers at **New Lebanon** by a spirit.

"Soon after, early in January, 1817, a letter was received from Elisha Smith, an outside Shaker," which declared that a Baptist elder had been working with the revivalists but that "he thought they were getting wild and needed help and that the Shakers could help them if anybody could" (White and Taylor, *Shakerism* 137). The new **Believers** formed their group with the guidance of Elder **Calvin Green**.

The reasons proffered for the closure of the community vary. In an account by a twentieth-century non-Shaker, gross and un-Shakerly behavior by the new Shakers, which caused Mother **Lucy Wright** no small amount of consternation, was at least one of the reasons:

> Controlling these small societies from New Lebanon was difficult. Believers at Savoy, whether native converts or imports from New Lebanon, were free from the more sever strictures that would have governed their lives at more solidly established Shaker villages, and they behaved accordingly. Ducks nested under the breakfast table and . . . brash young Brethren paraded in dooryards clad only in their shirts. (Brewer, *Shaker Communities* 38)

An account of the village by Shakers themselves, however, attributes the closing to unfavorable natural phenomena:

> They had a fine situation with a good water power, but a drouth in 1820, followed by a visitation of grasshoppers, affected their lands and they were reduced to great straits . . . and it was finally thought best to dispose of the property and transfer the family. (White and Taylor, *Shakerism* 138)

SAWYER, OTIS (18?–18?). In 1855, Brother Otis was appointed **lead elder** of the **Sabbathday Lake**, New Gloucester, Maine, community. One of his major contributions to the community was to rid it of unscrupulous **trustees** who had made financial deals in their own names, rather than in that of the community, and who simply stole money from transactions.

SEARS, ELIZABETH (18?–19?). In 1911, Sister Elizabeth, along with Brother Egbert Gillette, was involved in the infamous mercy killing of Sadie Marchant, another **Shakeress**, at the **Narcoossee**, Florida, colony, "who, in the last stages of tuberculosis, has asked for and received chloroform." Although criminal charges against Sears and Gillette were dismissed eventually, and although "it can scarcely be said that the Marchant case caused the abandonment of the Florida Shaker venture, . . . there was certainly little energy put into it after that time" (Anderson, "Shaker Community in Florida" 39, 42).

SECOND ADVENT. *See* MILLENNIUM.

SECOND COMING. *See* MILLENNIUM.

SENIOR CLASS/ORDER. Once **Shakers** satisfy all preliminary requirements for full membership in the Society, they are then "prepared to enter freely, fully, and voluntarily into a united and consecrated interest. These covenant and agree to devote themselves and services, with all they possess, to the service of God, and the support of the Gospel, forever." (Evans et al., *Compendium* 49–50). The Senior Class/Order literally comprised the Society itself because all other members were at various stages of **travel** toward total consecration. *See also* CHURCH FAMILY.

SEPARATION FROM THE WORLD. Along with principles and practices such as **celibacy**, **united interest**, and **confession of sin**, separation from **the world**—via Shakers constructing and residing in their own "towns"—is a cardinal element of institutional **Shakerism**. Since first settling in Niskayuna, New York, in 1776, until today at **Sabbathday Lake**, Maine, the United Society of Believers in Christ's Second Appearing has lived apart from the mainstream culture of the United States. However, as expressed in the following passage, spatial separation is neither the only nor necessarily the essential kind of separation:

> Christ's Kingdom and government can never be established on earth, among any people whatever, without a separation from the world; not indeed a separation from the natural creation, which is good in its or-

der, nor from anything in it which is virtuous, commendable or useful, to his true followers; but a separation from the follies, vanities, contaminating principles, and wicked practices of fallen man, under the reigning influence of a depraved human nature; and from all those things in which the great bulk of mankind seek their own honor and glory, instead of the honor and glory of God. (Green and Wells, *Summary View* 310)

SHAKER/SHAKERESS. *A.k.a. Believer.* A male/female member of the United Society of Believers in Christ's Second Appearing. Beginning with the leadership of **Joseph Meacham**, only the signers of the **Church Covenant** have been bona fide Shakers. (With the official closing of the covenant in 1965, a debate of sorts developed between the Canterbury and Sabbathday Lake communities—the only ones extant—over the latter's desire to add new members. Currently, because the Sabbathday Lake community is the only one peopled by **Shakers**, it adds members as it pleases, regardless of tradition and an **order** from the **Lead Ministry**.) Regarding the name "Shaker," a visitor to **New Lebanon** in the 1860s made the following comment: "Shaker being a term of mockery and reproach, like most of our religious names; one which the members meekly accept, and of which they are shyly proud" (Dixon, *New America* 301). The term very likely was derived from the so-called outward operations performed during Shaker worship. (For a more detailed discussion of Shaker ideology and practices, as well as a listing of other common appellations by which Shakers are called, *see* SHAKERISM.)

SHAKER (**JOURNAL; 1871–1872 and 1876–1877**). *See* LITERATURE.

SHAKER AND SHAKERESS (**JOURNAL; 1873–1875**). *See* LITERATURE.

"SHAKER BIBLE." The actual Bible of the **Shakers** is the 1611 King James Version. However, perhaps because **Benjamin S. Youngs's** *The Testimony of Christ's Second Appearing* (1808), which Marguerite Fellows Melcher calls "the most important of all the Shaker books" (*Shaker Adventure* 103), originally was possessed exclusively by the **elders**, it was alluded to by this nickname.

SHAKER CENTRAL TRUST FUND. A monetary fund established in 1959 by Eldress **Emma B. King** of the **Lead Ministry** of **Canterbury**, New Hampshire, "to provide for the care and needs of the covenanted members of the **Society**, to assist in the preservation of the Shaker heritage, and to promote the understanding of **Shakerism**" (Stein, *Shaker Experience* 366). The full nature of the trust fund was known by only the Canterbury ministry and the law firm that conducted its business. Now, however, since the Canterbury community is defunct, apparently only the law firm knows all the facts, such as the amount of the account and exactly how it is to be administered.

Presumably, the money was accumulated primarily from the sale of various properties as **villages** closed and, possibly, from stock market investments. A person might assume logically that the **Sabbathday Lake**, Maine, community inherited the funds upon the demise of the last Canterbury **Shaker**, but this seems not to be the case because friends of the Sabbathday Lake Shakers still contribute to the community's welfare by donating money and services to it, which it seems dearly to need.

SHAKER MANIFESTO (JOURNAL; 1878–1883). *See* LITERATURE.

SHAKER QUARTERLY (JOURNAL; 1961–). *See* LITERATURE.

SHAKER REVIVAL. *See* MOTHER ANN'S SECOND COMING.

SHAKERISM. Literally, the principles practiced—the beliefs acted upon—by all the members of the sect commonly called "**Shakers**": among the primary ones being **celibacy, confession of sin, separation from the world,** and **united interest** (also called, for example, **community of property** or **joint interest** or **Christian communism**). More generally, "Shakerism" denotes the name of the religion itself, and thus it embodies all adherents to its belief system as well. This sect and its members are known by a number of appellations, including:

Believers
Church of Christ's Second Appearing
Community of Shakers
Millennial Church
Shaking Quakers
Society of Shakers (often abbreviated, along with the last four names in this list, as "the Society")
True Believers
United Society of Believers
United Society of Believers in Christ's Second Appearing
United Society of Believers in the Second Appearing of Christ
United Society of Shakers (the name currently used by the **Sabbathday Lake** community)

All of these synonymous terms are interchangeably used, though some more often than others in certain contexts. For example, the "United Society of Believers in Christ's Second Appearing" is the most formal designation, and it is therefore used frequently in scholarly publications; less formal designations—most notably, simply "Shakers" or "Believers"—are employed more often in everyday parlance.

As an institutional system, Shakerism has been designed to be a total way of life—comprising, for example, religious, social, political, and economic systems that are inextricably bound together. To illustrate, since sin, ideologically to Shakers, lies in indulgence in the erotic pleasures of the flesh, salvation is predicated on ceasing such activity; hence, the Shakers have incorporated into their social system nonphysical intercourse between genders, of which celibacy is the extreme form.

From the beginning, Shaker apologists have made clear that Shakerism is not a fixed system but a progressive, ever-changing one:

> No creed can be framed to bind the progress of improvement in this institution. This would be incompatible with the true spirit of Christianity: for it is the faith of the Society, that the operations of divine light and wisdom are unlimited, and will forever continue to diffuse their benign and salutary influence, in extending divine knowledge and instruction, and bringing to perfection, in man, those principles which, in their Divine Source, are boundless as eternity. (Green and Wells, *Brief Exposition* 9–10)

Throughout its nearly 230 years of the history in America, Shakerism has been the object of much curiosity by people of "the world." In an effort to satisfy the requests of these people for information (and to promote their gospel), Shakers themselves have tendered in various types of publications numerous descriptions of the spiritual and temporal character of Shakerism. For example,

> Shakerism . . . is but another name for advanced Christianity. . . . It takes a whole man or woman to be a Shaker. For it means to cut off—to come to the end of the world in one's self. It means to leave kindred, home and people; to renounce worldly ambition and preferment; to renounce politics, to cast no party vote, to hold no political office in nation, state or city. It means to surrender one's whole life—time, talent, will; to give up one's own way; to work earnestly through all of life and have nothing of one's own to show, save character—the progress made in the work of redemption. (White and Taylor, *Shakerism* 379–80)
>
> *Shakerism as a system* is more varied in its elements, and complex and expansive in its character, than is any other purely *religious* system within our knowledge, and of course its adherents esteem it as the

most perfect and comprehensive; urging as a reason, that it takes possession and entire cognizance of the *whole* man; and, instead of attending *solely* to his *spiritual* necessities for only *one day in seven*, IT cares for and supplies all his *temporal* as well as *spiritual* wants *seven days a week*. (Evans et al., *Compendium* 25–26)

True Shakerism . . . is simply actualized Christianity . . . (Haskell, "What is Shakerism?" 21)

[Shakers espouse] virgin purity, peace, justice, love . . . celibate life, non-resistance, community of goods, universal brotherhood, . . . equality of the sexes, in all departments of life, equality in labor, . . . equality of property, . . . freedom of speech, . . . abolition of all slavery, . . . temperance in all things, . . . justice and kindness to all living beings, . . . practical benevolence, . . . [and] true democracy. [Furthermore, Shakers believe that] all life and activity animated by Christian Love is worship. Shakers adore God as the Almighty Creator . . . the Eternal Father-Mother. They recognize the Christ Spirit, the expression of Deity, manifested in fullness in Jesus of Nazareth, also in feminine manifestation through the personality of Ann Lee. Both they regard as Divine Saviors. [Also, Shakers live in] beautiful, comfortable Community Homes . . . [and are] free from debt, worry and competition. . . . The Head of the Shaker Order is Christ. . . . Spiritual leaders [are] of both sexes. (Shaker broadside, n.p., n.d.)

Such periodic descriptions were occasioned largely by what Shaker leaders perceived as scurrilous attacks on the nature and integrity of the Society, which they apparently felt obligated to defend:

Many erroneous opinions are entertained concerning the people generally known by the name Shakers, which are calculated to mislead the public mind, in respect to the true character of the Society. Many false reports and incorrect statements have been put in circulation, respecting the principles and practice of the Society, which have no foundation in truth. With a view to correct these erroneous opinions, and as far as in power, to remove prejudices and false impressions, we are induced from a principle of duty, to lay before the public a brief statement of facts respecting the principles, government, temporal order, and practical regulations of the Society. This duty we owe to ourselves and to our fellow creatures, for the information of the public, and the benefit of all concerned. (Green and Wells, *Brief Exposition* 3)

Besides expository disquisitions (sometimes very lengthy), Shakers have delineated the nature and principles of Shakerism in other forms of expression, such as in their poems and songs (poems performed, so to speak). For example, the virtue of humility and the paradoxical elevation spiritually of a humble person is expressed in the following verses:

I will bow and be simple.
I will bow and be free.
I will bow and be humble,
Yea, bow like the willow tree.

I will bow; this is the token.
I will wear the easy yoke.
I will bow and be broken.
Yea, I will fall upon the rock. (Patterson, *Shaker Spiritual* 339–340)

Whoever wants to be the highest
Must first come down to be the lowest.
And then ascend to be the highest
By keeping down, to be the lowest. (Elkins, *Fifteen Years* 22)

The value of Shakerism to humanity, along with the implicit expression of its creed, is contained in the following passage from the last great effort by Shakers themselves "to fit the principles embodied in this faith to the needs of the great world":

Shakerism presents a system of faith and a mode of life, which during the past century [the nineteenth], has solved social and religious problems and successfully established practical brotherhoods of industry, besides freeing woman from inequality and injustice. To this there must be added that it has banished from its precincts monopoly, immorality, intemperance and crime, by creating a life of purity, social freedom and altruistic industry. A system that has rendered such service to mankind merits attention from all thoughtful people, whatever may be their position in life. (White and Taylor, *Shakerism* 3)

SHAKING QUAKERS. The nickname of Quakers who became the original **Shakers**. Apparently, the name, devised by a non-Shaker, was first meant to be a derisive description of one of the worshipping habits of members who were wrought by so-called outward operations—shaking, that is, among other movements. *See also* SHAKERISM; WARDLEY, JAMES AND JANE.

SHEPHERD, JAMES (17?–18?). One of the original **Shakers** in America who arrived in New York with **Ann Lee** on August 6, 1774, James's role in the development of early **Shakerism** seems to have been negligible. Although he was an active participant in spreading the Shaker gospel with Mother Ann during her missionary journey to the eastern United States in 1781–1783, he, along with **John Partington**, refused to accept fellow English Shaker **James Whittaker** as the **lead** after the death of Ann Lee in 1784 and "then lost all relation to the work of God," soon thereafter leaving the Society (White and Taylor, *Shakerism* 69).

SHIRLEY, MASSACHUSETTS (1793–1908). *Spiritual name: Pleasant Garden.* Located only about seven miles west of the **Harvard** community, but in Middlesex County, Shirley had about 150 members in 1823; by 1875, it had only 2 **families**, composed of 12 children and 36 adults, of whom 30 were females (manifesting again, especially during the declining years, the phenomenon in Shaker **villages** of women far outnumbering men):

> As the old people died off, new members did not come in. They have not now [1875] many applications for membership; and of the children they adopt and bring up, not one in ten becomes a Shaker. Most of the members grew up in the society. . . . Like all the Shakers, they are long-lived—one sister, a colored woman, is eighty, and another eighty-eight—and their mortality rate is low. (Nordhoff, *Communistic Societies* 193–198)

As was its close neighbor Harvard, Shirley was a place of persecution of the **Shakers** during the time of **Ann Lee's** missionary work (1781–1783). Among the legends—the history, perhaps—is this incident: when Mother Ann was being harassed by a mob while staying at a Shaker's house in Shirley, "she was concealed in a narrow closet beside the chimney in the hall, a chest of drawers thrust before the door concealing the entrance. This was after known as 'Mother Ann's Closet.' " Another story involving the same mob entails the tree to which Father James Whittaker was tied while receiving "an inhuman whipping." He died soon after. "The blasted tree remained standing for many years, in silent yet eloquent testimony to the scenes it had witnessed" (White and Taylor, *Shakerism* 51–52).

Decline in membership due to apostasies and deaths and the opportunity to sell the property to the state of Massachusetts (to be used as an industrial school for boys) seem to have brought about the decision to close Shirley:

> The sale of Shaker properties in Shirley and in Lancaster for creation of the Shirley Industrial School was announced on October 3, 1908. . . . [T]he transaction involved 889 acres of land, together with twenty-six buildings. . . . The purchase price was $43,000.
>
> A Harvard diary entry for January 6, 1909, conveys the sense of loss: "Josephine Jilson, Laura Beal and Annie Bell Tuttle come here from Shirley, all there was left of a once promising society. . . . [P]oor sisters, they were heartbroken. . . . [T]hey had a hard time picking up and straightening out things. I hope they will get a home here." (Horgan, *Shaker Holyland* 146–147)

SISTER/BROTHER. *See* BROTHER/SISTER.

SLINGERLAND, JOSEPH (1854–1920). Besides "spearheading the financial reorganization of western Shakerism [by, for example, closing **North Union**, Ohio, in 1889] and the modernization of Union Village [Ohio], [by, for example, remodeling the Office building in the very un-Shaker Victorian style] in the 1890s" (Stein, *Shaker Experience* 281), Elder Joseph was much involved in land transactions and speculations—most notably, those regarding the short-lived Georgia colony at **White Oak**: "Purchases of land were recorded in the names of Joseph Slingerland, James K. Fennessy, Elizabeth Dowling, and Mary Gass 'trustees of and for the United Society of Believers at Union Village, Ohio' " (Vanstory, "Shakers" 361). The whole southern venture was not highly regarded by all **Shakers**: "Much doubt was felt in many minds of the advisability of these moves" because of the need of capital to support the northern communities (White and Taylor, *Shakerism* 213–214).

SMITH, COLONEL JAMES (17?–18?). Smith was "an ex-soldier of the Revolution, an ex-Presbyterian, an ex-New Light preacher, and an ex-Shaker" (Melcher, *Shaker Adventure* 77). After leaving the Society at **Union Village**, Ohio, he engaged in several vitriolic attacks on the **Shakers**. Among other activities, he "inserted in the public press . . . that they whip their underlings severely, and also their children; [and] that they count it no sin to have carnal knowledge of their own women" (MacLean, *Shakers of Ohio* 368). Also, on August 27, 1810, he was among the inciters of one of several mobs that plagued Union Village for over a decade thereafter. Furthermore, Smith produced two anti-Shaker pamphlets in 1810, *Remarkable Occurrences Lately Discovered among the People Called Shakers* and *Shakerism Detected*, which allege, among other charges, that the Shakers are treasonous and barbarous; if they are not prosecuted by the law, Smith argues, the militia ought to subdue them. Smith's son, James Jr., remained a Shaker after his father's apostasy.

SMITH, WAYNE (1963–). One of the two males residing in the extant **Sabbathday Lake** community in New Gloucester, Maine. Brother Wayne has been a **family** member since his late teenage years, even though he and the other **brother** did not sign the traditional **Church Covenant** due to its closure in 1965. His contribution to and role in the physical welfare of the **village** is what used to be called "farm **deacon**" in old Shaker parlance.

SOCIETY, THE. (Abbreviated form of several formal names by which Shakers are known.) *See* SHAKERISM.

SOCIETY OF SHAKERS. *See* SHAKERISM.

SODUS BAY, New York (1826–1836). Later moved to **Groveland**, New York, this community, situated beside Great Sodus Bay off Lake Ontario, was the last successful **village** to be established by the **Shakers**. Its founding was generated partly by religious revivalism in the area. On February 26, 1826, Shakers purchased about 1,300 acres on the Sodus Bay. The beginning of the community is actually dated as "March 13, 1826, when Joseph Pelham and his wife, Susanna, moved from their small farm in Galen [New York] into a communal dwelling, there to live separately for the rest of their lives" (Wisbey, *Sodus Shaker Community* 5).

Herbert A. Wisbey Jr. has provided an abridged chronology of the community as follows:

1826   May. Sodus ministry, appointed by New Lebanon, arrive. Process begins of clearing land, planting crops, setting out orchards, operating grist mill, saw, constructing buildings.

1829   January 1. Signed first covenant received from New Lebanon.

1831   July 17. Meeting house dedicated.

1832   June 27. . . . Improved methods of teaching introduced to school house by Seth Y. Wells.

1834   February 5. Moved into Church Family dwelling.

1836   Membership reached a high of 148. Nov. 21. Struck bargain with Sodus Canal Company to sell land. Dec. 6. Bought land in Groveland, Livingston County [New York].

1837   January 30. Began move to Groveland. (29).

The move from Sodus Bay to Groveland was occasioned by the Sodus Canal Company's being licensed by the New York legislature in 1829 to use whatever land it needed to build a canal from Sodus Bay to the Erie Canal. The Shaker tract lay in the way. The community had little choice but to vacate:

Local historians have explained the Shaker move . . . as an opportunity to profit from selling the improved land to the canal company at a good price and buying new property more cheaply in order to make a handsome profit. . . . Nothing could be more inaccurate. . . . When they [Shakers] purchased the land they expected to make a permanent communal home and were slow to recognize even the possibility that they might be forced to move. Certainly they were most reluctant to do so. (Wisbey, *Sodus Shaker Community* 19–20)

SONGS/POEMS. From the inception of **Shakerism**, singing has been a part of the sect's worshipping practices. Apparently, the earliest American **Shakers** not only sang so-called wordless songs but also sang spontaneously: "Some will be singing, each one his own tune; some without words . . . some tunes of their own making, in an unknown mutter, which they call new tongues" (Rathbun, *An Account* 11). Worded songs did not appear in **Meeting** until the first decade of the nineteenth century, by which time Meeting itself had evolved into a highly structured weekly event—and, apparently, a very entertaining one to the public. No longer seeming to be the product of a frenzy of fools, Meeting—as well as all of Shakerism—had become an orderly affair, as manifested, for example, by the performance of **dances/marches**, and **songs/poems**, all practiced to perfection. (Note that, to Shakers, "songs" and "poems" are synonymous, as a song is envisioned as a poem performed.)

The Shakers have been prolific composers of songs in various genres, such as ballads, hymns, and anthems. If indeed they produced "between one and two thousand songs and hymns" between 1837 and 1847—the period of **Mother Ann's Second Coming**—then they are likely to have written hundreds, maybe thousands, of verses for singing and reading during the rest of their history (White and Taylor, *Shakerism* 337).

SOULE, GERTRUDE (1895–1988). One of several elderly Shaker leaders to die between 1988 and 1990, Sister Gertrude entered the Society at **Sabbathday Lake**, Maine, when she was a child. She served as part of the **Lead Ministry** from 1957 onward, and as part of that governing body, she was involved in two major decisions intended to affect the future of **Shakerism**: the establishment of the **Shaker Central Trust Fund** in 1959 and the closing of the **Church Covenant** in 1965. Eldress Gertrude moved from Sabbathday Lake to **Canterbury**, New Hampshire, in 1971.

SOUTH UNION, Kentucky (1807–1922). *Spiritual name: Jasper Valley.* Located in Gasper (or Jasper) Springs, Logan County, about 15 miles northeast of Russellville, about 333 miles southwest of **Union Village**, Ohio, and about 135 miles southwest of **Pleasant Hill**, South Union had between 300 and 400 members in 1823 and about 700 total during its existence.

[It] was founded nearly on the scene of the wild "Kentucky Revival" in the year 1807, the gathering taking place on 1809. Some of the log cabins then built by the early members are still [1875] standing, and the first meeting house, built in 1810, bears that name on the front. . . . For many years there was a colored family, with a colored elder, living upon the same terms as the whites. . . . [S]ome of these fell away . . . but . . . a number . . . died in the faith. (Nordhoff, *Communistic Societies* 207)

Besides agriculture and the raising of livestock, among the other **industries** of the community was the silk culture:

in June, 1832, the sisters are reported as gathering the first crop of the season, 137 pounds of 110,285 cocoons. The most delicate and beautiful of silk handkerchiefs are still shown, the manufacture, by hand spinning, of Kentucky sisters. (White and Taylor, *Shakerism* 124)

As did Pleasant Hill, so did South Union suffer greatly from the Civil War. A **Shaker** alleged that it cost the community over $100,000 as a result of, among other things, destruction to buildings and their contents and the Shakers' charity with their food: "they served at least fifty thousand meals to Union and Confederate soldiers alike" (Nordhoff, *Communistic Societies* 210).

By the turn of the century, South Union, too, was in dire straits, and **Shakerism** in Kentucky was nearing its conclusion.

Slowly the little group diminished. Ten were alive in 1922, when it was decided to dispose of the property, now reduced from about 7,000 acres to 4,113 acres of fine farming land, with all the cattle, stock, farming implements and furnishings, the store and the hotel. The proceeds were to be divided among the surviving members of South Union and the parent society at New Lebanon, New York.

On September 26, 1922, the sale was held. One local newspaper account says 5,000 to 6,000 people attended it and that the average price of the land, divided into sixty farms, was about $56.00 per acre. At that rate at least $229,000 must have been realized from the land and buildings alone.

Three of the ten surviving Shakers decided to accept $10,000 each as their share of the money realized from the sale and to live in the nearby town of Auburn. Two of these married each other, contrary to their long-professed religious belief, and lived happily ever after. The other seven chose to end their days at . . . New Lebanon. (Coombs, "Shaker Colony" 171)

Today, South Union is one of several properties that have become museums of the Shaker experience in America. Unfortunately, very few original buildings are extant, but The Centre Family Dwelling, the Preservatory, and three and one-half acres were acquired by a nonprofit corporation in 1971 and thus the Shaker Museum at South Union was established. A testimony to the burgeoning interest in the Shakers by Americans of the late twentieth century is that "over 6000 persons visited the museum during the first season . . . 1972" (Richmond, *Shaker Literature* II, 119).

SPINNING, DAVID (18?–18?). "For thirty-six years North Union [Ohio] had the ablest type of leadership" (White and Taylor, *Shakerism* 88). One among those who contributed to this reputation was Brother David, **lead elder** of the community from 1832 to 1840. An effective preacher, Elder David

> was steeped in self-denial; he curtailed expenses, dieted and dressed cheaply and denied himself the simplest pleasures. The principle [*sic*] reason behind this frugality was . . . that there were so many poor . . . of whom he was ever conscious. He was simply obsessed by a desire to relieve suffering humanity. In spite of his personal frugality, North Union prospered under his guidance. (Piercy, *Valley of God's Pleasure* 96)

Among Spinning's activities was his direction to erect several buildings in 1832, 1836, 1837, and 1838, which served as workshops, barns, a sawmill, and a **dwelling house** (MacLean, *Shakers of Ohio* 124).

SPIRIT DRAWING. *See* INSPIRATIONAL DRAWING.

SPIRITUALISM. This concept has two dimensions in **Shakerism**. In one sense, the **Shakers** always have been spiritualists because the continuous development of the spiritual self is the essential principle of Shakerism. In all that they do everyday, they do the best that they can; thus, their striving for perfection in mundane matters such as making oval boxes and controlling their natural lasciviousness, say, is a manifestation—a symbol—of their efforts to perfect their spirits.

In another sense, spiritualism is the "conscious, continuous action and reaction between the worlds of spirit and sense" (White and Taylor, *Shakerism* 221). It involves, among other things, visions of the afterlife and visitations from spirits departed from the world. From the beginning—from the time of **Ann Lee**'s visits from the **Christ Spirit**—spirits manifesting themselves to humans have been a part of Shakerism and, indeed, "the inheritance of the Christian church" (Avery, "Spirit Manifestations," in Blinn, *Manifestation of Spiritualism* 64).

One period in Shaker history is singular for spirit manifestations. It is identified by several names, among them "**Mother Ann's Second Coming**" and "Mother's Work." Beginning August 16, 1837, at the **Watervliet**, New York, **village** and lasting until about 1847, the most profuse intercourse between the Shakers and the spirit world occurred. The glut of spiritualism began among the children (perhaps in connection somehow with the concern of the **elders** about the worldliness of the young people in the villages), but it spread to the older members as well. Probably typical of such experiences is the following account:

> While thus entranced these spirit messengers led them [children] on visionary journeys in the Spirit world, the scenes and incidents of which they, while entranced, would describe with all the graphic and enchanting minuteness of a most exquisitely gifted earthly traveler. Their trance journeys were made by gestures as of flying. . . . [T]he visionists met multitudes of spirits and often conversed with some of them as with mortals. (Avery, "Spirit Manifestations," in Blinn, *Manifestation of Spiritualism* 65–66)

Apparently, the experience of so-called visions was inadequate in itself to get Mother's Work done, so various members of the Society evolved, so to speak, into **instruments** (or mediums) whose role was, at least partly, to deliver messages—admonitions, often—from the spirit world to individual Shakers, many of whom were themselves claiming, among other things, reception of **gifts** from spiritual entities. The truthfulness of all the profuse alleged visions and gifts concerned the elders, who probably perceived that the nature and number of spiritual happenings betokened that things were getting out of hand; thus, eventually, spiritual experiences had to be "approved."

A Shaker historian of the period makes the following comment pertinent to this matter:

> The Shakers recognize the fact that when the avenues of spirit communication are opened to mortals . . .both good and evil spirits avail themselves of this open avenue; . . . therefore, impressible media are often ministered unto both by true and deceiving spirits, if entirely left to themselves and unguarded by the true Church of Christ. . . . If the mediumistic communications do not teach the overcoming of the worldly life, in every professed Christian, by self-denials (not self-indulgence), taught by Christ, then they are false teaching, and from evil spirits. (Avery, *A Defense* 3)

According to other Shaker historians, the remarkable period of spiritualism ended in 1847, when "the spirit visitors announced to the people that they were about to leave them and go out into the world . . . for the uplifting and enlightenment of humanity." However,

> The promise remained that in the fullness of time, a greater and more wonderful re-opening of the heavenly world would be given to the

people who had first received the endowment of spirit communication. Thus the Shaker Church may justly claim to be the parent of modern spiritualism. (White and Taylor, *Shakerism* 237–238)

SPIRITUAL NAME. *A.k.a.: religious name.* In 1842, as part of the unusual activity during the period known as "**Mother Ann's Second Coming**" (c. 1837–1847), **villages** were issued spiritual or religious names. For example, "Chosen Land" became the surrogate for **Sabbathday Lake**, Maine. Also during this period, all villages were instructed to build sites for special outdoor services held "one day in spring and one in autumn" (White and Taylor, *Shakerism* 230). Such places are called variously "holy ground" or "feast ground," where so-called mountain meetings occur, and they, too, were formally named, such as "Pleasant Grove" at **Canterbury**, New Hampshire. "Who gave these names . . . although I have persistently inquired, I have been unable to ascertain" (MacLean, *Shakers of Ohio* 407–408).

SQUARE HOUSE. The name given to the building that served as headquarters for **Mother Ann Lee** in Harvard, Massachusetts, during her 1781–1783 missionary work in Massachusetts and Connecticut. So named because of the shape of its roof, the house had been owned by **Shadrach Ireland**, who became a self-ordained reverend and rebel Congregationalist after he had attended a **New Light** revival meeting.

STANLEY, ABRAHAM (17?–17?). *Alt. sp.: Standerin, Standley.* The husband of **Ann Lee**, Abraham immigrated to America with her in 1774, which is somewhat enigmatic, for no evidence of his accepting any part of the Shaker gospel exists. Apparently, he and she parted permanently around 1775 while they were in New York City.

STEWART, PHILEMON (1804–18?). Among the **Shakers** from the time he was seven years old, Brother Philemon, a gardener for and a member of the **Church Family** of the **New Lebanon**, New York, community, achieved distinction initially during the era known as "**Mother Ann's Second Coming**," about 1837–1847. At Meeting early in 1838, he "delivered the first direct communication from Jesus and Mother Ann . . . [thus,] he was the first, and probably the most prominent of the Shaker 'instruments' " during this period of fantastical spiritual manifestations (Andrews, *People Called Shakers* 153).

> As an instrument . . . Philemon rapidly became a force to be reckoned with. . . . Whatever the impetus for Stewart's "gifts,"—whether genuine or feigned—they certainly put him on center stage. For the first time

he was in a commanding position within the sect. (Brewer, *Shaker Communities* 125–126)

What might be construed as evidence of Stewart's special position as an instrument, in 1843, acting as "a mortal instrument in the hands of Holy Angels" (219), he composed and the Society issued *A Holy, Sacred, and Divine Roll and Book* from the **Canterbury**, New Hampshire, **village**.

> The book is a product of the most intense spiritual manifestations among the Shakers, and its contents were believed to be a new revelation of the will of God. Later, when the Ministry decided that it did not represent a true revelation, the book was withdrawn from circulation. Its affinity with the Book of Mormon (1830) has often been noticed. (Richmond, *Shaker Literature* I, 192)

A traditionalist in Shaker politics, Stewart also continually feuded with the **Lead Ministry** over contemporary changes in the Society. For example, "he argued for a complete separation from worldliness; a stricter separation of the sexes . . . ; the prohibition of animal food and strong intoxicating liquors; [and] plainness in personal adornment" (Andrews, *People Called Shakers* 156).

SWEEPING GIFT. Introduced in 1842, during the era of **Mother Ann's Second Coming**, this ritual "through song and testimony was one of spiritual cleansing":

> Four Brethren and four Sisters were selected as mediums. Eight singers were appointed to accompany the Sweepers. This band marched in procession through every room in every building, and occupied more or less time in singing and speaking. . . . Eight days were occupied in these exercises [performed once a year for eight years], and the sixteen persons were released from all temporal duties, during this term, and gave themselves to meditation and prayer. (Blinn, *Manifestation of Spiritualism* 37–39)

Conjunctive with the purification accomplished by spiritual "sweeping" was the literal sweeping and cleansing of the entire **village** in preparation for visits from **Holy Mother Wisdom**.

-T-

TALCOTT, JEREMIAH (17?–18?). Elder Talcott was among the missionaries sent from **New Lebanon**, New York, in 1825 to deliver "instruction in the principles of Shakerism" to the people in Lyons, New York, who had requested it. The mission resulted in the founding of the **Sodus Bay**, New York, community in 1826 (White and Taylor, *Shakerism* 154).

TAYLOR, AMOS (17?–18?). Another of the early **apostates**, Taylor published in 1782, at his own expense, a pamphlet of 23 pages stating his perceptions of the first American **Shakers** and his disaffection with them. They ought, he said, "to be guarded against" because, among other things, their leaders'—"a few Europeans"—control over the members "saps the foundation of Independency," the primary principle for which the American Revolution occurred (Taylor, *Narrative* 3). An itinerate teacher and poet, Taylor's early experiences with the Shakers happened at **Harvard**, Massachusetts. Some of his allegations, such as that about the early Shakers' frantic behavior at **Meeting**, complement those of other early apostates, for example, **Valentine Wightman Rathbun Sr.**

TAYLOR, LEILA S. (18?–19?). Among other significant activities, Eldress Leila of **New Lebanon**, New York, was one of the female leaders of the Society in the latter nineteenth and early twentieth centuries; she was an heir, so to speak, of Elder **Frederick W. Evans**, one of the dominant spokespersons of the era who were advocating, for example, that the Society become more involved with **the world**. Her support of gender parity—and not that of just Shaker people—and her knowledge of the Society's history and **theology**, as well as the quality of her thought are manifested in *Shakerism: Its Meaning and Message* (1904), which she co-authored with Eldress **Anna White**, also of the New Lebanon community. The volume has become the last attempt by **Shakers** themselves to render a somewhat comprehensive account of the Shaker pilgrimage (although its usefulness suffers from its lack of proper documentation). After an account of the past, the authors conclude their work with, among other thoughts, a surmise that **Shakerism** will be everlasting:

> Are the Shakers dying out? Yea! dying out and up. Men and women die—advance, go to higher planes, to spheres of greater radius than earth, where we hear of them actively engaged along the same lines as on earth—the spread of truth among humanity.
>
> Is Shakerism dying? Nay! not unless God and Christ and eternal verities are failing.
>
> Thought, spiritual life, move in spirals; each greater spiral returning on itself, yet ever higher, ever onward. . . . As in physical nature, so in spiritual life, organizations obey the tidal law of ebb and flood, the spiral law of retrogression and fresh advance. (389)

TESTIMONY(IES). Autobiographical accounts of experiences related to religion were often presented by **Shakers**. Early in the nineteenth century, testimonies by **Believers** who had been in the company of Mother **Ann Lee** 30 years earlier, during her missionary trip in New England (1781–1783), for example, began to be collected and recorded for posterity, especially for the inspiration and edification of current and future Shakers. Besides individual published autobiographies, collections of the testimonies of eighteenth-century Shakers were published several times during the nineteenth century—with each subsequent edition possessing some remarkable differences in its version of the "same" testimony rendered in an earlier edition, making, in these cases, the historical value of the testimony suspect. Variations of the word "testimony" appear in the title of several Shaker publications.

THEOLOGY. Regarding God's nature, God's attributes, and God's relationship to the universe, among other matters, **Shakerism** is in the mainstream of Judeo-Christian thought—especially the Christian part of it. For one thing, the sect reveres an almighty creator—a "father"—of all things who is loving, merciful, and forgiving (but only to a certain point, apparently). This is evidenced by His matchless sacrifice in "allowing," so to speak, the **Christ Spirit**—His "son"—to inhabit a carnal form in order to suffer human physical pain and death as a surrogate reprisal of God for humanity's willful sins and as a promise of a heavenly eternal life to humans who follow the admonitions and ways of Christ as manifested in/through Jesus. (Jesus himself is not to be confused with Christ—according to the Shaker perspective, of which the **Shakers** are ever re-mindful. Jesus the human being played only a superficial role in the first appearance of the Christ Spirit.)

However, as do all sects of the Christian religion, so the Shakers have their own particular, peculiar, and unique principles and practices, as witnessed by, for example, their belief that God has both male and female attributes, which is perfectly logical to them because all of generative nature also has these characteristics. God's dual nature is the source of the master metaphor of institutional Shakerism: **leads**, equal numbers of males and females when possible, are the "**fathers**" and "**mothers**" of "**families**" peopled by "sons" and "daughters"—spiritual "**brothers**" and "**sisters**." All members work in **union** to create a heaven on earth, a "home," by virtue of their efforts to reach spiritual perfection via, among other ways, subduing their carnal (i.e., human) nature by practicing **celibacy**.

Another peculiarity of the Shaker theology, also stemming from the concept of a dual-gendered deity, is the belief that although the appearance of the Christ Spirit in/through Jesus was not the end of God's plan to redeem fallen humanity, the **Millennium** was to be (or *is*, in Shaker thought) quite different from the first Advent:

> There was to be a second coming of the Christ Spirit *in his glory—not* of *Jesus* but of *Christ*, manifest *in* and *through the female—*woman, the *glory of man*; thus, redeemed man, in dual character the *glory of God.* (Avery, *Sketches of Shakers* 14)

Since God is both male and female, for the sake of **gender parity**, logic insists that the Second Advent or Second Coming be accomplished in/through a female. Englishwoman **Ann Lee**, founder of the Shakers around the middle of the eighteenth century, was regarded by her followers as the human in/through whom the Christ Spirit was making Its second appearance (hence the sect's formal title: the United Society of Believers in Christ's Second Appearing). Although Ann Lee conducted her adult life in the same humble manner as did Jesus, the Christ Spirit seemingly did not work through her in as dramatic a fashion as It did through Jesus, albeit she suffered terrible mental and physical persecution and is believed to have died from wounds she received on a missionary trip. Simply put, to the Shakers, Mother Ann's intense and, apparently, powerful testimony of love for God and mankind, her fierce deprecation of her carnal self, and her inexhaustible desire for spiritual perfection clearly manifested the appearance of the Christ Spirit in/through her.

If she could affect those around her with these attributes, and they, in turn, could affect others with them, and so on, then the Christ Spirit would be present eventually in all humans. (This is much akin to the modern Catholic Church tenet that Christ works through individual persons.) The Second Coming, therefore, would not be sudden and ubiquitous. Rather, like a sunrise, it would be gradual and not everywhere simultaneously. Humanity would be saved, but redemption might take a good long time. The New Creation would exist sooner or later, depending entirely on humans themselves. Part of the salvation philosophy of the Shakers is couched in the following paraphrase of a saying alleged to have been spoken by Ann Lee: "Do all the good you can, in every way you can, for everybody you can, as often as you can."

In the beginning, Shaker theology was what Ann Lee said it was. Although she was illiterate, according to accounts of her by witnesses, she evidently knew the Bible, especially the New Testament, very well and preached her understanding of it. In a sense, she was Shakerism, but posterity knows her virtually only from the memories of some of her followers, many of them very far along in years when Shaker chroniclers trying to preserve their heritage asked them to recall their times with Mother Ann.

The first written and printed statement of Shaker theology has been attributed to **Joseph Meacham**, the organizer of institutional Shakerism. His *A Concise Statement of the Principles of the Only True Church* (1790) promulgated, among other thoughts, that Christ was in His second appearance—that the Millennium was in progress. Thus, unlike the case of Christ and Jesus, Christ did not go away when Ann Lee died. Christ still is present, is "alive," working salvation through **True Believers**.

Undoubtedly, the most definitive exposition of Shaker theology is that which scholars have attributed to Shaker **Benjamin S. Youngs**. His *Testimony of Christ's Second Appearing* (1808) is a typical Shaker tour de force of biblical knowledge in the course of his exposition of the sect's faith and principles. Sometimes called (erroneously) the **"Shaker Bible"** by **the world**, this work put into writing what mostly had been communicated orally, but, if scholars are correct, the text is not the work of only Youngs. It is probably a composite of the thought of other prominent Shaker theologians, such as **Richard McNemar**, all of whom apparently conceded that Youngs was the best qualified to do the composition.

Common members of the Society are encouraged to study on their own the Old and New Testaments and the writings on Shakerism by their fellow Shakers. However, as is often the case, especially with such a diverse demographic character as that of the Shakers during the nineteenth century, most of the common members' experience with and knowledge about Shaker theology comes at **Meeting**, where they are read to, sometimes preached at, sing songs celebrating their faith, and render personal **testimonies** about the ongoing work to achieve spiritual perfection. (In the old days, the brothers and sisters danced symbolically and engaged in **operations**— making evident in both activities that they were involved in matters of the spirit.)

In the late nineteenth and early twentieth centuries, Shakers were still defining their theology as it continued to develop into "higher and higher more perfect" condition through revelations to **Believers** and their so-called spiritual **travel** in the gospel. *A Summary View of the Millennial Church* (Green and Wells, 1823), the journal *Manifesto* (1871–1899, during which time it was published under various names), and *Shakerism:*

Its Meaning and Message (White and Taylor, 1904) are examples of the Shakers' continuing efforts to delineate their faith.

See also BAPTISM; CELIBACY/MARRIAGE; CHRIST SPIRIT; CONFESSION OF SIN; CROSS; DANCES/MARCHES; ELDER/ELDRESS; FATHER/MOTHER DEITY; FEAST GROUND; GIFT; HEAVENLY FATHER; HOLY MOTHER WISDOM; INSTRUMENT; LEAD MINISTRY; LORD'S SUPPER; MEETING; MILLENNIUM; MOTHER ANN'S SECOND COMING; RESURRECTION; SHAKERISM; SPIRITUALISM.

TRANCE-GOER. In Shaker parlance, this term denotes any person "who would be absent for hours at a time" on a visit to the spirit world (*see also* INSTRUMENT; VISIONIST):

> When they returned . . . they would relate many wonderful sights and scenes realized, mostly of a pleasurable character, but often they met with very painful experiences, spirits in darkness and prison, suffering great distress in consequence of their past sinful lives here on earth. (Blinn, *Manifestation of Spiritualism* 78)

TRAVEL. **Shakers** have used this old metaphor to concretize progress in spiritual development, as in the phrase "travel in the gospel." Lack of such progress—or even regression—is expressed by **backsliding** (not exactly a metaphorical negative of traveling).

TRUE BELIEVER. A synonym, along with just **Believer** or **Shaker**, for a member of the **Church Family**.

TRUSTEE. *A.k.a.: office deacon.* A member of the sect responsible for managing the temporal matters on behalf of the community—with the proviso, of course, that a trustee's acts are in **union** with the welfare of the **Church** or Society in general. Groups of such members, equal in number per gender whenever possible, in effect supervise all of the material wealth of the communities at their own discretion; trustees mostly transact business with **the world**, such as buying and selling land and making contracts. *See also* CHURCH COVENANT.

TURNOFF. *See* APOSTATE.

TYRINGHAM, MASSACHUSETTS (1792–1875). *Spiritual name: City of Love.* Along with **Hancock**, Massachusetts, and **Enfield**, Connecticut, Tyringham composed the Second Bishopric. It was situated in Berkshire County, about 16 miles south of Hancock. In the 1840s and 1850s, it had about 100 members. Regarding its location, a remarkable place was chosen for this village. The country is mountainous and the mountain rises several hundred feet above the buildings, while the valley in which was found their best tillage is many hundred feet below. Some of the houses, entered from the roadway, were two stories in front and four stories in the rear, being built against the side of a mountain. (White and Taylor, *Shakerism* 97)

When Tyringham was closed in 1875,

it still had seven sisters between the ages of twenty and forty, two more forty to sixty, six above the age of sixty. Among the Believers a young woman could find loving friends, a decent primary education, training in useful work, and the opportunity—almost unknown in the world— to hold a leadership position. (Burns, *Shaker Cities* 160)

After the community property was sold, the members moved to Hancock or Enfield.

-U-

UNION. Shakers seek to be together in their efforts to eradicate sin (theirs and that of others), among other goals, and, hence, advance spiritually. Thus, the concept of union appears often in their statements of both spiritual and temporal matters, as in those concerning **union meeting.** That everything, such as social relationships between the genders, be in accord with the principles of the pilgrimage to perfection of the spirit not only is necessary to the realization of that condition, but also being in union is itself an expression or manifestation of perfection.

UNION BRANCH. *See* GROVELAND, NEW YORK.

UNION MEETING: Because "the business side of communistic life required the cooperation of brethren and sisters . . . a spiritual union . . . [of them] was always sought" (White and Taylor, *Shakerism* 80). To this end, union meetings were established in 1793 by Father **Joseph Meacham**. They were "such a source of intellectual and spiritual satisfaction, that they were continued for over a century" (White and Taylor, *Shakerism* 80). Regarding numbers, procedures, and the value of these meetings, some disagreement among reporters exists.

According to an observer from **the world** in 1841, who probably was speaking of the **New Lebanon**, New York, community because of the large number of **Shakers** mentioned ("six hundred"), union meetings took the following course:

A few minutes past nine [every day?], work is laid aside; the females change, or adjust, as best suits their fancy, their caps, handkerchiefs, and pinners, with a precision which indicates that they are not *altogether* free from vanity. The chairs, perhaps to the number of a dozen, are set in two rows, in such a manner that those who occupy them may face each other. At the ringing of a bell, each one goes to the chamber where either he or she has been directed by the elders, or remains at home to receive company. . . . They enter the chambers *sans ceremonie*, and seat themselves—the men occupying one row of chairs, the women the other. Here, with their clean, checked, home-made pocket-handkerchiefs spread in their laps, and their spitboxes standing in a row between them, they converse about the raising of sheep and kine [e.g., cows), herbs and vegetables, building wall and raising corn, heating the oven and paring apples, killing rats and gathering nuts, spinning tow and weaving sieves, making preserves and mending the brethren's clothes,—in short, every thing they do will afford some little conversation. But beyond their own little world, they do not appear to extend scarcely a thought. And why should they? Having so few resources of information, they know not what is passing beyond them. They however make the most of their own affairs, and seem to regret that they can converse no longer, when, after sitting together from half to three-quarters of an hour, the bell warns them that it is time to separate, which they do by rising up, locking their hands across their breasts, and bowing. Each one then goes silently to his own chamber. ([C. B.], "A Shaker Visit" 195–196)

The account of union meetings rendered by an **apostate** Shaker in 1853 is instructive of the fact in historiography that the truth depends partly and often on who is relating it:

[At **Enfield**, New Hampshire,] three evenings in the week are set apart for worship, and three for "union meetings." Monday evenings all may retire to rest at the usual meeting time, an hour earlier than usual. For the union meetings the brethren remain in their rooms, and the sisters, six, eight, or ten in number, enter and sit in a rank opposite to that of the brethren's, and converse simply, often facetiously, but rarely profoundly. In fact, to say "agreeable things about nothing," when conversant with the other sex, is as common there as elsewhere. And what of dignity or meaning could be said? where talking of sacred subjects is not allowed, under the pretext that it scatters those blessings which should be carefully treasured up; and bestowing much information concerning the secular plans of economy practiced by your own, to the other sex, is not approved; and where to talk of literary matters would be termed bombastic pedantry, and small display, would serve to exhibit accomplishments which might be enticingly dangerous. Nevertheless, an hour passes away very agreeably and even rapturously with those who there chance to meet with an especial favorite; succeeded soon, however, when soft words, and kind, concentrated looks become obvious to the jealous eyes of a female espionage, by the agonies of a separation. For the tiding of such reciprocity, whether true or surmised, is sure before the lapse of many hours to reach the ears of the elders; in which case, the one or the other party would be subsequently summoned to another circle of colloquy and union. (Elkins, *Fifteen Years* 26)

Yet another version of this social ritual is that rendered by a twentieth-century historian:

Following a prescribed order set by the Ministry, an equal number of brethren and sisters met two evenings a week and twice on Sundays in certain retiring rooms; sat facing each other in two ranks about five feet apart; and conversed for about an hour, each with the person opposite him or her, on topics of mutual but impersonal interest. Sometimes the gathering was turned into a singing meeting. (Andrews, *Gift to Be Simple* 12)

UNION VILLAGE, Ohio (1806–1912). *Spiritual name: Wisdom's Paradise.* The community was located in Warren County, about 4 miles west of the town of Lebanon and about 30 miles northeast of Cincinnati. A direct product of the so-called **Kentucky Revival**, it was the oldest and largest Shaker community in what the **Shakers** labeled the "southwest" at the time and the seat of the **bishopric** of the area. As of 1823, it had nearly 600 members. In 1875, the village consisted of 4 **families** and about 215 persons, 95 being males (Nordhoff, *Communistic Societies* 200). In 1907, a reporter states that

the Shakers number about forty-five, who take life quietly, and enjoy all the luxuries they desire. The office, where resides the ministry, is one of the finest executive buildings in America, and furnished more luxuriously than any business office in the state. Notwithstanding the fact that here we may find nearly every desire that an upright mind might demand, yet the community is growing less, and apparently its days are numbered. (MacLean, *Shakers of Ohio* 59)

Besides suffering a continuous decline in membership, Union Village had a plethora of other problems, such as several mob attacks—the most infamous one occurring on August 27, 1810:

An armed mob of five hundred strong, led by a Presbyterian minister, marched against the village, for the avowed purpose of releasing the women and children who were said to be detained there against their will. . . .

> To the demand that they leave the country, the Shakers replied that they were living on their own lands purchased with their own money and they were entitled to the liberties allowed by the laws of the land, liberty of conscience included. [After a committee of the mob searched the premises, it reported] that everything was orderly, neat and attractive and every one seemed happy, contented and well cared for. (White and Taylor, *Shakerism* 120–121)

Another problem of Union Village was indebtedness: "in 1835 they suffered from the defalcation of a trustee, to the amount of between forty and fifty thousand dollars" (Nordhoff, *Communistic Societies* 202). In the 1860s, though membership had significantly declined, it purchased more land, which it could not properly manage, and ran up a debt of about $20,000. To these financial woes were added others, for example, the closure of the woolen factory in 1869 because it could not compete with mills of **the world** and the loss to fire by an alleged arsonist in 1870 of a grain and stock barn worth about $25,000 (MacLean, *Shakers of Ohio* 103).

Among the innovations in traditional Shaker practices was the Lyceum in operation at Union Village in the 1870s. It was

> a kind of debating club which . . . [met] once a week, for the discussion of set questions, reading, and the criticism of essays written by the members. The last question discussed was, "Whether it is best for the Shaker societies to work on cash or credit."
>
> This Lyceum [opposed at first by the eastern ministry] has produced another meeting in the Church Family . . . once a week, [for] all the members. . . . [Among other benefits] these weekly meetings are found to give the younger members a greater interest in the society . . . "and we feel [said one of the older and official members] that we must do something to make home more pleasant for our young people—they want more music and more books, and shall have them; they are greatly interested in these weekly business meetings; and I am in favor of giving them just as much and as broad an education as they desire." (Nordhoff 203)

In 1867, another attempt at innovation was unsuccessful:

> A proposition was advanced to make the society a corporate body, introducing the voting system into the government. This was severely rebuked by the Eastern Ministry, as introducing a worldly form of government, entirely subversive of the principles of Gospel Order. (White and Taylor, *Shakerism* 122)

In a short periodical article published in 1907, the Union Village **Shakers** receive the following compliments:

These old people are cheery and good. They are liked by all who know them. They go about their tasks with a spirit that is beautiful. They read papers and good books, and love to talk of the noble characters of great men and women. They love the beauties of Nature, and their hearts throb with the joys that beat in bosoms of purity. In a very few years the story of the Shakers will be a tale of the past. When they are gone, there will remain their beautiful home . . . and there will remain that splendid estate, worth hundreds of thousands of dollars.

May I presume to wonder what monument will be erected there to Shakerism. (Berry, "Last of the Shakers" 18)

Another short history of Union Village published five years before it was closed contains the following concluding remarks:

Owing to the paucity of their [Shaker] numbers, public meetings are no longer held and their Meeting House is practically abandoned. Religious services are now conducted in the chapel of the Center House [or **Center Family** dwelling]. There appears to be a general feeling among the Shakers of Union Village that the days of their existence as a Community are drawing to a close. The Shakers of the United States, from a membership of 4,000 in 1823, have dwindled to less than 600 in 1901. (MacLean, *Shakers of Ohio* 111)

UNITED INHERITANCE. *See* UNITED INTEREST.

UNITED INTEREST. *A.k.a.: Christian communism, community of property, joint interest, united inheritance.* "United interest," a term that appeared in the **Church Covenant** of 1795, is a cardinal principle of **Shakerism**. "Communism" is, by definition, a matter of common interest: whatever belongs to the community belongs equally to and is shared equally by all the members. If **Shakers** are equal spiritually—**brothers** and **sisters**, sons and daughters of the **Father/Mother Deity**—then they are equal in temporal matters, too, so says Shaker logic.

At the very beginning of the Shaker pilgrimage in America, the scattered and mostly destitute members had no opportunity to exercise the principle of united interest. However, according to two Shaker historiographers, the opportunity to do so was not long in coming.

An early document referring to the family at Niskeyuna . . . shows the beginning of the communistic life in the Shaker Order. . . . The Church at Niskeyuna held the property as a joint interest. After we became acquainted with them and believed their testimony, they gave what they gained by their industry, with the use and improvement of their farm, for the benefit of the whole society, to be improved in the following manner, viz.: There should be a free table and other necessaries for the entertainment of those who went to see them, that the poor have an equal opportunity of the Gospel with the rich. All who were able had liberty to contribute according to their faith, toward supporting table and other expenses and the poor. None were compelled or even desired to contribute, but such as could do it freely, believing it to be their duty: and they were often cautioned, taught to deal justly with all, and were often examined as to whether they were in debt, or whether their families were in need of what they offered to give. The teaching plainly implied that those who went to visit the Church, who were able to support themselves should do so, or give as much as they received. And those who were able to give more ought to give more than sufficient to support themselves. It is well known that many poor people came who were not able to support themselves while there, not even to bear their own expenses back to their families. Many poor came for alms and none were sent away. None had liberty to work there but those who would freely give their services as a matter of their own faith. (White and Taylor, *Shakerism* 301)

The principle of united interest did not appear in writing until 1795, when the **Church Family** of each community all gathered together into "gospel order" and began to sign the **Church Covenant**. One chronicler speculates that Shakers subsequent to **Ann Lee**, who was herself "impressed with some of . . . [**Shadrach Ireland**'s] works" at the **Square House** in Harvard, Massachusetts (her "headquarters" during her missionary work), may well have "absorbed the idea for the Christian necessity of communal living" from Ireland himself, whose **New Lighters**, whom he fashioned into a society, "put themselves and much of their goods into his hands" (Webber, *Escape to Utopia* 50–51, 38). The above quotation, alleged by **Anna White** and **Leila S. Taylor** to be the work of **Calvin Harlow**, who accompanied **Joseph Meacham** in 1780 on his visit to the Shakers at Niskayuna (**Watervliet**), suggests that Harlow was describing the Shakers as he saw them in the beginning of his experience with them. Thus, apparently, before Mother Ann's trip commenced in 1781, the Shakers had already begun practicing united interest. (For a statement of the principle, see Article VI, Section 1, of The Covenant or Constitution of the Church at Hancock, reprinted in appendix B.)

UNITED SOCIETY OF BELIEVERS IN CHRIST'S SECOND APPEARING. *See* SHAKERISM.

UNITED SOCIETY OF BELIEVERS IN THE SECOND APPEARING OF CHRIST. *See* SHAKERISM.

UNITED SOCIETY OF SHAKERS. *See* SHAKERISM.

UNITED SOCIETY OF SHAKERS, INC. A nonprofit corporation established in 1971 by the **Sabbathday Lake Shakers**, it is for the welfare of the community and for ministering to the knowledge of and appreciation for the Society.

-V-

VALE OF PEACE. *See* WATERVLIET, OHIO.

VILLAGE. Although some early **Shakers** gathered with their own families and other groups of various sizes for worship and fellowship, the Society commonly is cited as formally having founded 24 communistic villages or communities between 1787 and 1898, one surviving only four years (**White Oak**, Georgia) and one still remaining, as of early 2000 (**Sabbathday Lake**, Maine). Descriptions and judgments by Shakers and non-Shakers about both the entire system of communities and the individual villages are bountiful. For example, a former Shaker renders the following material about some of the daily routine of the village to which he once belonged (**Enfield**, Connecticut):

> All rise simultaneously every morning at the signal of the bell, and those of each room shall kneel together in silent prayer, strip from the beds the coverlets and blankets, lighten the feathers, open the windows to ventilate the rooms, and repair to their places of vocation. Fifteen minutes are allowed for all to leave their sleeping apartments. In the summer the signal for rising is heard at half-past four, in the winter at half-past five. Breakfast is invariably one and a half hours after rising—in the summer at six, in the winter at seven; dinner is always at twelve; supper at six. These rules are, however, slightly modified upon the Sabbath. They rise and breakfast on this day half an hour later, dine lightly at twelve, and sup at four. Every order maintains the same regularity in regard to their meals. (Elkins, *Fifteen Years* 24)

Because of the many similarities among the various villages, the following account of a particular village most likely expresses the general aura of all Shaker communities in the 1860s:

> Life appears to move on Mount Lebanon [i.e., **New Lebanon**] in an easy kind of rhythm. Order, temperance, frugality, worship—these are the Shaker things which strike upon your sense first; the peace and innocence of Eden, when contrasted with wrack and riot of New York [City]. Everyone seems busy, everyone tranquil. No jerk, no strain, no menace, is observed, for nothing is done, nothing can be done in a Shaker

settlement by force. Everyone here is free. Those who have come into
union came unsought; those who would go out may retire unchecked.
No soldiers, no police, no judges, live here . . . peace reigns. (Dixon,
New America 306)

According to the eyewitness account of another visitor from **the world**,
a journalist who visited 18 of the communities in 1874,

> in their buildings, their customs, their worship, their religious faith, their
> extreme cleanliness, their costume, and in many other particulars, they
> are all nearly alike; and the Shaker in Kentucky does not to the cursory
> view differ from his brother in Maine. (Nordhoff, *Communistic Com-
> munities* 179)

Yet another observer in 1878 records the following about the real estate
and wealth of the Shaker communal system:

> They all have large home farms, ranging from one thousand acres up-
> ward, and many of them own additional tracts of land in the Western
> and Southern States. . . . It is not easy to ascertain the aggregate landed
> estate; but it must nearly or quite reach one hundred thousand acres.
> They were long under the land-mania, and . . . now regret their past
> policy in this respect. They find themselves burdened with investments
> that yield small returns, and call themselves "land poor." . . . Of the
> wealth of the Shaker Societies it is impossible to speak with definite-
> ness. [Charles] Nordhoff estimated the wealth of all the American Com-
> munities at twelve million. I have reason to believe that the wealth of
> the Shaker Societies alone approximates this amount. (Hinds, *American
> Communities* 81–83)

Ordinarily, villages have been composed of more than one family.
Covenanted members usually reside with the Centre or **Church Family**. The other families commonly have borne names that reflect their
geographical relationship to the Centre Family; thus, villages often have
had, for example, a West Family, an East Family, and a North Family,
such as that at **Pleasant Hill**, Kentucky. These families often consist of
would-be Shakers at various levels of spiritual progression. The North
Family of Pleasant Hill, for example, was composed of **novitiates** and
was commonly called the "Novitiate Family" or "Gathering Order." Each
of these families has had its own **dwelling house**.

Shaker villages have existed in 10 states—as far east and north as
Maine, as far south as Florida, and as far west as Indiana:

> In the beginning of the year 1780, the Society consisted, in all, of but
> 10 or 12 persons, all of whom came from England. Early in the spring
> of that year, the people in this country, having heard their testimony,

began to gather to them; and from this time, there was a gradual and extensive increase in numbers, until in the year 1787, when those who had received the faith, and had been faithful from the beginning, and who were the most fully prepared, began to collect at New-Lebanon. Here the church was established. . . . This still remains [1848] as the Mother-Church. . . . [F]rom 1787 to 1792, regular Societies were formed and established upon the same principles of order and church government, in the various parts of the eastern states. . . . [P]ersecutions in the western states [during the Kentucky Revival] produced inquiry. . . which generally led to a knowledge of truth; consequently the testimony of the truth prevailed, and believers were multiplied. . . . The testimony has mostly prevailed in the states of Ohio, Kentucky and Indiana, where Societies have been established. (Green and Wells, *Summary View* 75–76, 83)

Few, if any, physical vestiges of some of the communities still exist. However, those with facilities that have been preserved have been used in various ways by their new owners. For example,

Alfred [Maine] was sold to the Brothers of Christian Instruction . . . ; Enfield, New Hampshire, was obtained by the Brothers of La Salette, and South Union [Kentucky] by the Order of St. Benedict. . . . Union Village [Ohio] went to the Otterbein Church. . . . Shirley [Massachusetts] and Enfield, Connecticut, are state penal institutions. . . . Hancock [Massachusetts] and Pleasant Hill [Kentucky] are museum-restorations, while Watervliet, Ohio, was until very recently the farm for a state mental hospital. Its namesake in New York is in part a county home for the indigent, in part the Albany County Airport, and in part privately owned. Harvard [and] Tyringham [Massachusetts], and Whitewater [and] North Union [Ohio] are in private hands [—the North Union property becoming Shaker Heights, a posh residential area about eight miles southeast of Cleveland]. (Horgan, *Shaker Holyland* xx–xxi)

For further details on specific Shaker villages, see the individual listings herein.

VISIONIST. Some **Shakers** experienced, among other **gifts**, visitations to the spiritual sphere, after which they "often gave vivid representations of all that came under their observation." "As a general thing these visionists were entranced only a few hours, but instances are recorded of forty and sixty and eighty hours, and the longest term was one hundred and forty-four hours, or a period of six days" (Blinn, *Manifestations of Spiritualism* 28). Visionists were most numerous and most operative during the era called "Mother Ann's Second Coming." *See also* INSTRUMENT; TRANCE-GOER.

-W-

WARDLEY, JAMES (17?–17?) and JANE (17?–17?). *Alt sp.: Wardlaw, Wardleigh.* Former Quakers who lived near Manchester, England, the Wardleys organized and conducted the religious society nicknamed the "**Shaking Quakers**," which **Ann Lee** joined in 1758, at 22 years of age, apparently because of, among other concepts, the Wardleys' belief that the **Millennium** was imminent. By 1770, the Wardleys acknowledged Ann as the leader of the sect because she had the most "light," as manifested by her visions, especially that of the lust between Adam and Eve, which was the original sin and, thus, the cause of their own fall from grace as well as their progeny's fallen nature. The only remedy for this sin is for the individual being to crucify his or her flesh—to take up a **cross** against carnal pleasures, in Shaker parlance. Neither of the Wardleys accompanied Mother Ann to America in 1774.

WATERVLIET, NEW YORK (1787–1938). *Spiritual name: Wisdom's Valley.* Formerly named "Niskayuna" (now the Town of Colonie), Watervliet was the original location in 1776 of the first Shaker community organized by the original **Shakers** in America. Several principal Shakers are buried there, among them **Ann Lee**, **William Lee**, **Lucy Wright**, and **Benjamin S. Youngs**. Watervliet was situated "about 7 miles northwest from the city of Albany. . . . This was established soon after the church at New-Lebanon, and now [1848] contains upwards of 200 members" (Green and Wells, *Summary View* 76). By 1875,

> the society there has now four families, containing two hundred and thirty-five persons, of whom sixty are children and youth under twenty-one. Of the adult members, seventy-five are men and one hundred women. In 1823 it had over two hundred members; between 1837 and 1850 it had three hundred and fifty.
>
> It has in its home estate twenty-five hundred acres . . . and owns besides about two thousand acres in the same state, and thirty thousand in Kentucky. Its chief industry is farming. . . . [T]hey raise large crops of broom-corn and sweet corn . . . they put up fruits and vegetables in tin cans, and also sell garden seeds . . . they make in their own shops, for use of the society, shoes, carpets, clothing, furniture, and almost all the articles of household use they require.
>
> They had formerly a good many colored members; and have still some, as well as several mulattoes and quadroons.
>
> They are careful to have thorough drainage and ventilation, and pay attention to sanitary questions.

They take a number of newspapers, and have a library of four hundred volumes, but the people are not great, and are fonder of religious books and works of popular science than of any other literature.
(Nordhoff, *Communistic Societies*)

One of the longest-lived communities, the closure of Watervliet in 1938 was part of the seemingly inevitable fate long established for Shaker **villages**:

In 1849 there had been 285 members distributed among the four families; by 1875 membership was down to 166 and that included 22 hired hands. The North Family closed in 1892 when the last eight members moved to the Church Family; but then their buildings were taken over by the Shaker Groveland Community which moved there from western New York when their community was closed. By 1905 the four families totaled only 77 including hired hands. At the West Family, Elder Isaac Anstatt died in 1913, the sole remaining Shaker sister moved to the Church Family, and the property was sold. The North Family closed again in 1919 and the remaining members moved to the South Family. . . . By 1925 there were less than ten Shakers at Watervliet. (Shaver and Pratt, *Watervliet Shakers* 23)

WATERVLIET, OHIO (1806–1910). *Spiritual name: Vale of Peace.* Organized in the same year as was **Union Village**, Ohio, from which it was 22 miles north, "the extinct Shaker community, called Watervliet, was located about six miles east by south of Dayton, on sections 13 and 14, VanBuren Township, Montgomery County" (MacLean, *Shakers of Ohio* 190). In 1823, it had about 100 members. In 1875, it had 2 families, containing 55 members; 1,300 acres, farmed mostly by tenants; and a wool factory, its only manufacturing enterprise. At that time also, the community was prosperous, had no debt, and owned money earning interest (Nordhoff, *Communistic Societies* 206).

"In the early Shaker documents . . . the society is variously called Beaver Creek, Beulah and Mad River" (MacLean, *Shakers of Ohio* 190). It was always small and subordinate to Union Village (which itself was always subordinate to **New Lebanon**), and although economically successful generally, it was not exempt from various internal problems, as evidenced by the following example:

In 1827 an unfortunate schism broke out among the young and ambitious. They contended for a division of the property, which meant the end of the community. Being defeated in their designs, quite a few withdrew from the Society; which however did not take place until 1832.

They were mostly young people of both sexes. (MacLean, *Shakers of Ohio* 203)

In the estimate of two Shaker chroniclers, Watervliet was distinguished from other Shaker communities by virtue of "its immunity from persecution" (White and Taylor, *Shakerism* 126). Its relationship with the town of Dayton generally was amicable, especially after two **brothers** allegedly rode through the streets declaring that God had blessed the town and its citizens: "There were farmers who now believed . . . [that] the town would become prosperous. Some rented and others sold their farms and moved to the town, giving it an impetus which has ever continued" (MacLean, *Shakers of Ohio* 201).

Some curiosity exists about the closure of Watervliet. Although its official closing date is usually stated as 1910, suddenly and for no apparent reason "in the year 1900, the society was merged with Union [V]illage" (White and Taylor, *Shakerism* 128), even though "the members were fully able to manage their domain" (MacLean, *Shakers of Ohio* 224).

WELLS, FREEGIFT (1786–1871). Far less than reticent and inactive, Elder Freegift was a **Shaker** for more than 50 years, mostly at the **Watervliet**, New York, community, where he also is buried. Besides being a superb chairmaker, among his contributions to the Society was compiling the ***Millennial Laws*** (1821), a book of orders and regulations that previously had existed primarily only in oral form throughout the Society during the administrations of **Joseph Meacham** and **Lucy Wright**. Furthermore, regarded highly by the **New Lebanon** ministry, he was appointed head **elder** of **Union Village**, Ohio, in 1836, a position left vacant upon the death of Father **David Darrow**; in effect, the position also made Brother Freegift the **lead** of all the Ohio and Kentucky communities. He served in this capacity until 1843.

Throughout his life, Wells was involved in various issues and controversies within the Society. Among other matters, he adversely criticized elders for being ineffective models for common **Believers** and argued against severe dietary reforms (such as vegetarianism), upon which he placed part of the blame for the loss of membership.

WELLS, SETH YOUNGS (1767–1847). A member of the Wells family of Long Island, New York, Brother Seth, his parents, and nine siblings all joined the Society around 1800. He "was an Educator of some note, and Principal of a High School in Albany, [New York,] before he joined the Shakers at Watervliet, N[ew] Y[ork]" (Hollister, in Wells, *Thomas*

Brown 1). In 1807, Elder Seth (nephew of Elder **Benjamin S. Youngs**) was appointed **elder** of the Gathering Order at the **Watervliet** community.

In 1821, his most significant contribution to the Society was made by Mother **Lucy Wright**, who "strongly felt the necessity of a thorough education for the children in the Shaker homes." She thus appointed Elder Wells, "a man of sterling integrity, intellectual ability and possessing a classical education," to the post of "General Superintendent of Believers' Literature, Schools, etc. in the First Bishopric, which included Watervliet, Hancock [Massachusetts] and Mount Lebanon [New York]" (White and Taylor, *Shakerism* 132–133). With this appointment and his accompanying release from all other duties, Elder Seth became

> the most important single feature in Shaker educational history. . . . For approximately three decades (circa 1815–1844) he unified the Shaker curriculum, trained teachers, established schools and traveled to all the eastern communities to publicize and promote Shaker education. He believed that the Lancastrian System, a monitorial method [developed by Joseph Lancaster, Southwark, England] in which students were trained to help teach other students, was particularly adaptable to the Shakers' needs. . . . In Wells' view, the emphasis of education should be on character building and on promoting kindness. (Taylor, *Analysis* 285–286)

Other of Elder Wells's major contributions to the Society were his writings on Shaker principles and history and his editing, along with Brother **Calvin Green**, of the early publications of the **Shakers**, such as *Testimonies* (1827). Their *Summary View of the Millennial Church* (1823), authorized by Mother Lucy, might be regarded as the finely "polished" version of early Shaker history.

WEST, BENJAMIN (17?–18?). Another of the early **apostates** who published attacks on the **Shakers**, West—with the public's interest in mind—wrote a tract in 1783 "at the request of many serious minded persons." Based upon his own "sorrowful experience . . . with the new, false and strange religion [**Shakerism**]," he warns of the "inchanting influence" of, for example, the Shakers' claim that "a new dispensation had taken place." "But alas," he says, "I found myself awfully deceived" by "those that call themselves perfect," because, among other reasons, they actually carried on "the horrid sin of adultery" in addition to breaking "the most tenderest ties of nature between a man and his wife"—which leads to women becoming "monsters" who rule over men, to whom they should be submissive (West, *Scriptural Cautions* 1, 12–13, 7).

WEST UNION, INDIANA (1810–1827). The westernmost Shaker community, West Union (at Busro, Busroe, or Busserow)—"west" because of its relationship to **Union Village**, Ohio, the center of western Shakerdom—was in Knox County "on Busseron Creek, near its confluence with the Wabash, about 16 miles above Vincennes" (Green and Wells, *Summary View* 83). In 1809, it was yet another area visited by Shaker missionaries, from Union Village in this case, because "a great revival had been in progress, thus preparing the soil for Shakerism" (White and Taylor, *Shakerism* 117). The extremely difficult weather conditions encountered by the missionaries during their 16-day, 235-mile journey is a testimony of their faith and devotion to their cause. (**Issachar Bates Sr.**, one of the missionaries, wrote "The Sixteenth Day of January," a ballad of 128 lines that describes the journey.) As of 1823, the community had about 200 members.

The shortness of West Union's history has been attributed to extreme factors other than any loss of membership, for example:

> For several years [beginning around 1814] the plucky little company held the ground, suffering from disaster by tornado, violent and extreme weather, sickness, robbery and incendiary fire, with malarial fever, the scourge of the new, rich western land. . . . At one time, one hundred and twelve were sick, two brethren only being able to work. (White and Taylor, *Shakerism* 119)

Also, the community suffered from persecution by local mobs, and its location put it in danger during the so-called War of 1812. On November 19, 1826,

> Elder Elezar [pseud. of **Richard McNemar**] gathered all the people and after speaking a few sentences, he proceeded to read a letter. . . . The substance of which . . . was this—That it was universally thought and felt best, for all the people to rise once more and move away from Busro, and so abandon the place forever! (MacLean, *Shakers of Ohio* 324)

Thus, the community was divided into three companies, one going to Union Village and one each going to **South Union** and **Pleasant Hill**, the two Shaker **villages** in Kentucky.

WHITCHER, BENJAMIN (17?–18?). Somewhat well-to-do, Whitcher joined with the **Believers** in 1782 at Canterbury, New Hampshire. The Shaker community at **Canterbury**, organized in 1792, was made possible by **Brother** Benjamin's "having generously donated his fine farm of one hundred acres, then valued at $1250 to the Society." He and Mary, his wife, had for ten years most generously and conscientiously opened their doors in welcome to all who came to seek the truth. On the formation of the communistic relation, Benjamin Whitcher was appointed [in 1794] one of the presiding Elders, while his companion, Mary, was chosen one of the directors of the temporal interests of the community. (White and Taylor, *Shakerism* 91)

In 1827, the *Testimonies concerning the Character and Ministry of Mother Ann Lee and the First Witnesses of the Gospel of Christ's Second Appearing* was published. The text "paints Mother Ann and Elders as warm, simple, and kindly, making real and credible their spiritual parenthood toward their followers" (Melcher, *Shaker Adventure* 108). Elder Whitcher's name is among those editors **Seth Youngs Wells** and **Calvin Green** included in the volume.

WHITE, ANNA (1831–1910). "Having received a liberal education, Anna White, at the age of eighteen, after much opposition and disinheritance by her uncle . . . united with the Shakers, entering the North Family at Mount Lebanon, in October, 1849." She advanced in the Society to become "the cheery, vigorous Head of the North Family" (White and Taylor, *Shakerism* 172).

Eldress Anna also was among the so-called progressive female leaders of the sect in the latter decades of the nineteenth and early twentieth centuries; she advocated, among other reforms, more contact by the **Shakers** with **the world**, via their involvement, for instance, in an international disarmament movement, and she strongly supported (along with **Frederick W. Evans**, and others) a vegetarian diet—as opposed to the "depraved diet" of **Believers** who eat "blood and . . . dead carcasses" (*Manifesto* 25, no. 1 [1895]: 6).

Regarding Shaker history and **theology**, Sister Anna's major contribution to posterity is her *Shakerism: Its Meaning and Message* (1904), which she co-authored with Sister **Leila S. Taylor**. The work has been called "the crowning intellectual achievement by Shaker women" of the authors' era (Stein, *Shaker Experience* 266). It is the most recent attempt by Shakers themselves to render a comprehensive account of the Shaker pilgrimage.

WHITE OAK, GEORGIA (1898–1902). The Shaker community of **Union Village**, Ohio, financed this warm-weather site, the shortest-lived of all the Shaker communities. In 1898, it purchased, first, "about ten thousand acres of magnificent land. . . . For the entire holdings the Shakers paid $30,000." Later in the year, it purchased "51,000 acres of undeveloped land in Pierce, Charlton, and Ware Counties" (Vanstory, "Shakers" 360). In October 1899, the following article appeared in the Shaker journal:

> Sept. 1899. To-day the first brick of our enlarged Southern home was laid by a son of Ham, and we are glad to record progress and increasing prosperity. . . . We have already proved that our home farm is capable of raising 50 bu. of corn per acre, and 300 lbs. of pumpkin per vine, and sweet potatoes to astonish even New Jersey. Asparagus equals anything North, and melons, well—they are at home here, and just enjoy growing "big and beluscious" as the darkey declares. On another branch of our possessions [Glynn County], a $10,000 crop of excellent rice is being harvested, and this will very materially help to raise the new and conveniently modern 90 x 40 two-story extension to our home. (*The Manifesto* 29, no. 10 [October 1899]: 160)

Although the Georgia venture apparently was designed not only to provide a more pleasing climate overall for members but also to increase the ever-decreasing membership and meager financial base of the **Society**, it was not regarded with wholehearted favor by all **Shakers**. For example,

> Much doubt was felt in many minds of the advisability of these moves. It was felt by many, that concentration rather than scattering of force was demanded by the condition of the societies; that empty buildings and untilled fields in the north hardly called for new territories and the erection of new dwellings and store-houses in distant states. . . . Perhaps it is too soon [1904] to say whether . . . true wisdom prompted the . . . attempt. (White and Taylor, *Shakerism* 213–214)

With virtually no success in doing what needed to be done to develop a new community (never having more than about 20 members, for example), "on September 19, 1902, [Shaker] trustees . . . transferred their 'bond for title' or contract to James W. Schley. . . . [T]hey disposed of all their holdings—apparently some 7,145 acres . . . and the Georgia venture was over" (Anderson, "Shaker Communities" 168–169).

WHITEWATER, OHIO (1824–1907). *Spiritual name: Lonely Plain of Tribulation.* Located in Hamilton County and about 22 miles northwest of Cincinnati, Whitewater was the last Shaker community organized in both Ohio and in what the **Shakers** called the "southwest." Its early membership stemmed largely from another religious movement and a failed Shaker community. Members of "the Christian (New Light) Church . . . from Connecticut and Rhode Island settled on Darby Plains, Union Township, Union County, Ohio" (MacLean, *Shakers of Ohio* 229–230). After visits starting in 1820 from Shaker missionaries from **Union**

Village, "the leaders of the Darbyites became inoculated with Shaker beliefs, which were, in fact, an advance upon their own." However, the soil at Darby "was found to be unhealthy, the lands disputed by military claims and liable to endless litigation." These factors, plus the small number of new Shakers there, were causes enough for the Society to unite the Darby people with the small Shaker settlement that it was developing at Whitewater. The merger created a community of 65 members. The Whitewater settlement was further enlarged in 1827 by the addition of some of the members from the failed **West Union**, Indiana, community (White and Taylor, *Shakerism* 128–129).

The following entry from the diary of a **New Lebanon** Shaker visiting the Shaker communities in the western region is informative of various aspects of the **village** in the 1840s (the era of **Mother Ann's Second Coming**):

> [September] 2nd: We reached Whitewater at half past 7 in the evening 20 miles from Cincinnati. The reason for our starting so early this morning [about 12:00 a.m.] was the dogs and men made such a racket there was no rest for us. So we arose & departed.
>
> [September] 3rd: We are now at Whitewater among the Advents — pretty fine times, and joyful feelings we have found here, there are about 60 of the Advents and in all 140 **Believers**. They appeared pleased to see us but some of them seem a little backward about making much parade, and we are glad of it and love them just as well.
>
> [September] 5th: After breakfast we visited the brethren, and a very likely company we saw. A number of them are middle aged, smart men, strong in body and in mind, and very promising; they have built a brick house for a wash house and weave shop this season, without hiring, besides doing their harvest. . . . This afternoon at 1 o'clock we attended meeting at the meeting house with both families, we had a very wonderful meeting; the people were all alive, they sung many beautiful songs and labored in the works of God until they were wet with sweat. . . . We gave them a great bundle of good gospel love, which pleased them much and they gave us much love in return.
>
> [September] 6th: We went to the chosen square [holy ground] with nearly all the sisters, had a good visit with them, and a little good meeting; exchanged love &c. This place is a very beautiful spot of Ground, thickly shaded by forest trees, the yard is four square rods each way, the fountain is 18 by 14 feet. The Brethren and Sisters here are so near feeling and kind that no Believer can hesitate to love them. We had a good visit in both families. (Morrell, "Account" 87–88)

In 1875, Whitewater was reported to have had 3 families, 140 members (15 of them under 21), with the females outnumbering the males 60 to

40. It then owned 1,500 acres, had no debt, put up garden seeds, sold brooms, raised stock, and farmed much, among other activities (Nordhoff, *Communistic Societies* 206).

However, fewer than 100 **Believers** remained in all of Ohio at the advent of the twentieth century. In 1907, Whitewater, too, suffered the inevitable dissolution.

WHITTAKER, JAMES (1751–1787). *A.k.a., Father James.* Designated in the *Compendium* as one of the founders of the Shaker Society—along with **Ann Lee**, **William Lee**, **John Hocknell**, **Joseph Meacham**, and **Lucy Wright**—James was among the original **Shakers** who immigrated to America in 1774. In England, he already had had a lengthy association with Mother Ann, whom he knew from the religious society of the **Wardleys**, of which his natural mother was a member. Possibly as a testimony to the respect then being given to Ann Lee by the society, James was placed under her tutelage, about which James said: "I was brought up in the way of God by my Mother [Ann], and I knew no unclean thing" (in Evans et al., *Compendium* 161). (Thus, his early life contrasted remarkably to that of fellow Shaker William Lee, who as a young adult devoted himself to gaiety and finery.)

Prior to coming to America, James had visions of it and the future of **Shakerism** there. For example, while on a 20-mile trip to **Meeting** at night—to avoid persecution—he and others sat by the side of the road to eat:

> While I was sitting there I saw a vision of America; and I saw a large tree, and every leaf thereof shone with such brightness as made it appear like a burning torch, representing the church of Christ, which will yet be established in this land. (Quoted in Green and Wells, *Summary View* 50)

In America, "being greatly gifted in public speaking, [James] was instrumental in gathering many souls to the gospel" (Green and Wells, *Testimonies* 276).

According to Shaker chroniclers, after the death of Mother Ann in September 1784 and, consequently, Elder James's assumption of **lead** (disapproved of by English Shakers **John Partington** and **James Shepherd**, who left the Society), James continued to make significant contributions to the early development of Shakerism. For one thing, "evidently called, of God, to be Mother Ann's successor, in the ministry" (Green and Wells, *Testimonies* 278), he was immediately confronted with the tribulations of members greatly disheartened by her death, which posited that their faith centered more on her than on what she had preached. Realizing danger to the welfare of the Society on this account, he constantly encouraged, consoled, and warned distraught **Believers** not to lose their faith. While doing so, "he visited all the different places in the land where the Gospel had been planted—some of them several times" (Evans et al., *Compendium* 177). Apparently, he was successful enough to arrest damaging apostasy. Also, James was instrumental in the origin of the concept of Shaker communal living based on **united interest**:

> His instructions to the Elders who afterward succeeded him, relative to gathering, building, and establishing the Church in gospel order, might, with great propriety, be likened to the instructions of David to Solomon, concerning the building of the temple. (Green and Wells, *Testimonies* 294)

(The **elder** most responsible for building the "temple" was Joseph Meacham, James's immediate successor.)

James's other contributions to the development of early Shakerism included his ordering of the first house of worship, or **Meeting house**, built in 1785 at **New Lebanon** by **Moses Johnson** and, in conjunction with it, his issuing of the Believers' first so-called gospel orders, among which was the regulation that males would enter west doors and that females would enter east doors, a practice that would be extended to all structures public to both genders.

As were Ann Lee and William Lee, so was James firm and undaunted in censoring sinful ways. Furthermore, he is said to have had a great **gift** for understanding the particular problem of the individual Believer and, thus, was able to minister to the souls of people with a wide range of difficulties, such as the lost, the careless, the ignorant, the weak, the buffeted, and the brokenhearted. Albeit gifted with leadership ability, James was forever humble. He often abased himself to other Believers:

> I am more mean than any of you, my parents were mean, and poor. I am a very mean man! When I look around upon you all, I consider your parentages to be more honorable than my own. . . . I am but a poor worm of the dust, and a very little one too. (Green and Wells, *Testimonies* 281)

Although James reproved all sin, indulgence in sexual pleasures seemed to be of special concern to him, and he addressed the topic often. A lifelong sexual virgin ("I never had carnal knowledge of any woman"), James applauded and encouraged the **celibacy** of other Believers in utterances such as, "Blessed are those who are not defiled by women.

Blessed are all those young virgins who were never defiled by men" (Green and Wells, *Testimonies* 292).

James Whittaker, "having laid the foundation for the establishment of order, and finished the work which was given him to do, departed this life at Enfield, in Connecticut, July 20th, 1787" (Green and Wells, *Summary View* 31). At his death, leadership of the United Society of Believers in Christ's Second Appearing passed out of the hands of the original Shakers in America into those of Joseph Meacham, Mother Ann's "first-born son in America."

WICKERSHAM, GEORGE (17?–18?). Among the plethora of Shaker inventors, Brother George has been alleged to have invented, for example, the turbine water wheel (White and Taylor, *Shakerism* 311).

WILSON, DELMAR (1873–1961). The last **Shaker** male to have signed the traditional **Church Covenant**, officially closed by the **Lead Ministry** in Canterbury in 1965, Brother Delmar was among the Shakers from 1882 until the "close [of his] earthly journey." At the **Sabbathday Lake**, New Gloucester, Maine, community, where he resided exclusively, he had charge of the dairy herd from the age of 14. By his early adult years, he also had become "a skilled worker with wood"—specializing in the famous Shaker oval box, of which he made thousands—"as well as an able horticulturalist. . . . Through his efforts the Shaker orchards and their fruits became widely known throughout the state." Among other services to the Society, Brother Delmar was appointed **trustee** in 1927 and was "raised to the Elder's lot of the Church at Sabbathday Lake" in 1931 ("In Memoriam," *Shaker Quarterly* 1, no. 4 [Winter 1961]: 135–137). *See also* CONFESSION OF SIN.

WINTER SHAKERS. A term used by **Shakers** to describe the people who "joined" (used) the Society to enjoy its warmth and generosity during the cold season but deserted it with the coming of spring.

WISDOM'S PARADISE. *See* UNION VILLAGE, OHIO.

WISDOM'S VALLEY. *See* WATERVLIET, NEW YORK.

WOODS, JOHN (1780–18?). Joining the **Shakers** around 1807 after participating in the **Kentucky Revival**, Woods, who for a while served as schoolmaster at **Union Village**, Ohio, "lived with them about seventeen years" before abjuring the Society and then writing an "unfriendly attack" on it (Richmond, *Shaker Literature* I, 211). He describes his

Shakerism Unmasked (1826) as a "narrative shewing the entrance of the Shakers into the western country." Also, he "shews" the absurdities of the Shakers—"their strategems and devices"—which caused him to become an **apostate**. Among other foibles, the **elders** and members of the ministry treated themselves to privileges not allowed the "common people." For example,

> Bread, such as the children ate, was not fit for the ministry, Fruits, sweet meats, tea, coffee, dried fish, oysters . . . were thought necessary for father, and mother, and the ministry. Good spirits and wine were privately procured for them by some in office; and who expected to continue in office by keeping their favor. The elders and eldresses in each family supported and justified the ministry, and [the] ministry supported and justified them. (32–33)

WORLD, THE. In Shaker parlance, everything outside of Shaker **villages** and outside of **Shakerism** in general is alluded to by this term. As perceived by the **Shakers**, the ways of the world are everything that they seek to avoid: greed, carnality, deceit, selfishness, and so on. However, the ironies of the relationship between the Shakers and the world seem endless. For instance, during the nineteenth century especially, with their economic enterprises such as furniture making, the success of which depended on the world as customers, they violated their principle of **separation from the world** to such a degree that they became nearly bankrupt because their cottage **industries** could not compete with the rest of the country's capitalist economy after the Civil War.

Of course, the ultimate irony seems to be that the world today—via its magazine articles, books, scholarship, historical societies, television, movies, audio recordings, lectures, museums, and the like—has engendered a heretofore unknown appreciation of the Shakers as a national treasure. Whether the Society continues in its traditional form or ceases to be extant, the world itself has ensured that Shakerism will be acknowledged as a significant portion of every American's cultural heritage.

What led to the decline of the Shakers probably always will be debated, but little argument can occur over the contention that among the major reasons for their failure is their violation of their principle of separation, instituted from the beginning in the forest of Niskayuna in 1776. Perhaps, if the Shakers had cultivated self-reliance with the same zeal that they lavished on **celibacy**, say, **Pleasant Hill**, Kentucky, would still be a viable community instead of merely a museum.

WORLD'S PEOPLE, THE. A general term for non-Shakers.

WORLEY, MALCOLM (17?–18?). *Alt. sp.: Malcham.* When Shaker missionaries **Issachar Bates Sr.**, **John Meacham**, and **Benjamin S. Youngs** emerged from the forest at the end of their journey to the so-called southwest from **New Lebanon**, New York, on March 22, 1805, they did so near the home of Worley in Turtle Creek, Ohio. "They were welcomed with true pioneer hospitality" by soon-to-be Brother Malcolm, "a man of large means, generous hospitality, a deep thinker of great themes, well educated, intensely and actively interested in religious matters" (White and Taylor, *Shakerism* 114).

Deep into the **Kentucky Revival**, Worley, a leader among the **New Lights**, invited revivalist preachers—**Richard McNemar**, for example—to his home to listen to the Shaker gospel. Worley and his wife, parents of nine children, "formally accepted the message of the Shakers" on March 27 (MacLean, *Sketch* 68). The land that Worley consecrated to the Society was the foundation of what was shortly to become **Union Village**. However, views on Worley differed. For example, the **apostate John Woods**, who helped with the care of the children at **North Union**, accused Brother Malcolm of, among other faults, living "sumptuously" while the children "lived on coarse food" (Woods, *Shakerism Unmasked* 54).

WORSHIP. *See* MEETING.

WRIGHT, LUCY (1760–1821). *A.k.a.: Mother Lucy.* At the age of 21, Lucy, of Pittsfield, Massachusetts, and her husband joined the Society. She is designated in the *Compendium* as one of the six founders of the Shaker Society—along with **Ann Lee**, **William Lee**, **James Whittaker**, **John Hocknell**, and **Joseph Meacham**. She

> was possessed of a high order of native talent and intellectuality, and a refined education, cojoined to a solid religious experience, and a pure devotional spirit; all of which combined, fitted her for becoming the external leader, and a spiritual mother of the new creation into which God had so providentially called her. (Evans et al., *Compendium* 186)

Although just exactly how Father Joseph came to appoint Sister Lucy and just exactly how she was received by the membership are not altogether clear, she apparently was so highly regarded by Ann Lee and other **Shakers** that she was the "logical" choice to succeed Mother Ann as "the first leading character in the female line" as the Shakers in 1788 continued to gather into "gospel order" and shape Shakerdom into a system of highly structured communities (Green and Wells, *Summary View* 31). With her appointment by Father Joseph, she became the first American-born female leader of the sect and one of the very few females who have been honored with the appellation "Mother" of the whole sect.

Although Lucy receives universal praise in publications by many Shaker authors, the early chroniclers render few specifics about her contributions to the development of **Shakerism** in America—other than that she, "tho' of the weaker sex" (Bishop, *Collection of Writings* 91), along with Joseph Meacham, was significant in creating institutional Shakerism. Perhaps the most ardent account of her is that rendered by two early twentieth-century female Shakers, **Anna White** and **Leila S. Taylor**. They applaud Mother Lucy's significance in developing not only **Shakeresses** but also some gender parity in the top-to-bottom structure of the Shaker system:

> At the age of twenty-eight . . . she had before her a long, laborious and delicate task to train, discipline and inspire the sisters and girls under her charge, educating them in the unfolding principles of the new spiritual Order to **obedience**, self control and unselfish devotion. . . . [H]eroically did Lucy lead the way in all hard and distasteful toil, lifting drudgery to duty, then to delight, as the consecrated heart gift; subduing, controlling, directing by inspiration of "pure heavenly love." Natural thoughts and feelings, old beliefs and prejudices centuries old had to be overthrown and demolished, and these women, conservative in their very life blood, brought up to the standard of a New Heaven upon earth where Woman, Daughter of God, should stand side by side in ability, authority and responsibility with Man, Son of God. Nobly did Lucy Wright do her difficult work; well did she earn the title . . . of "Mother." (White and Taylor, *Shakerism* 108–109)

After Joseph Meacham's death in 1796, Mother Lucy conducted the Society for 25 years, until her death in 1821. (She did not appoint a male member to serve as the **"father"** portion of the "visible" spiritual parents, and the **lead** of the Society never again has been vested so largely in a single person.)

According to the estimates of various modern researchers, Mother Lucy made other notable contributions to the progress of Shakerism. For one thing, her emphasis on missionary work, which along with revivalists and other disgruntled Christians still looking for heaven on earth, helped increase the Society's membership not only in New England but also in what the Shakers called the "southwest"—the locus of the **Kentucky Revival**—where seven new communities were developed in Ohio,

Indiana, and Kentucky between 1806 and 1824. Furthermore, in conjunction with the influx of members from varied backgrounds, Mother Lucy was instrumental in the introduction of the **novitiate** or the so-called Gathering Order for new members during their introduction to Shakerism. Also as a consequence of the mounting membership during the first two decades of the nineteenth century, Mother Lucy fostered the development of standards or rules of conduct (they eventually were called "laws" when published in 1821, after Mother Lucy's death), so that all Shakers were one Shaker, so to speak. Certainly, not the least of her executive decisions was her appointment of **Seth Youngs Wells** as "General Superintendent of Believers' Literature . . . [and] Schools" (White and Taylor, *Shakerism* 133), making him "chiefly responsible for the philosophy and content of Shaker education" (Andrews, *People Called Shakers* 328). On a less lofty plane, Mother Lucy is usually credited with introducing hand movements during **songs/poems** and **dances/marches** performed during **Meeting**. She died while on one of her "fact-finding" tours for the **Society** and is buried beside Mother Ann in the Shaker cemetery located in what used to be the Niskayuna (then **Watervliet**) Shaker community, the area known today as the "Town of Colonie," Albany County, New York.

Although "in her lifetime she had been opposed to written compilations of any sort circulating among Believers," after her death, "many felt that the words of strength and encouragement which she had uttered should be gathered and distributed for benefit of all Believers" (Carr, "Mother Lucy's Sayings" 102–103). The following are some of these adages:

Such as you call little orders you pass by. . . . But I want you to remember that such things are not allowed; we do not allow disorder.

I desire there be none . . . but that labor to be peacemakers. You had better sacrifice a great deal, than not to keep peace.

I expected to give up pride, covetousness, deceit, lying and every bad thing if I ever went to heaven. And if you can give away to backbiting, anger, crabbed and crooked ways and whatever an evil nature may lead you to and think you are going to Heaven, I want no such Heaven.

You ought to be very careful how you speak to each other; speak lovingly one to another according to the simplicity of the gospel.

Believers are held together in union, by a golden chain, this chain is composed of the gifts and orders of God; and every order is a link in this chain; and if you break any of these orders you break this chain and are exposed to be led astray.

Due in large part to the influence of Lucy Wright, study of the female's role in the Shaker system, especially the issue of **gender parity**, has burgeoned in the latter half of the twentieth century (which is no surprise, of course). See, for example, the works by the following authors listed in the bibliography: D'Ann Campbell, Lawrence Foster, Louis Kern, Marjorie Procter-Smith, Jean Humez, Beverly Gordon, Rosemary Gooden, and Karen and Pamela Nickless.

-Y-

YEARLY SACRIFICE. As was **Meeting** at the **feast ground**, for example, so was this ritual of worship distinguished from weekly Sabbath services:

> The followers of Ann Lee, Believers in the coming of the Maternal Spirit of Christ in Woman, have one unique, strangely sweet and wonderfully effective custom. It is called the "Yearly Sacrifice"; sometimes it is also the "Christmas Gift." On the Saturday evening before the Sabbath that is to be the "Day of Sacrifice," the spiritual heads of each family, at the hour of worship, in a few solemn, tender words, explain the meaning and importance of the gift, call on all to enter heartily into its humiliations and its blessings, and, charging all to withdraw quietly in a silence that shall leave each soul alone with its God, dismiss the brethren and sisters to rest.
>
> Sabbath morning comes to a strangely quiet house. . . . Morning duties performed, all retire to their rooms, and each withdraws into his or her own soul, searching the heart, scanning the life of the months past. (White and Taylor, *Shakerism* 284)

Another chronicler summarizes the ritual in the following manner:

> At this time all the people would confess their sins, the men to men and the women to women, and adjust all things that had not been right among themselves. These are said to have been seasons of great spiritual rejoicing, and that words unfitly spoken, and that deeds known and unknown, but of a wrong character, were confessed, forgiveness asked, and all spiritual life brought down to date without sin or iniquity, open of concealed. (Phillippi, *Shakerism* 21)

YOUNG BELIEVER'S ORDER. No one became a **Shaker** instantly. The Society's institution of this **order** is testimony to the circumspection with which it developed itself: "This order was instituted . . . as an introduction step of entrance in the Society. Into this order is received all *new* *comers* by the usual method—confession of sin" (Haskett, *Shakerism Unmasked* 152). *See also* NOVITIATE.

YOUNGS, BENJAMIN S. (1774–1855). Less than 20 years after he had joined the Society in 1794, Elder Benjamin became one of the most significant adherents of **Shakerism**. For one thing, along with **Issachar Bates Sr.** and **John Meacham**, he took the Shaker gospel from **New Lebanon**, New York, southwestward in the spring of 1805. He served as an itinerate preacher through parts of Ohio, Kentucky, and Indiana, thus contributing to the **in-gathering** (*see* GATHERING/IN-GATHERING) of members who eventually founded seven Shaker colonies in this region. Brother Benjamin also served as **lead elder** of **South Union**, Kentucky, from 1811 until 1836, at which time he was recalled to the East, where he lived the remainder of his life and was buried at **Watervliet**, New York.

Another of Elder Benjamin's major contributions to the Shaker pilgrimage was his writings. Foremost of these is his *Testimony of Christ's Second Appearing* of 1808 (although the work is unsigned, other than the preface, scholars regard it as his). Said by one modern auditor of the Society to be "the most important of all the Shaker books" (Melcher, *Shaker Adventure* 103), the 600-page volume is the "authoritative statement of Shaker theology. . . . [It was] sanctioned by the Society, and was written to [among other purposes] correct slanderous and prejudiced information being circulated about the sect and its practices" (Richmond, *Shaker Literature* I, 1470). Also, Elder Benjamin's account of the founding and growth of South Union from 1804 to 1836 is contained in what copyist **Harvey L. Eads** designated as *Shaker Record A*, a volume of 640 pages that "contains an unrivaled account of Shaker life and an almost day-by-day history of South Union" (Coombs, "Shaker Colony" 157–158).

A tribute to Youngs was made by his fellow missionary Issachar Bates Sr. in his autobiographical sketch:

> But as I was with Little Benjamin, (now Elder Benjamin) from the beginning; I always felt safe with him; for you know, he the son of the right hand; but whom I always esteemed as the Father of my right hand in all matters. We have traveled many thousands of miles together, through tribulations & suffering—Many were the snow banks & deep waters we waded through together; & love & union were always our staff—Beside I am persuaded, there were never many Davids and Jonathans whose hearts were more closely knit together: and I learned many good things of him. (Bates, *Sketch* 19)

YOUNGS, ISAAC N. (1793–1865). Younger biological brother of **Benjamin S. Youngs,** Elder Isaac was, among other things, one of a plethora of **Shakers** who possessed many skills and, thus, could contribute much to the welfare of the Society. For example, if he did not invent the metal pen (nib), he made many pens, was a clockmaker, a tailor, a farmer, a blacksmith, a tinker, a mason, a schoolteacher, and, along with **Russell Haskell,** developer of the Shaker system of music notation (which was based on the first seven letters of the alphabet).

Isaac N. Youngs usually has not been noted particularly as a prominent Shaker theologian or apologist. On the other hand, the records he kept of his and the Society's pilgrimage have been of great service to posterity. Virtually all unpublished, his personal journals and his accounts of and commentaries on various events, issues, and persons have been precious to auditors of the sect. For instance, Shaker historian Edward D. Andrews bases a good deal of chapter 8 of his *The People Called Shakers* (1953) on "A Concise View of the Church of God (1856–1860)," one of Brother Isaac's manuscripts, and Priscilla J. Brewer refers to Youngs on 21 pages of her *Shaker Communities, Shaker Lives* (1986).

-Z-

ZION. Literally, the place or religious community of or devoted to God. In **Shaker** contexts, Zion is both the spiritual heaven—the abode of God—and God's heaven or kingdom on earth. On earth, **Shakerism** is metaphorically God's kingdom; thus, **Believers**—"the children of Zion"—are its citizens. Until its closure in 1947, the **New Lebanon,** New York, community—long the center of Shakerdom—was spoken of as "the Spiritual Mount Zion, whence the Law and Gospel went forth to Believers" (White and Taylor, *Shakerism* 77).

Appendix A
Passages from *Millennial Laws*

The following are passages from the *Millennial Laws*, or orders "concerning intercourse between the sexes." The much larger number of "laws" issued in 1845 apparently reflects the contemporary concern of the **Church** leaders about such relations.

1821

1st. The Gospel of Christ's second appearing strictly forbids all private union between the two sexes.

2nd. One Brother and one Sister must not be together alone, except it be long enough to do a short and necessary errand, nor touch each other unnecessarily.

3rd. Brethren & Sisters must not work together, except on special occasions, and then it must be by the permission of the Elders.

4th. Brethren and Sisters are not allowed to make presents to each other in a private manner.

5th. It is contrary to good order for Brethren and Sisters to pass each other on the stairs.

6th. It is contrary to good order for members of the family to stop on broad stairs, or on the walks, or in the streets with those of our own order, or any other order, longer than to do some necessary errand or messages or to enquire after the welfare of our friends &c. If any longer time be necessary to talk among ourselves, or with our neighbors we are taught to do it within some of our buildings.

7th. Brethren & Sisters must not go to each others [*sic*] apartments without a just and lawful occasion.

8th. Brethren & Sisters must not go into each others [*sic*] apartments after evening meeting; except on needful occasion.

9th. When Brethren have occasion to go into Sisters [*sic*] apartments, or Sisters into Brethrens [*sic*] apartments they must knock at the door & go in by liberty.

10th. The Brethren must all leave their rooms when the Sisters go in to make the beds or clean the room, unless prevented by sickness or infirmity.

11th. When Sisters walk out into the fields, or to the barns, or to the hen roost, or even to the Brethrens' shops, there must be at least two in company; for it is considered unbecoming for one Sister to go alone on such occasions, unless by the special liberty of the Elders of their own sex.

1845

[1.] The Gospel of Christ's Second Appearing, strictly forbids all private union between the two sexes, in any case, or under any circumstances, in doors or out.

2. One brother and one sister, must not be together, alone, at any time, longer than to do a short and necessary duty or errand; and must not have private talk together at all, which they desire to have unknown to the Elders. Neither should brethren and sisters touch each other unnecessarily.

3. Brethren and sisters must not work together, except on special occasions, and then by liberty from the Elders.

4. Brethren and sisters may not make presents to each other in a private manner.

5. Brethren and sisters may not write for each other nor to each other, without liberty from the Elders.

6. If brethren and sisters need instruction in reading, writing, or music, or any other branch of literature or science, they must receive it from those of their own sex, or by such persons as the Elders may appoint.

7. Brethren and sisters may not pass each other on the stairs.

8. Brethren and sisters may not shake hands together.

9. It is contrary to order for Believers to offer to shake hands with apostates; and if brethren shake hands with women of the world, or if sisters shake hands with the men of the world, they must open it to their Elders before meeting.

10. Brethren and sisters may not go to each other's apartments, without a just and lawful occasion; but when they do go, they should rap at the door, and go in by liberty.

11. When brethren go to brethren's rooms, or sisters to sister's [sic] rooms, they should ask if they may come in, but this is not the order or duty of Ministry or Elders.

12. There must not be any sitting or standing on the outside steps, railing

or platforms, nor in the doors, or halls to hold lengthy conversations, either of brethren with brethren, sisters with sisters, or of brethren and sisters together.

13. Brethren and sisters must not go into each other's apartments, after evening meeting at night, except on some very needful occasion.

14. The brethren must all leave their rooms, while the sisters are doing the necessary chores therein; unless prevented by sickness or infirmity.

15. Sisters must not mend, nor set buttons on brethren's clothes, while they have them on.

16. Sisters should not use cloths that have their own initials on to do up brethren's clothes in, nor keep the brethren's clothes with their's [*sic*], neither hang them side by side, nor together.

17. Brethren and sisters must not wear each other's clothes, nor be trying them on, on any occasion whatever.

18. When brethren and sisters come together to support union, their conversation should be open and general, and not whispering or blinking may be done at such times; and blinking should never be practised [*sic*].

19. None should sit crosslegged nor in any awkward posture, in the time of any meeting for worship; and in union, or singing meeting there should be at least five feet distance, between the seats of brethren and sisters, when there is sufficient room to admit it.

20. No fans, cologne water, or any kind of perfumery, may be used in time of union meetings, or any other meeting, neither should any one or ones, scent themselves with perfumes, immediately before attending such meetings.

21. All are required to attend union meetings at the appointed times, unless special duty requires them to be absent; and each absence should be by liberty of the Elders. Real flesh hunters, are generally willing to be absent from an orderly union meeting, and to meet their particular favorites in private.

22. None should leave union meetings, or any meeting for worship, only on necessary duties, which should seldom occur, requiring such absence.

23. Brethren's and sister's [*sic*] shops, should not be under one and the same roof, except those of the Ministry.

24. When sisters walk out into the fields, to the barns, or out buildings, or even to the brethren's shops, there should be at least two in company, for it is considered improper for one sister to go alone on such occasions, unless by special liberty of their Elder sisters.

25. Brethren and sisters must not take opportunities to come together to settle difficulties or make reconciliation with each other, without liberty from the Elders; neither should they accept for company at such times, a youth under eighteen years of age.

26. It is not allowable for brethren to go to sisters' shops, to partake of melons, fruits, or nuts; neither should they go to the kitchen for that purpose, except at meal times. Neither may sisters go to brethren's shops for a like purpose.

27. Brethren and sisters may not lend things to each other; intending never to take them back, without the liberty of the Deacons and Deaconesses, each sex in their own order.

28. Sisters must not take a girl that lives in the children's order, to be their only companion, when they go to brethren's shops on errands.

29. It is disorderly for brethren and sisters to spend much time in making conveniences or articles of manufacture for each other, save such as come within the regular line of business, done by brethren and sisters in general, except by direction of the Deacons and Deaconesses, each sex in their own order.

Appendix B
The Covenant or Constitution
of the Church at Hancock

PREAMBLE

We, the brethren and sisters of the United Society of Believers, (called Shakers) residing in the County of Berkshire and Commonwealth of Massachusetts, being connected together as a religious and social community, distinguished by the name and title of THE CHURCH OF THE UNITED SOCIETY INT HE TOWN OF HANCOCk, which, for many years, has been established and in successful operation under the charge of the Ministry and Eldership thereof; and feeling the importance not only of renewing and confirming our spiritual covenant with God and each other, but also of renewing and improving our social compact, and amending the written form thereof, Do adopt, ordain and declare the following articles of agreement as a summary of the principles, rules and regulations established in the Church of the said United Society, which are to be kept and maintained by us, both in our collective and individual capacities, as a Covenant or Constitution, which shall stand as a lawful testimony, of our religious and social compact before all men, and all cases of question and law, relating to the possession and improvement of our united and consecrated interest, property and estate.

ARTICLE I. OF THE GOSPEL MINISTRY

Section 1. Their Origin, Call and Institution.

We solemnly declare to each other, and to all whom it may concern. That we have received, and do hereby acknowledge, as the foundation of our faith, order and government, the testimony or gospel of Christ, in his first and second appearing; and we do hereby solemnly agree to support and maintain the true primitive faith and Christian principles, the morals, rules and manners pertaining to the said gospel, as ministered by the founders of this Society, and kept and conveyed thro a regular order of ministration

175

down to the present day; and altho, as a religious society, we are variously associated, with respect to the local situations of our respective communities; yet we are known and distinguished as a peculiar people, and consider and acknowledge ourselves members of one general community, possessing one faith, and subject to one united parental and ministerial administration, which has been regularly supported from the first foundation pillars of the institution, and which continues to operate for the support, protection and strength of every part of said community.

Section 2. Their Order and Office.

We further acknowledge and declare, That for the purpose of promoting and maintaining union, order and harmony throughout the various branches of this community, the primary administration of parental authority has been settled in the first established Ministry at New Lebanon, there to rest and remain as the center of union to all who are in gospel relation and communion with the Society. The established order of this Ministry includes four persons, two of each sex.

Section 3. Perpetuity of Their Office, and How Supplied.

We further acknowledge and declare, That the said primary administration of parental authority, has been and is perpetuated as follows, namely; That the first in that office and calling possesses the right given by the sanction of DIVINE AUTHORITY, thro the first founders of this Society, to prescribe or direct any regulation or appointment which they may judge most proper and necessary respecting the Ministry, or any other important matter which may concern the welfare of the Church subsequent to their decease. But in case no such regulation or appointment be so prescribed or directed, then the right to direct and authorize such regulations and appointments devolves upon the surviving members of the Ministry, in counsel with the Elders of the Church or others, as the nature of the case, in their judgment, may require. Such appointments being officially communicated to all concerned, and receiving the general approbation of the Church, are confirmed and supported in the Society.*

---

*This is agreeable to the examples recorded in the scriptures, and continued by the first founders of this Society, and is the order and manner which has been regularly practiced, acknowledged and maintained in the community from the beginning.

Section 4. Of The Ministerial Office in the Several Societies or Communities.

We further acknowledge and declare, covenant and agree, That the ministerial office and authority, in any society or community of our faith, which has emanated or which may emanate in a regular line of order from the center of union aforesaid, is, and shall be acknowledged, owned and respected as the spiritual and primary authority of such society or community, in all matters pertaining to the ministerial office: And in case of the decease or removal of any individual of said Ministry, in any such society, his or her lot and place shall be filled by agreement of the surviving ministers, in counsel with the Elders and others, as the nature of the case may require, together with the knowledge and approbation of the primary ministerial authority at New Lebanon aforesaid, to which they are responsible.

Section 5. Powers and Duties of the Ministry.

The Ministry being appointed and established as aforesaid, are vested with the primary authority of the Church and its various branches. Hence it becomes their special duty to guide and superintend the spiritual concerns of the Society as a body of people under their care and government, and in connection with the Elders in their respective families and departments, who shall act in union with them, to give and establish such orders, rules and regulations as may be found necessary for the government and protection of the Church and Society within the limits of their jurisdiction, and also to counsel, advise and judge, in all matters of importance whether spiritual or temporal. The said Ministry are also invested with authority, to nominate and appoint to office, ministers, elders, deacons and trustees; and to assign offices of care and trust to such brethren and sisters as they, the said Ministry and Elders, shall judge to be best qualified for the several offices to which they may be appointed: And we do hereby covenant and agree, That such nominations and appointments being made and especially communicated to those concerned, and receiving the general approbation of the Church, or of the families concerned, shall thenceforth be confirmed and supported until altered or revoked by the authority aforesaid.

ARTICLE II. INSTITUTION OF THE CHURCH

Section 1. The Object and Design of Church Relation.

We further acknowledge and declare, That the great object, purpose and design of our uniting ourselves together as a Church or body of people in social and religious compact, is faithfully and honestly to occupy, improve and diffuse the various gifts and talents, both of a spiritual and temporal nature, with which Divine Wisdom has blessed us, for the service of God, for the honor of the gospel, and for the mutual protection, support, comfort and happiness of each other, as brethren and sisters in the gospel, and for such other pious and charitable purposes as the gospel may require.

Section 2. Who Are Not Admissable Into Church Relation.

As the unity, stability and purity of the Church essentially depend on the character of its members and their qualifications, and as it is a matter of importance that it should not be encumbered with persons who are under any involvements or incapacity, natural or moral: Therefore, no member of any company or association in business or civil concern; no co-partner in trade; no person under any legal involvement or obligation of service; no minor; no slave or bond servant; no insane person; no profance [profane?] person; nor any person who lives in the willful violation of the known and acknowledged principles of moral conduct, shall be deemed qualified for admission into the covenant relation and communion of the Church.

Section 3. Preparation for Admission Into Church Relation.

In order that Believers may be prepared for entering into the sacred privilege of church relation, it is of primary importance that sufficient opportunity and privilege should be afforded under the ministry of the gospel, for them to acquire suitable instruction in the genuine principles of righteousness, honesty, justice and true holiness and also that they should prove their faith and Christian morality by their practical obedience to the precepts of the gospel, according to their instructions. It is also indispensably necessary for them to receive the one uniting Spirit of Christ, and become so far of one heart and one mind, that they are willing to sacrifice all other relations for this sacred one. Another essential step is to settle all just and equitable claims of creditors and filial heirs; so that whatever property they may possess, shall be justly their own. When this is done, and they feel themselves sufficiently prepared to make a deliberate and final choice to devote themselves with all they possess, wholly to the service of God, without reserve, and it shall be deemed proper by the leading authority of the Church, after examination and due consideration, to allow them to associate together in the capacity of a Church, or a branch thereof, in gospel order, they may then consecrate themselves, and all they possess, to the service of God forever, and confirm the same by signing and sealing a written covenant predicated upon the principles herein contained, and fulfilling on their part all its obligations.

Section 4. Admission of New Members.

As the door must be kept open for the admission of new members into the Church, when duly prepared, it is agreed that each and every person who shall, at any time after the date and execution of the Church covenant, in any branch of the community, be admitted into the Church, as a member thereof, shall previously have a fair opportunity to obtain a full, clear and explicit understanding of the object and design of the Church covenant, and all the obligations it enjoins upon the members. For this purpose he or she shall, in the presence of two of the Deacons or acting Trustees of the Church, read or hear the same distinctly read, so as to be able freely to acknowledge his or her full approbation and acceptance thereof, in all its parts. Then he, she or they, as the case may be, shall be at liberty to sign the same; and having signed and scaled it, and being subject to all the obligations required of the original signers, shall thenceforth be entitled to all the benefits and privileges hereunto appertaining; and the signature or signatures, thus added, shall be certified by the said deacons or trustees, together with the date thereof.

Section 5. Concerning Youth and Children.

Youth and children, being minors, cannot be received as members of the Church, possessing a consecrated interest in a united capacity; yet it is agreed that they may be received under the immediate care and government of the Church, at the desire or consent of such person or persons as have a lawful right to, or control over such minors, together with their own desire or consent. But no minor under the care or protection of the Church can be employed therein for wages of any kind.

ARTICLE III. OF THE TRUSTEES

Section 1. Appointment, Qualifications and Powers of Trustees.

It has been found necessary for the establishment of order in the Society, in its various branches, that superintending deacons and deaconesses should be appointed and authorized to act as trustees or agents of the temporalities of the Church. They must be recommended by their honesty and integrity, their fidelity in trust, and their capacity for the transaction of business. Of these qualifications the Ministry and Elders must be the judges. The official Trustees of the Church are generally known among us by the title of Office Deacons, of which there must be two or more; and being appointed by the authority aforesaid, they are invested with power to take the general charge and oversight of all the property, estate and interest dedicated, devoted, consecrated and given up for the benefit of the Church; to hold in trust, the fee of all the lands belonging to the Church; also all gifts, grants and donations which have been, or may hereafter be dedicated, devoted, consecrated and given up as aforesaid; and the said property, estate, interest, gifts, grants and donations, shall constitute the united and consecrated interest of the Church, and shall be held in trust by the said Deacons, as acting Trustees, in their official capacity, and by their successors in said office and trust forever.

Section 2. Duties of the Trustees.

It is, and shall be the duty of the said Deacons or acting Trustees, to improve, use and appropriate the said united interest for the benefit of the Church, in all its departments, and for such other religious and charitable purposes as the gospel may require; and also to make all just and equitable defense in law, for the protection and security of the consecrated and united interest, rights and privileges of the Church and Society, jointly and severally, as an associated community, so far as circumstances and the nature of the case may require. Provided nevertheless, That all the transactions of the said Deacons or acting Trustees, in the use, management, protection, defense and disposal of the aforesaid interest shall be for the benefit and privilege, and in behalf of the Church or Society, as aforesaid; and not for any private interest, object or purpose whatever.

Section 3. Trustees to Give Information and Be Responsible to the Ministry & Elders.

It shall also be the duty of the Trustees to give information to the Ministry and Elders of the Church, of the general state of the temporal concerns of the Church and Society committed to their charge; and also to report to said authority all losses sustained in the united interest thereof, which shall come under their cognizance: And no disposal of any of the real estate of the Church, nor any important contract, shall be considered valid without the previous approbation of the authority aforesaid, to whom the said Deacons and Trustees are, and shall, at all times, be held responsible in all their transactions.

Section 4. Books of Account and Record to be Kept.

It is, and shall be the duty of the Deacons or acting Trustees to keep, or cause to be kept, regular Books of account, in which shall be entered the debit and credit accounts of all mercantile operations and business transactions between the Church and others; all receipts and expenditures, Bonds, Notes and Bills of account, and all other matters that concern the united interest of the Church: And also a Book or Books of Record, in which shall be recorded a true and correct copy of this covenant, also all appointments, removals and changes in office of ministers, elders, deacons and trustees; all admissions, removals, departures and decease of members, together with all other matters and transactions of a public nature which are necessary to be recorded for the benefit of the Church, and for the preservation and security of the documents, papers and written instruments pertaining to the united interest and concerns of the Church committed to their charge. And the said records shall be annually inspected by the leading authority of the Church, who, together with the Trustees, shall be the official auditors of the same; and the signature of one or more of said creditors, with the date of inspection and approval, shall be deemed sufficient authority for the correctness and validity of the facts and matters so recorded.

Section 5. Trustees to Execute a Declaration of Trust.

For the better security of the united and consecrated interest of the Church to the proper uses and purposes stipulated in this Covenant, it shall be the duty of the Trustee or Trustees who may be vested with the lawful title or claim of the real estate of the Church, to make and execute a declaration of trust, in due form of law, embracing all and singular, the lands, tenements and hereditaments, with every matter of interest pertaining to the Church which, at the time being, may be vested in him or them, or that may in future come under his or their charge of office, during his or their Trusteeship. The said declaration shall state expressly, that the said Trustee or trustees hold all such lands, tenements, hereditaments, and all the personal property of every description, belonging to the Church or Society, in trust, for the uses and purposes expressed in, and subject to the rules, conditions and regulations prescribed by the Covenant and Constitution of the said

Church or Society, or any amendments thereto which shall hereafter be adopted by the general approbation of the Church, and in conformity with the primitive faith and acknowledged principles of the Society; And the said declaration shall be in writing, duly executed under his or their hands and seals, and shall be recorded in the Book of Records provided for in the preceding Section.

Section 6. Vacancies In Certain Cases How Supplied.

We further covenant and agree, That in case it should at any time happen in the course of Divine Providence, that the office of trustee should become wholly vacant by the death or defection of all the Trustees, in whom may be vested the fee of the lands or real estate belonging to the said Church or Society, then, and in that case, one or more successors shall be appointed by the constitutional authority recognized in this Covenant, according to the rules and regulations prescribed by the same: And the said appointment being duly recorded in the Book of Records provided for in this article, shall be deemed and is hereby declared to vest in such successor or successors all the rights, interest and authority of their predecessors, in respect to all such lands, property and estate belonging to the Church or Society as aforesaid.

ARTICLE IV. OF THE ELDERSHIP

Section 1. Choice and Appointment of Elders.

The united interest and objects of Believers, established in gospel order, require that Elders should be chosen and appointed for the spiritual protection of families; whose business it is to take the lead in their several departments, in the care and government of the concerns of the Church, and of the different families established in, and pertaining to the Society. Their number and order should correspond with that of the Ministry. They are required to be persons of good understanding, of approved faithfulness and integrity, and gifted in spiritual administration. They must be selected and appointed by the Ministry who are to judge of their qualifications.

Section 2. Duties of the Elders.

As faithful watchmen upon the walls of Zion, it becomes the duty of the Elders to watch over their respective families; to instruct the members in their respective duties; to counsel, encourage, admonish, exhort and reprove, as occasion may require; to lead the worship; to be examples to the members of obedience to the faith, principles and orders of the gospel, and to see that the orders, rules and regulations pertaining to their respective families and departments are properly kept.

ARTICLE V. OF FAMILY DEACONS & DEACONESSES

Section 1. Their Qualifications and Appointment.

The office of family Deacons and Deaconesses has long been established in the Church, and is essentially necessary for the care, management and direction of the domestic concerns in each family, order or branch of the Church. They are required to be persons of correct and well grounded faith in the established principles of the gospel; faithful in duty; closely united to their Elders, and of sufficient capacity in business. Of these Qualifications the Ministry and Elders, by whom they are chosen and appointed, must be the judges. Their number in each family is generally two of each sex; but may be more or less, according to the size of the family and the extent of their various duties.

Section 2. Their Duties and Obligations.

The Deacons and Deaconesses of families are entrusted with the care and oversight of the domestic concerns of their respective families. It is their duty to make proper arrangements in business; to maintain good order; to watch over, counsel and direct the members in their various occupations, as occasion may require; to make application to the office deacons, or trustees for whatever supplies are needed in the several departments of the family: to maintain union, harmony and good understanding with the said office deacons, and to report to their Elders the state of matters which fall under their cognizance and observation. But their power is restricted to the domestic concerns of their respective families and departments, and does not extend to any immediate or direct correspondence with those without the bounds of the Church. They have no immediate concern with trade and commerce; therefore, it is not their business to buy and sell, nor in any way to dispose of the property under their care, except with the counsel and approbation of the Trustees.

ARTICLE VI. PRIVILEGES & OBLIGATIONS OF MEMBERS

Section 1. Benefits & Privileges of Members In Church Relation.

The united interest of the Church having been formed and established by the freewill offerings and pious donations of the members respectively, from the commencement of the Institution, for the objects and purposes already stated, it cannot be considered either as a joint tenancy or a tenancy in common; but as a consecrated whole, designed for, and devoted to the uses and purposes of the gospel forever, agreeable to the established principles of the Church; Therefore, it shall be held possessed and enjoyed by the Church, in their united capacity, as a sacred and covenant right; that is to say, all and every member thereof, while standing in gospel union, and maintaining the principles of this Covenant, shall enjoy equal rights, benefits and privileges, in the use of all things pertaining to the Church, according to their several needs and circumstances; and no difference shall be made on account of what any one has contributed and devoted, or may hereafter contribute and devote to the support and benefit of the Institution.

Section 2. Proviso.

It is nevertheless provided, stipulated and agreed, that the benefits, privileges and enjoyments secured by this Covenant to the members of the Church, shall not be considered as extending to any person who shall refuse to comply with the conditions of this association, or who shall refuse to submit to the administration and discipline of the constituted authority of the Church, or who shall willfully depart from the principles and practice of those religious and moral obligations which have been established in the Church, agreeable to the primitive faith and distinguished principles of this institution, of which refusal or non-compliance the leading authority acknowledged in the first Article of this Covenant shall be the proper and constitutional Judges.

Section 3. Obligations of the Members.

As subordination and obedience is [*sic*] the life and soul of every well regulated community, so our strength and protection, our happiness and prosperity in the capacity of Church members, must depend on our faithful obedience to the rules and orders established in the Church, and to the institutions, counsel and advice of its leaders: Therefore, we do hereby covenant and agree, That we will receive and acknowledge as our Elders in the gospel, those members in the Church who are, or may be chosen and appointed, for the time being, to that office and calling, by the authority aforesaid, and also, that we will, as faithful brethren and sisters in Christ, conform and subject ourselves to the known and established faith and principles of our community, and to the counsel and direction of the Elders who shall act in union as aforesaid; and also to all the orders, rules and regulations which are, or may be given and established in the Church, according to the principles and by the authority aforesaid.

Section 4. Duties of the Members.

The faithful improvement of our time and talents in doing good, is a duty which God requires of man as a rational, social and accountable being; and this duty is indispensable in the members of the Church of Christ; Therefore it is, and shall be required of all and every member of this institution, unitedly and individually, to occupy and improve their time and talents to support and maintain the interest of the Society; to promote the objects of this Covenant, and discharge their duty to God and each other, according to their several abilities and callings, as members in union with one common lead; so that the various gifts and talents of all may be improved for the mutual benefit of each other and concerned.

Section 5. Concerning Wages and Removals.

As we esteem the mutual possession and enjoyment of the consecrated interest and privileges of the Church a valuable consideration, fully adequate to any amount of personal interest, labor or service devoted or consecrated by any individual; We therefore covenant and agree, In conformity with an established and well known principle of the Church, that no person whatever, under its care and protection, can be employed for wages of any kind, on his or her individual account; and that no ground is or can be afforded for the recovery of any property or service devoted or consecrated as aforesaid: And it is also agreed, that in case of the removal of any member or members from one family, society or branch of the Church to another, his, her or their previous signature or signatures to the Church or family Covenant from whence such member or members shall have removed, shall forever bar all claims which are incompatible with the true intent and meaning of this Covenant, in the same manner as if such removal had not taken place: yet all who shall so remain, in union with the authority aforesaid, shall be entitled to all the benefits and privileges of the family or order in which they shall then be placed, so long as they shall conform to the rules and regulations of the same.

ARTICLE VII. DEDICATION & RELEASE.

Section 1. Dedication and Consecration of Person, Property and Service.

According to the faith of the gospel which we have received, and agreeable to the uniform practice of the Church of Christ, from its first establishment in this Society, We covenant and agree to dedicate, devote, consecrate and give up, and by this Covenant we do, solemnly and conscientiously, dedicate, devote, consecrate and give up ourselves and services, together with all our temporal interest, to the service of God, and the support and benefit of the Church of this community to which we are united, and to such other pious and charitable purposes as the gospel may require, to be under the care and direction of such Elders, Deacons and Trustees as are, or may be established in the Church by the authority aforesaid.

Section 2. Declaration and Release of Private Claim.

Whereas, in pursuance of the requirements of the gospel, and in the full exercise of our faith, reason and understanding, we have freely and voluntarily sacrificed all self-interest, and consecrated and devoted our persons, services and property, as aforesaid, to the pious and benevolent purposes of the gospel: Therefore, we do hereby solemnly and conscientiously, unitedly and individually, for ourselves, our heirs and assigns, release and quitclaim, to the Deacons or acting Trustees of the Church, for the time being, for the uses and purposes aforesaid, all our private personal right, title, interest, claim and demand of, in and to the estate, interest, property and appurtenances, so consecrated, devoted and given up: And we hereby jointly and severally promise and declare, in the presence of God, and before these Witnesses, That we will never hereafter, neither directly nor indirectly, under any circumstances whatever, contrary to the stipulations of this Covenant, make nor require any account of any interest, property, labor or service, nor any division thereof, which is, has been, or may be devoted by us, or any of us, to the uses and purposes aforesaid; nor bring any charge of debt or damage, nor hold any claim nor demand whatever, against the said Deacons or Trustees, nor against the Church nor Society, nor against any member thereof, on account of any property, or service given, rendered, devoted or consecrated to the aforesaid sacred and charitable purposes.

In confirmation of all the aforesaid statements, covenants, promises and articles of agreement, we have hereunto subscribed our names and affixed our seals, commencing on this twenty-fifth day of December in the year of our Lord and Saviour one thousand eight hundred and thirty.

Appendix C
A Chronological Bibliography of Imaginative Literature Featuring Shakers

1824   Sedgwick, Catherine Maria. *Redwood: A Tale* 2 vols. New York: E. Bliss and E. White.

1829   K. "The Shakeress." *Miscellany* (Pittsfield, Mass.) 1 (July 14): 1–2.

1831   [Unsigned.] "The Shaker and the Deacon." *Free Enquirer* (New York) 3, 17 (February): 133–134.

1833   Hawthorne, Nathaniel. "The Canterbury Pilgrims." *Token and Atlantic Souvenir*, 153–166. Also in *The Snow Image and Other Twice-Told Tales*. Boston: Ticknor, Reed, and Fields, 1852, 145–158.

1837   Hawthorne, Nathaniel. "The Shaker Bridal." *Twice-Told Tales.* Boston: American Stationers Co. and John B. Russell. Also in the *Token and Atlantic Souvenir* (1838): 117–125.

        Mayo, Sarah C. Edgarton. "Eleonora, the Shakeress." *Selections from the Writings of Mrs. Sarah C. Edgarton Mayo: With a Memoir, by Her Husband.* Boston: A. Tompkins, 1849, 262–287.

1839   Hentz, Caroline Lee. "The Shaker Girl." *Lady's Book* 18 (February): 49–58.

1848   Thompson, Daniel Pierce. "The Shaker Lovers." In *The Shaker Lovers and Other Tales.* Burlington, Vt: C. Goodrich and S. B. Nichols. Also in *May Martin and Other Tales of the Green Mountains.* Rev. ed. Boston: Benjamin B. Mussey and Co., 1852.

        [Unsigned.] "The Shakeress." In *The Moss Rose, for 1848,* Alfred A. Phillips, ed. New York: Nafis and Cornish.

        Lamson, David R. "Story of Mary Williams and William Wright." Embedded in *Two Years' Experience among the Shakers.* West Boylston [Mass.]: By the author. Reprinted New York: AMS Press, 1971.

1849   Sedgwick, Catherine Maria. "Magnetism among the Shakers." *Berkshire Culturalist and Weekly Family Gazette* 2 (May 16): 157–158. Johnson, Samuel D. *The Shaker Lovers: A Drama in One Act.* Boston: William V. Spencer.

1853   Elkins, Hervey. ["Urbino and Ellina: or, the Triumph of Shaker Piety."] Embedded in *Fifteen Years in the Senior Order of Shakers: A Narration of Facts, concerning that Singular People. . . .* Hanover, N.H.: Dartmouth Press, 1853. Reprinted New York: AMS Press, 1973.

1857   Guild, Caroline [Hetty Holyoke, pseud.] *Never Mind the Face: Or, The Cousin's Visit.* New York: Scribner.

1861   Browne, Charles Farrah [Artemus Ward, pseud.] "On the Shakers." *Vanity Fair* (February 23, 1861): 94–95.

1872   Raffensperger, E. B. "Shaker John," *Atlantic Monthly* 30 (December): 734–743.
        [Unsigned.] ["Minette and Theo".] Embedded in "Fifteen Years a Shakeress," *Galaxy* (New York) 13 (January–April): 29–38, 191–201, 337–346, 460–470.

1873   [Unsigned.] "Why a Woman Joined the Shakers." *Frank Leslie's Illustrated Newspaper* 37 (September 13): 10.

1878   Scudder, Horace Elisha. "A House of Entertainment." *Atlantic Monthly* 42 (September/October): 305–319, 438–452. Reprinted in *Stories and Romances.* Boston: Houghton Mifflin Co., 1880.

1879   Woolsey, Sarah Chauncey [Susan Coolidge, pseud.] *Eyebright, a Story.* Boston: Roberts Bros.

1880   Howells, William Dean. *The Undiscovered Country.* Boston: Houghton Mifflin Co.

1891   McGlasson, Eva Wilder. "A Shaker Wooing." *Harper's Weekly* 35 (June 20): 457–458.
        [Brodhead] McGlasson, Eva Wilder. *Diana's Livery.* New York: Harper and Bros.

1893   Howells, William Dean. *The World of Chance.* New York: Harper and Brothers.

1894   McGlasson, Eva Wilder. "The Shaker Baby." *Youth's Companion* 68 (December 13): 602.

1895   Haight, Charles Sherman. "A Shaker Romance." *Munsey's Magazine* 12 (March): 625–632. Also in *Werner's Small Pieces.* New York: Werner, 1905.
        Howells, William Dean. *The Day of Their Wedding.* New York: Harper and Bros.

1896   Howells, William Dean. *A Parting and a Meeting*. New York: Harper and Bros.

1901   Norris, Zoe Anderson. *They, Too: A Shaker Love Story*. Harrodsburg, Ky: *Harrodsburg Herald*, Inc., 1987. Copyrighted by Mary Chelf Jones, Norris's granddaughter, as an unpublished work.

1909   Holden, Marietta E. *The Story of Martha: Or, Love's Ordeal*. Boston: American Printing Co. First published in 1904 as *Uncovered Ears and Opened Vision*. New York: Broadway Publishing Co.
       Wiggin, Kate Douglas. *Susanne and Sue*. Boston: Houghton Mifflin Co.

1910   Deland, Margaret. *The Way to Peace*. New York: Harper and Bros.

1912   Thomas, T. J. "A Shaker Romance." *Wide World Magazine* 28, No. 166 (February): 390–395.

1920   Mills, Fanny, "The Passing of the Shakers." *Watch Tower* 3, No. 6 (May): 13–18, 31.
       Howells, William Dean. *The Vacation of the Kelwyns: An Idyl of the Middle Eighteen-Seventies*. New York: Harper and Bros.

1922   Sears, Clara Endicott. *The Romance of Fiddler's Green*. Boston: Houghton Mifflin Co.

1923   Rosenthal, Carla F. *The Little Shakeresses*. Chicago: Old Tower Press.

1937   McCullough, Robert. *Me and Thee*. New York: Lothrop, Lee, and Shepard.

1943   Cameron, Leslie Georgiana [Ann George Leslie, pseud.] *Dancing Saints*. Garden City, N.Y.: Doubleday, Doran, and Co.

1945   Piercy, Caroline Behlen. *Sylvia, the Shaker Maid*. Cleveland, Ohio: By the Author. (Accompanied by a doll, Sylvia, alleged to look like a Shaker girl.)
       Cramer, Miriam Anne. *More Love, Brother: A Play in Three Acts about the People Called Shakers, with Incidental Songs and Dances*. Shaker Heights, Ohio: Shaker Historical Society, photocopy.

1957   Giles, Janice Holt. *The Believers: A Novel of Shaker Life*. Boston: Houghton Mifflin Co.

1970   Jonas, Gerald. "The Shaker Revival." *Galaxy Magazine* 29 (February): 4–33.

1973   Silverberg, Selma K. *Matt's Real Adventure*. N.p. Reprinted Solon, Ohio: Evans Printing Co., 1991; distributed by the Shaker Historical Society, Shaker Heights, Ohio.

1978   Howard, Elizabeth. *Out of Step with the Dancers*. New York: William Morrow and Co.
1981   Yolen, Jane. *The Gift of Sarah Barker*. New York: Viking Press.
1982   Sprigg, June. "Rachael: A Fictional Account of a Shaker Woman." *Berkshire Magazine* 1, no. 2 (Autumn): 33–37.
1987   Ray, Mary Lyn. *Angel Baskets*. Sanborton, N. H.: Martha Wetherbee Books.
1992   McGaughey, R. H. *Molly of the Shakers, a Story of Love and Tragedy*. Paducah, Ky: Turner Publishing Co.
       Harper, Karen. *Circle of Gold*. New York: Dutton.
       Smith, Gregory Blake. *The Divine Comedy of John Venner.* New York: Poseidon.
1994   Ray, Mary Lyn. *Shaker Boy.* San Diego, Calif.: Browndeer Press/Harcourt.
1995   Gaeddert, Louann. *Hope.* New York: Atheneum Books for Children.
1997   Turner, Ann. *Shaker Hearts.* New York: HarperCollins Publishers.
       Woodworth, Deborah. *Death of a Winter Shaker.* New York: Avon Books, Inc.
1998   Woodworth, Deborah. *A Deadly Shaker Spring.* New York: Avon Books, Inc.
1999   Woodworth, Deborah. *Sins of a Shaker Summer: A Sister Rose Callahan Mystery.* New York: Avon Books, Inc.

Appendix D
Selected Museums and Libraries with Shaker Collections

Edward Deming Andrews Memorial Shaker Collection, Henry Francis du Pont Winterthur Museum, Winterthur, Delaware 19735

Filson Club, 118 West Breckenridge Street, Louisville, Kentucky 40203

Hancock Shaker Community, Inc., Pittsfield, Massachusetts 01201

Library of Congress, Washington, District of Columbia, 20540

New York Public Library, New York City, New York 10028

Ohio State Historical Society, Columbus, Ohio 43211

Shaker Historical Society, 16740 South Park Boulevard, Shaker Heights, Ohio 44120

The Shaker Library, Sabbathday Lake, New Gloucester, Maine 04274

Shaker Museum and Library, Old Chatham, New York 12136

Shaker Village at Canterbury, Inc., East Canterbury, New Hampshire 03224

Shakertown at Pleasant Hill, Inc., Harrodsburg, Kentucky 40330

Shakertown at South Union, Inc., South Union, Kentucky 42283

University of Kentucky, Lexington, Kentucky 40506

Western Kentucky University, Bowling Green, Kentucky 42101

Western Reserve Historical Society, 10825 East Boulevard, Cleveland, Ohio 44106

Williams College, Williamstown, Massachusetts 01267

Selected Bibliography

Although posterity's knowledge of **Shakers** has suffered because **Ann Lee**, the founder of the **United Society of Believers in Christ's Second Appearing**, left no written commentary about her life, a plethora of information about her and her sect exists and continues to be developed. For one thing, when the sect was institutionalized in 1787, after her death, Shakers became very prolific record keepers. Who sold packages of mustard seeds to **the world**; how many oval boxes Brother **Delmar Wilson** made one winter; which **Believer** from **Pleasant Hill**, Kentucky, was recently "translated" to the spirit world; how many board feet of white pine were harvested at **Enfield**, New Hampshire; who "absconded" from **New Lebanon**—seemingly, all such matters have been recorded, and most of the records are available (though not always easily and inexpensively) to researchers. Most of this material has remained in manuscript form, much of it owned by historical organizations, such as the Western Reserve Historical Society, Cleveland, Ohio.

Besides the thorough and somewhat mundane information provided by Shaker scribes, the sect has had numerous and intelligent theologians, historians, and apologists. Even cursory readings of, for example, **Benjamin S. Youngs**'s *The Testimony of Christ's Second Appearing* (1808), **Seth Youngs Wells** and **Calvin Green**'s *Testimonies Concerning the Character and Ministry of Mother Ann Lee* (1827), and **Frederick W. Evans**'s *Auto biography of a Shaker* (1869) are edifying. To a large degree, these works together define **Shakerism**.

Another large source of material about the Shakers is that rendered by **apostates** and other people who either disliked or feared them. Their revelations of the "facts," so to speak, of Shakerism largely conflict with the Shakers' accounts of themselves (and those of people who respected them) and, thus, provide readers with another perspective on "the people so wondered at." Did Ann Lee and the earliest Believers get drunk, dance naked, and fornicate in the moonlight of the primitive forest of Niskayuna, New York? Extremes in this body of material are exemplified in the accounts

195

rendered by **Valentine Wightman Rathbun Sr.** (in the negative) and **Hervey Elkins** (in the positive), both of whom had once eagerly embraced Shakerism.

Posterity also has an ever-increasing wealth of material about the Shakers that has been produced by people who seem more interested in truth than in judgment, although preference creeps into so-called objective accounts of the Society, for, after all, even a scientist—a university professor of sociology, say—has a self, which is hard to subdue in all matters. Nevertheless, the discoveries, observations, and connections made by modern scholars have been bountiful. Beginning with Marguerite Fellows Melcher's *The Shaker Adventure* (1941), the first attempt by a non-Shaker to produce something akin to a comprehensive account of the Shaker experience, scholarship has burgeoned for nearly 60 years. It and appreciation of the contributions of the Shakers to the cultural heritage of all Americans have become inextricably bound. The most recent and seemingly definitive history of the sect is Stephen Stein's *The Shaker Experience in America: A History of the United Society of Believers* (1992), which may be said to supersede Edward D. Andrews's *The People Called Shakers: A Search for the Perfect Society* (1953), which itself superseded Melcher's work. On a lesser scale, an absolute plethora of works exist, Suzanne Skees's *God Among the Shakers: A Search for Stillness and Faith at Sabbathday Lake* (1998) being among the most recent.

Finally, no study of Shakerism would be complete without notice of its delineations in imaginative works by non-Shaker authors. The Shakers themselves have been prolific composers of **songs/poems** and expository prose about their spiritual experiences and their religion, but they seem not to have published or even to have written a single work of imaginative narrative or dramatic fiction about themselves (although Brother Frederick McKechnie did write and publish "Professor Comstock's Experience" in 1902, a small tale that derides vivisection). However, authors of "the world" have not been reluctant to use the Shakers as grist for various modes of imaginative literature, especially so-called historical fiction.

Throughout the nineteenth and the twentieth centuries, Shakers and Shakerism have been delineated continually in short stories and novels (but, strangely, they virtually have been ignored by playwrights and poets). Most of these narratives pay some homage to various elements of the Shaker way, but, generally, they treat Shakerism quite negatively. Accordingly, among other things, they are instructive of the values and principles of the mainstream culture and, hence, its causes for opposition to the Shaker counterculture. Even so, since around 1945—the publication date of Caroline

Behlen Piercy's *Sylvia, the Shaker Maid*—a new trend has developed in the way Shakers are appropriated by non-Shaker authors. Not only does the new literature tread very lightly upon Shakerism, but also it is more historically accurate and more comprehensive of the Shaker pilgrimage. Moreover, it is directed at a different audience: the young readers of the mainstream culture, who are being encouraged in classrooms and elsewhere to appreciate all of their cultural heritage. A bibliography of imaginative literature comprises appendix C.

UNPUBLISHED WORKS BY SHAKERS

Bates, Betsy. *A Journal of Events.* Western Reserve Historical Society (hereafter WRHS) V B 128. New Lebanon, N.Y., 1833–1835.

Bathrick, Eunice, comp. *Testimonies and Wise Sayings, Counsel and Instruction of Mother Ann and the Elders.* WRHS VI B 10–13. Harvard, Mass., 1869.

Bishop, Rufus, comp. *A Collection of the Writings of Father Joseph Meacham Respecting Church Order and Government.* WRHS VII B 59. New Lebanon, N.Y., 1850.

Blakeman, Elisha D. *The Boys' Journal of Work.* WRHS V B 59. New Lebanon, N.Y., 1844–1865.

Blanchard, Jemima. "Testimony." WRHS VII B 107. Harvard, Mass., n.d.

A Book of Orders Given by Mother Lucy for All that Belong to the Children's Order. Edward Deming Andrews Memorial Shaker Collection, SA 1262, Henry Francis du Pont Winterthur Museum, Winterthur, Delaware (hereafter Andrews Collection). New Lebanon, N.Y., 1840–1842.

Brethren's Journal of Domestic Occurrences. WRHS V B 63–71. New Lebanon, N.Y., 1790–1860.

Eads, Harvey, comp. *Shaker Record A [of South Union].* Bowling Green: Western Kentucky University, 1870.

Gates, Benjamin. *A Day Book of Journal of Work and Various Things.* Andrews Collection, SA 1030. New Lebanon, N.Y., 1827–1838.

Green, Calvin. "Biography of Elder Henry Clough." WRHS VI B 24. New Lebanon, N.Y., 1860.

———. "Biographic Memoir of the Life, Character and Important Events in the Ministration of Mother Lucy Wright." WRHS VI B 24. New Lebanon, N.Y., 1861.

Harris, Sally. *A Journal Kept by Sally Harris for the Benefit of the Sisters at the West Family, [1854–1855] . . . Pleasant Hill, Mercer County, Ky.* Harrodsburg, Ky.: Harrodsburg Historical Society, photocopy.

A History of the Society of Believers at Sodus and Port Bay, N.Y., 1822–1838. WRHS, V-B: 22 and V-B: 21. New Gloucester, Maine: Shaker Library and Wayne County, N.Y.: Wayne County Historical Society, photocopies.

Hollister, Alonzo G., comp. *Autobiography of the Saints.* 2 vols. WRHS VI B 36–37. New Lebanon, N.Y., 1872.

Letter from the New Lebanon, New York, Ministry to the West Union, Ohio, Ministry, dated July 30, 1825. WRHS IV A 35.

Letter from the New Lebanon, New York, Ministry to the West Union, Ohio, Ministry, dated July 12, 1826. WRHS IV A 35.

Prescott. Hannah. "Testimony." WRHS IV A 11. N.p., n.d.

Prescott, James. *History of North Union.* Shaker Heights, Ohio: Nord Library, The Shaker Historical Library, 1870.

Rankin, John. "Autobiography," *Shaker Record A.*, Harvey Eads, comp. Bowling Green: Western Kentucky University, 1870.

Wells, Freegift. *Journal regarding Charges of Misconduct.* WRHS V A 14. Watervliet, N.Y., 1849.

Wells, Seth Youngs. "A Plain Statement of the Custom and Manner of Receiving, Managing, Teaching, Governing and Disciplining Children, in the Society of People Called Shakers." WRHS VII B 62. N.p., 1825.

———. "Remarks on Learning and the Use of Boks [*sic*]." WRHS VII B 173. N.p., March 10, 1836.

Youngs, Isaac N. *Personal Journal.* Shaker Museum and Library, No. 10, 509. Old Chatham, N.Y., 1837–1857.

———. *A Concise View of the Church of God and of Christ on Earth Having Its Foundation in the Faith of Christ's First and Second Appearing.* Andrews Collection, SA 760. New Lebanon, N.Y., 1856–1860.

PUBLICATIONS BY SHAKERS

Allen, Catherine. *A Century of Communism: The History of the People Known as Shakers.* Pittsfield, Mass.: Eagle Publishing Company, 1902.

Avery, Giles Bushnell. "A Defense of Shaker Friends." *Mind and Matter* 2 (January 3, 1880): 3–4.

———. "Spirit Manifestations." *Progressive Thinker* (Chicago) (November 25, 1880): 64–76.

———. *Sketches of "Shakers and Shakerism": Synopsis of Theology of United Society of Believers in Christ's Second Appearing.* Albany, N.Y.: Weed, Parsons, and Co., 1883.

———. "Spiritual Life." *Manifesto* 18 (November 1888): 241–243.

———. "The New Creation." *Manifesto* 19 (June 1889): 28–30.

———. *Autobiography by Elder Giles B. Avery, of Mount Lebanon, N.Y.* East Canterbury, N.H., 1891.

Barker, Ruth Mildred. "A History of 'Holy Land'—Alfred, Maine." *Shaker Quarterly* 3 (Fall/Winter 1963): 75–95, 107–127.

———. "History of Union Branch, Gorham, Maine, 1784–1819." *Shaker Quarterly* 7 (Summer 1967): 64–82.

———. *The Sabbathday Lake Shakers: An Introduction to the Shaker Heritage.* Sabbathday Lake, Maine: Shaker Press, 1985.

Bates, Issachar. "A Sketch of the Life and Experience of Issachar Bates." *Shaker Quarterly* 1 (Fall/Winter, 1961): 98–118, 145–163; 2 (Spring 1962): 18–35.

———. "A Ballad by Elder Issachar Bates." *Shaker Quarterly* 2 (Summer 1962): 60–66.

Bates, Paulina. *The Divine Book of Holy and Eternal Wisdom, Revealing the Work of God; Out of Whose Mouth Goeth a Sharp Sword . . . Written by Paulina Bates . . . Including Other Illustrations and Testimonies. . . .* Canterbury, N.H.: United Society Called "Shakers," 1849.

[Bishop, Rufus, and Seth Youngs Wells, eds.] *Testimonies of the Life, Character, Revelations, and Doctrines of Our Ever Blessed Mother Ann Lee, and the Elders with Her; through Whom the Word of Eternal Life as Opened in This Day of Christ's Second Appearing: Collected from Living Witnesses, by Order of the Ministry, in Union with the Church. . . .* Hancock, Mass.: J. Tallcott and J. Deming, Junrs., 1816.

Blinn, Henry Clay. *The Life and Gospel Experience of Mother Ann Lee.* Canterbury, N.H., 1882.

———. "Florida." *Manifesto* 25 (March 1895): 69–70.

———. *Advent of the Christ in Man and Woman.* East Canterbury, N.H., 1896.

———. "A Journey to Kentucky in the Year 1873: Parts I–IX." *Shaker Quarterly* 5 (1965): 3–19, 37–55, 69–79, 107–133; 6 (1966): 22–30, 53–72, 93–102, 135–144; 7 (Spring 1967): 13–23.

———, ed. *The Manifestation of Spiritualism among the Shakers, 1837–1847.* East Canterbury, N.H., 1899.

———, comp. *A Sacred Repository of Anthems and Hymns, for Devotional Worship and Praise. . . .* Canterbury, N.H., 1852.

[———.] *A Collection of Hymns and Anthems Adapted to Public Worship. Published by the Shakers. . . .* East Canterbury, N.H., 1892.

Brief Account of Shakers and Shakerism: Several Pages of Shaker Music are also Added that Have Never Before Been Published. Canterbury, N.H., [1875].

Briggs, Nicholas A. "Forty Years a Shaker." *Granite Monthly* (Concord, N.H.) 52 (1920): 463–474; 53 (January/March 1921): 19–32, 56–65, 113–121.

Carr, Frances A. *Growing Up Shaker.* [Sabbathday Lake, Maine]: United Society of Shakers, 1995.

———, ed. "Mother Lucy's Sayings Spoken at Different Times and under Various Circumstances." *Shaker Quarterly* 8 (Winter 1968): 99–106.

Cumings, Henry. *What Shall I do to Become a Shaker?* [Enfield, N.H.?], 1879, broadside.

A Declaration of the Society of People (Commonly Called Shakers) Shewing Their Reasons for Refusing to Aid or Abet the Cause of War and Bloodshed, by Bearing Arms, Paying Fines, Hiring Substitutes, or Rendering Any Equivalent for Military Service. Albany, N.Y.: E. and E. Hosford, 1815.

Doolittle, Mary Antoinette. *Autobiography of Mary Antoinette Doolittle Containing a Brief History of Early Life Prior to Becoming a Member of the Shaker Community, Also an Outline of Life & Experience among the Shakers.* Mount Lebanon, N.Y., 1880.

Dunlavy, John. *The Manifesto: or, A Declaration of the Doctrines and Practices of the Church of Christ. . . .* Pleasant Hill, Ky.: P. Bertrand, 1818.

———. "The Shakers: The Nature and Character of the True Church of Christ, Proved by Plain Evidences and Showing Whereby It May Be Known from All Others. . . ." *Nineteenth Century* (Philadelphia) (April 1848): 350–353.

Eads, Harvey. "The Shaker Problem, No. 2." *Phrenological Journal* (August 1873): 111–115.

———. *Shaker Sermons: Scripto-Rational. Containing the Substance of Shaker Theology. Together with Replies and Criticisms Logically and Clearly Set Forth. . . .* Albany, N.Y.: Weed, Parsons, and Co., 1879.

———. *Discourses on Religion, Science, and Education.* South Union, Ky.: N.p., 1884.

Evans, Frederick W. "Celibacy. Letter from a Shaker." *American Phrenological Journal* 43 (June 1866): 177–178.

———. *Autobiography of a Shaker.* [Albany, N.Y.: Charles Van Benthuysen and Sons], 1869.

———. "Shakerism and Spiritualism in Their Moral Aspects." *Shaker* 1 (July 1871): 49–51.

———. *Religious Communism.* London: J. Burns, 1871.

———, et al. *Shakers: Compendium of the Origin, History, Principles, Rules and Regulations, Government, and Doctrines of the United Society of Believers in Christ's Second Appearing. With Biographies of Ann Lee, William Lee, Jas. Whittaker, J. Hocknell, J. Meacham, and Lucy Wright. . . .* New York: D. Appleton and Co, 1859.

Fraser, Daniel. "An Analysis of Human Society: Declaring the Law Which Creates and Sustains a Community Having Goods in Common." *Shaker*, 7 (March–June 1877): 18–19, 44.

[———.] *The Music of the Spheres. . . .* Albany, N.Y.: Weed, Parsons, and Co., 1887.

———. "Shakerism: Is Celibacy Contrary to Natural and Revealed Law?" *Manifesto* 19 (April 1889): 78–80.

Frost, Marguerite. "The Prose and Poetry of Shakerism." *Philadelphia Museum Bulletin* 57 (Spring 1962): 67–82.

Gentle Manners: A Guide to Good Morals. East Canterbury, N.H., 1899.

The Gospel Monitor: A Little Book of Mother Ann's Word to Those Who Are Placed as Instructors & Care-takers of Children; Written by Mother Lucy Wright, and Brought by Her to the Elders of the First Order, on the Holy Mount, March 1, 1841. Copied by Inspiration at Mother Ann's Desire, March 2, 1841. Canterbury, N.H., 1843.

Green, Calvin. "Biographical Account of the Life, Character & Ministry of Father Joseph Meacham . . . 1827." *Shaker Quarterly* 10 (Spring/Summer/Fall 1970): 20–32, 58–68, 92–102.

[Green, Calvin, and Seth Youngs Wells.] *A Summary View of the Millennial Church, or United Society of Believers (Commonly Called Shakers): Comprising the Rise, Progress, and Practical Order of the Society; Together with the General Principles of Their Faith and Testimony. Published by Order of the Ministry, in Union with the Church.* Albany, N.Y.: Packard and Van Benthuysen, 1823.

[———.] *A Brief Exposition of the Established Principles and Regulations of the United Society Called Shakers. . . .* Albany, N.Y.: Packard and Van Benthuysen, 1830.

[———, eds.] *Testimonies of the Life, Character, Revelations and Doctrines of Mother Ann Lee and the Elders with Her.* 2nd ed. Albany, N.Y.: Weed, Parsons, and Co., 1888.

Haskell, Delia. "What is Shakerism?" *Shaker Quarterly* 1 (Spring 1961): 21.

Haskell, Russell, comp. *A Musical Expositor: Or, A Treatise on the Rules and Elements of Music; Adapted to the Most Approved Method of Musical Writing.* New York: George W. Wood, 1847.

"History of the Church of Mt. Lebanon, NY." *Manifesto* 19 (July–December 1889): 145–148, 169–171, 193–196, 217–220, 241–243, 265–267; 20 (January–November 1890): 3–4, 25–28, 49–51, 73–75, 97–100, 121–123, 145–169, 193–195, 217–218, 241–242.

Hodgdon, Charles C. *Just Published, Hodgdon's Life and Manners of Living among the Shakers. . . .* Concord, N.H.: By the Author, 1838.

Hollister, Alonzo Giles, and Calvin Green. *Pearly Gate of the True Life and Doctrine for Believers in Christ. . . .* Mount Lebanon, N.Y., 1894.

Hulings, Martha A. *Shaker Days Remembered.* Albany, N.Y.: Shaker Heritage Society, 1983.

Johnson, Julia H. "Among the Shakers: Some Peculiar Spirit Manifestations." *Progressive Thinker* (n.d.).

Johnson, Theodore E. *Life in the Christ Spirit: Observations on Shaker Theology.* Sabbathday Lake, Maine: United Society of Shakers, 1969.

———, ed. "The 'Millennial Laws' of 1821." *Shaker Quarterly* 7 (Summer 1967): 35–58.

———, ed. "Rules and Orders for the Church of Christ's Second Appearing. Established by the Ministry and Elders of the Church, Revised and Reestablished by the Same, New Lebanon, New York, 1860." *The Shaker Quarterly* 11 (Winter 1971): 139–165.

A Juvenile Guide, Manual of Good Manners. Consisting of Counsels, Instructions & Rules of Deportment, for the Young. By Lovers of Youth. In Two Parts. . . . Canterbury, N.H., 1844.

Leonard, William. *A Disclosure on the Order and Propriety of Divine Inspiration and Revelation, Showing the Necessity Thereof, in All Ages, to Know the Will of God. Also, a Discourse on the Second Appearing of Christ, in and through the Order of the Female. And a Discourse on the Propriety and Necessity of a United Inheritance in All Things, in Order to Support a True Christian Community.* . . . Harvard, Mass.: United Society, 1853.

Lindsay, Bertha. "The Canterbury Shakers: 1792–1967." *Shaker Quarterly* 7 (Fall 1967): 87–95.

Lomas, George Albert. "Shaker Criticism." *Oneida Circular*, n.s., 6 (February 21, 1870): 389.

———. "The Shaker Problem, No. 1." *Phrenological Journal* (July 1873): 42–44.

———. "Decay of Shaker Institutions." *American Socialist* 1 (June 1, 1876): 75–76.

———. *Plain Talks upon Practical Religion: Being Candid Answers to Earnest Inquirers, Including an Answer to the Inquiry "What Shall I Do to Be a Shaker?".* . . . 4th ed. Watervliet, N.Y.: Office of the *Shaker Manifesto*, 1878.

Lyford, James Otis. "The Canterbury Shakers," *History of the town of Canterbury, New Hampshire, 1727–1912.* I: 350–369. Concord, N.H.: Rumford Press, 1912. 2 vols. illus.

[Mace, Aurelia Gay.] *The Aletheia: Spirit of Truth.* . . . Farmington, Maine: Knowlton, McLeary and Co., 1899.

Mace, Fayette. *Familiar Dialogues on Shakerism, in which the Principles of the United Society Are Illustrated and Defended* . . . Portland, Maine: Charles Day and Co., 1837.

Manifesto (New Lebanon, N.Y.) 13–29 (1883–1899).

Marcia, Sister. "Recollections of My Childhood." *Good Housekeeping* 43 (August 1906): 126–129.

McCool, Elsie. "Gleanings from Sabbathday Lake Journals, 1872–1884." *Shaker Quarterly* 6 (Fall/Winter 1966): 103–112, 124–134.

McKechnie, Frederick. "Professor Comstock's Experience." New Lebanon, N.Y., 1902. Short story.

McNemar, Richard. *The Kentucky Revival: Or, A Short History of the Late Extraordinary Out-Pouring of the Spirit of God, in the Western States of America, Agreeably to Scripture-Promises, and Prophecies concerning the Latter Day: With a Brief Account of the Entrance and Progress of What the World Call Shakerism.* . . . Cincinnati, Ohio: John W. Brown, 1807.

[———, comp.] *Investigator: Or A Defense of the Order, Government & Economy of the United Society called Shakers, against Sundry Charges & Legislative*

Proceedings. Addressed to the Political World. By the Society of Believers at Pleasant Hill, Ky. . . . Lexington, Ky.: Smith and Palmer, 1828.

[————.] *The Constitution of the United Societies of Believers (Called Shakers) Containing Sundny* [sic] *Covenants and Artcles* [sic] *of Agrement* [sic], *Definitive of the Legal Grounds of the Institution.* . . . Watervliet, Ohio: 1833.

[———— (Philos Harmoniae, pseud.).] *A Selection of Hymns and Poems; for the Use of Believers. Collected from Sundry Authors* . . . Watervliet, Ohio, 1833.

[Meacham, Joseph.] *A Concise Statement of the Principles of the Only True Church, according to the Gospel of the Present Appearance of Christ.* . . . Bennington, Vt: Haskell and Russell, 1790.

Merrill, Althea. *Shaker Girl.* South Portland, Maine: Pilot Press, Inc., 1987.

Morrell, Prudence. "Account of a Journey to the West in the Year 1847." *Shaker Quarterly* 8 (Summer/Fall 1968): 37–60, 82–96.

Myrick, Elijah. "The Celibate Shaker Life." *Manifesto* 11 (December 1881): 266–267.

Offord, Daniel. *Seven Travails of the Shaker Church.* Mt. Lebanon, N.Y., [1889].

[————, et al.] *Original Shaker Music Published by the North Family, of Mt. Lebanon.* . . . N.Y.: Wm. A. Pond, 1893.

Offord, William. "'Cause and Cure of Evil'—A Shaker's View." *Spiritual Telegraph* (New York) 7 (November 14, 20, 1858): 283–285, 291–293.

Pelham, Richard W. *The Shaker's Answer to a Letter, from an Inquirer.* Union Village, Ohio, 1868.

————. "A Sketch of the Life and Religious Experience of Richard W. Pelham." *Shaker Quarterly* 9 (Spring/Summer/Fall 1969): 18–32, 53–64, 69–96.

Prescott, James Sullivan. "The Social Evil," *Shaker* (May 1871), 34–35.

Rankin, John N., and Harvey Lauderdale Eads. "To the Honorable Abraham Lincoln, President of the U.S., Kind Friend;—Strike, but Hear." *Manifesto* 25 (March 1895): 50–52.

"Remarks of Mother Lucy Wright." *Manifesto* 26 (April, July, November 1896): 65–66, 113–114, 169–170; 27 (January 1897): 5–6.

Sawyer, Otis. "Alfred, Me [Maine]." *Manifesto* 15 (January–May 1885): 9, 11–12, 33–34, 58–59, 79–81, 105–107.

Sears, Chauncy Edward. *Shakers: Duality of the Deity: Or, God as Father and Mother.* Rochester, N.Y.: *Daily Democrat* Steam Printing House, 1867.

————. *A Short Treatise on Marriage.* Rochester, N.Y.: *Daily Democrat* Steam Printing House, 1867.

Shaker (New Lebanon, N.Y.) 1–2 and 6–7 (1871–1872 and 1876–1877).

Shaker and Shakeress (New Lebanon, N.Y.) 3–5 (1873–1875).

Shaker Church Covenant. . . . Canterbury Shaker Village, N.H., 1889.

Shaker Manifesto (New Lebanon, N.Y.) 8–12 (1878–1882).

Shaker Quarterly (Sabbathday Lake, New Gloucester, Maine) 1961–Present.

The Shaker's Covenant (Never before Published) with a Brief Outline of Shaker History by Roxalana L. Grosvenor. . . . Boston: W. C. Allen, 1873.

"The Shakers." *Christian Spectator* (New Haven, Conn.) 6 (July 1824): 351–359.

Sherburn, Trudy Reno. *As I Remember It: Being a Detailed Description of the North Family of the Watervliet, N.Y., Shaker Community.* Holland, Mich.: World of Shaker, 1987.

"The Shirley Shakers." *Manifesto* 23 (December 1893): 273–276.

[Slater, Catherine Ann.] "Fifteen Years a Shakeress." *Galaxy* (New York) 13 (January–April 1872): 29–38, 191–201, 337–346, 460–470.

"South Union." *Manifesto* 23 (November–December 1893): 249–250, 276–279; 24 (1894): 3–6, 25–28, 53–56, 77–81, 101–104, 125–127, 149–151, 173–176, 197–199, 221–225, 245–248, 269–271; 25 (January–April): 3–5, 25–28, 49–52, 73–77.

[Stewart, Philemon.] *A Holy, Sacred, and Divine Roll and Book; from the Lord God of Heaven, to the Inhabitants of Earth: Revealed in the United Society at New Lebanon. . . .* Canterbury, N.H.: United Society, 1843.

Wells, Seth Youngs. *Thomas Brown and his Pretended History of Shakers.* [Mount Lebanon, N.Y., 1848?].

———, comp. *Millennial Praises, Containing a Collection of Gospel Hymns, in Four Parts; Adapted to the Day of Christ's Second Appearing. Composed for the Use of His People.* Hancock, Mass.: Josiah Tallcott Jr., 1812.

[Wells, Seth Youngs, and Calvin Green, eds.] *Testimonies Concerning the Character and Ministry of Mother Ann Lee and the First Witnesses of the Gospel of Christ's Second Appearing; Given by Some of the Aged Brethren and Sisters of the United Society. . . .* Albany, N.Y.: Packard and Van Benthuysen, 1827.

West, Arthur. "Reminiscences of Life in a Shaker Village." *New England Quarterly* 9 (June 1938): 343–360.

Whitcher, Mary. *Mary Whitcher's Shaker House-Keeper.* Boston: Weeks and Potter, [c. 1882].

[White, Anna, comp.] *Affectionately Inscribed to the Memory of Elder Frederick W. Evans, by His Loving and Devoted Gospel Friends. . . .* Pittsfield, Mass.: Eagle Publishing Co., 1893.

[———.] *Mount Lebanon Cedar Boughs.* Buffalo, N.Y.: Peter Paul Book Co. 1895.

White, Anna, and Leila S. Taylor. *Shakerism: Its Meaning and Message. Embracing an Historical Account, Statement of Belief, and Spiritual Experience of the Church from Its Rise to the Present Day.* Columbus, Ohio: Fred J. Heer, 1904.

Wickersham, George M. *How I Came to Be a Shaker.* East Canterbury, N.H., 1891.

Wickliffe, Robert. *The Shakers. Speech of Robert Wickliffe. In the Senate of Kentucky—Jan. 1831. On a Bill to Repeal an Act of the General Assembly of the Senate of Kentucky, Entitled, "An Act to Regulate Civil Proceedings against Certain Communities having Property in Common."* Frankfort, Ky.: A. G. Hodges, 1832.

Wilson, Delmar. "The Diary of a Maine Boy: Delmar Wilson—1887." *Shaker Quarterly* 8 (Spring 1968): 3–22.

Youngs, Benjamin Seth. *The Testimony of Christ's Second Appearing Containing a General Statement of All Things Pertaining to the Faith and Practice of the*

Church of God in This Latter-day. . . . . Lebanon, Ohio: John M'Clean, Office of the *Western Star,* 1808.

———. "An Expedition against the Shakers." *Ohio Archaeological and Historical Society Publications* 21 (1912): 403–415.

Youngs, Isaac Newton. *A Short Abridgement of the Rules of Music. With Lessons for Exercise, and a Few Observations; for Beginners.* New Lebanon, N.Y., 1843.

PUBLICATIONS BY EX-SHAKERS AND ANTI-SHAKERS

Baily, John. *Fanaticism Exposed: Or, The Scheme of Shakerism Compared with Scripture, Reason, and Religion and Found to Be Contrary to Them All.* Lexington, Ky.: W. W. Worsley, Office of the *Reporter, 1811.*

[Bourne, George.] *Marriage Indissoluble: And Divorce Unscriptural.* . . . Harrisonburg, Va: Davidson and Bourne, 1813.

A Brief Exposition of the Fanaticism, False Doctrines, and Absurdities, of the People Called Shakers: Contained in Their Own Religious Creed, or Confession of Faith, as Published by Themselves. By an Enquirer after the Truth. Poughkeepsie, N.Y.: Office of *The Observer,* 1822.

Brown, Samuel. *A Countercheck to Shakerism.* Cincinnati, Ohio: Looker and Reynolds, 1824.

Brown, Thomas. *An Account of the People Called Shakers: Their faith, doctrines, and Practice, Exemplified in the Life, Conversations, and Experience of the Author during the Time He Belonged to the Society. To Which Is Affixed a History of Their Rise and Progress to the Present Day.* Troy, N.Y.: Parker and Bliss, 1812.

Chapman, Eunice. *An Account of the Conduct of the People Called Shakers: In the Case of Eunice Chapman and Her Children, since Her Husband Became Acquainted with That People, and Joined Their Society. Written by Herself.* . . . Albany, N.Y.: By the Author, 1817.

Dyer, Mary Marshall. *A Portraiture of Shakerism, Exhibiting a General View of Their Character and Conduct, from the First Appearance of Ann Lee in New-England, down to the Present Time, and Certified by Many Respectable Authorities.* . . . Haverhill, N.H.: Sylvester T. Gross, 1822.

Elkins, Hervey. *Fifteen Years in the Senior Order of Shakers: A Narration of the Facts, concerning That Singular People.* . . . Hanover, N.H.: Dartmouth Press, 1853 (repr. New York: AMS Press, 1973).

Haskett, William J. *Shakerism Unmasked: Or, The History of the Shakers; Including a Form Politic or Their Government as Councils, Orders, Gifts, with an Exposition of the Five Orders of Shakerism, Ann Lee's Grand Foundation Vision, in Sealed Pages.* . . . Pittsfield, Mass.: By the Author, 1828.

Holloway, Joanna. "Corruptions of Shakerism." *Voice of Truth* (Rochester, N.Y.) (April 7, 1847).

Lamson, David Rich. *Two Years' Experience among the Shakers: Being a Description of the Manners and Customs of That People, the Nature and Policy of Their Government, Their Marvellous Intercourse with the Spiritual World, the Object and Uses of Confession, Their Inquisition, in Short, a Condensed View of Shakerism as It Is*. West Boylston, Mass.: By the Author, 1848 (repr. New York: AMS Press, 1972).

Rathbone [Rathbun], Reuben. *Reasons Offered for Leaving the Shakers*. Pittsfield, Mass.: Chester Smith, 1800.

Rathbun, Valentine Wightman, Sr. *An Account of the Matter, Form, and Manner of a New and Strange Religion, Taught and Propagated by a Number of Europeans, Living in a Place Called Nisqueunia, in the State of New-York. . . .* Providence, R.I.: Bennett Wheeler, 1781.

———. *Some Brief Hints, of a Religious Scheme, Taught and Propagated by a Number of Europeans, living in a Place Called Nisqueunia, in the State of New York*. Norwich, Conn.: John Trumbull, 1781.

Smith, James. *Remarkable Occurrences Lately Discovered among the People Called Shakers; Of a Treasonous and Barbarous Nature, or Shakerism Developed*. Carthage, Tenn.: William Moore, 1810.

———. *Shakerism Detected. Their Erroneous and Treasonous Proceedings and False Publications, Contained in Different News-papers, Exposed to Public View, by the Depositions of Ten Different Persons Living in Various Parts of the States of Kentucky and Ohio. . . .* Paris, Ky.: John R. Lyle, 1810.

Taylor, Amos. *A Narrative of the Strange Principles, Conduct, and Character of the People Known by the Name of Shakers: Whose Errors Have Spread in Several Parts of North-America, but Are Beginning to Diminish, and Ought to Be Guarded Against. . . .* Worcester, Mass.: By the Author, 1782.

West, Benjamin. *Scriptural Cautions against Embracing a Religious Scheme, Taught by a Number of Europeans, Who Came from England to America in the Year of 1776. . . .* Hartford, Conn.: Basil Webster, 1783.

Whitbey, John. *Beauties of Priestcraft; Or, a Short Account of Shakerism*. New Harmony, Ind.: Office of *New Harmony Gazette*, 1826.

Woods, John. *Shakerism Unmasked: Or, A Narrative Shewing the Entrance of the Shakers in the Western Country, Their Stratagems and Devices, Discipline and Economy, Together with What May Seem Necessary to Exhibit the True State of That People. By John Woods: Who Lived with Them Seventeen Years. . . .* Paris, Ky.: Office of the *Western Observer*, 1826.

PUBLICATIONS BY NON-SHAKERS

Abram, Norm, and David Sloan. *Mostly Shaker, from the New Yankee Workshop*. Boston: Little, Brown and Co. 1992.

Anderson, Russell H. "The Shaker Community in Florida." *Florida Historical Quarterly* 37 (July 1959): 29–44.

————. "The Shaker Communities in Southeast Georgia." *Georgia Historical Quarterly* 50 (June 1966): 162–172.

Andrews, Edward Deming. *The Community Industries of the Shakers.* Albany, N.Y.: University of the State of New York, 1933 (repr. Philadelphia: Porcupine Press, 1972).

————. "Shaker Songs." *Musical Quarterly* 23 (October 1937): 491–508.

————. "The Dance in Shaker Ritual." *Dance Index* 1 (April 1942): 56–67.

————. *The People Called Shakers: A Search for the Perfect Society.* New York: Oxford University Press, 1953.

————. *The Gift to Be Simple.* New York: Dover Publications, 1962.

————. *A Shaker Meeting House and Its Builder.* Hancock, Mass.: Shaker Community, Inc., 1962.

Andrews, Edward and Faith Andrews. *Shaker Furniture: The Craftsmanship of an American Communal Sect.* New York: Dover Publications. 1964.

————. *Work and Worship Among the Shakers.* New York: Dover Publications, 1982.

Applebee, Arthur N. *Tradition and Reform in the Teaching of English: A History.* Urbana, Ill.: National Council of Teachers of English, 1974.

Bach, Marcus. *Strange Sects and Curious Cults.* New York: Dodd, Mead, and Co., 1961.

Baker, Jean Havey. "Women in Utopia: The Nineteenth Century Experience." In *Utopias: the American Experience,* Gardner B. Moment and Otto F. Kraushaar, eds. Metuchen, N.J.: Scarecrow Press, 1980.

Barnes, Sherman Bisbee. "Shaker Education." *Ohio Archaeological and Historical Quarterly* 62 (January 1953): 67–76.

[Bates, Barnabus.] *Peculiarities of the Shakers, Described in a Series of Letters from Lebanon Springs, in the Year 1832, Containing an Account of the Origin, Worship, and Doctrines, of the Shaker's Society. By a Visitor. . . .* New York: J. K. Porter, 1832.

Beers, W. H., and Co. *The History of Warren County, Ohio.* Chicago: W. H. Beers and Co., 1882.

Benedict, David. *A History of All Religions, as Divided into Paganism, Mahometanism, Judaism, and Christianity. . . .* Providence, R.I.: John Miller, 1824.

Berry, G. W. "The Last of the Shakers." *Ohio Magazine* (Columbus) 3 (July 1907): 14–18.

Bestor, Arthur Eugene. *Backwoods Utopias: The Sectarian and Owenite Phases of Communitarian Socialism in America, 1663–1829.* Philadelphia: University of Pennsylvania Press, 1950.

Blake, Nelson M. "Eunice against the Shakers." *New York History* 41 (October 1960): 359–378.

Brewer, Priscilla J. *Shaker Communities, Shaker Lives.* Hanover, N.H.: University Press of New England, 1986.

————. " 'Tho' of the Weaker Sex': A Reassessment of Gender Equity among the Shakers." In *Women in Spiritual and Communitarian Societies in the United*

States. Wendy E. Chmielewski, Louis J. Kern, and Marlyn Klee-Hartzell, eds. Syracuse, N.Y.: Syracuse University Press, 1993.

Buchanan, Rita. *The Shaker Herb and Garden Book.* Boston: Houghton Mifflin Co., 1966.

Burns, Amy Stechler. *The Shakers: Hands to Work, Hearts to God.* New York: Aperture Foundation, Inc., 1987.

Burns, Deborah E. *Shaker Cities of Peace, Love, and Union: A History of the Hancock Bishopric.* Hanover, N.H.: University Press of New England, 1993.

[C. B.] "A Second Visit to the Shakers." In *American Life in the 1840s,* Carl Bode, ed. New York: New York University Press, 1967.

Campbell, D'Ann. "Women's Life in Utopia: The Shaker Experiment in Sexual Equality Reappraised—1810 to 1860." *New England Quarterly* 51, no. 1 (March 1978): 23–38.

Campion, Nardi Reeder. *Ann the Word: the Life of Mother Ann Lee, Founder of the Shakers.* Boston: Little, Brown, and Co., 1976,

Chandler, Isaac. *A Summary View of America: Comprising a Description of the Face of the Country, and of Several of the Principal Cities; and Remarks on the Social, Moral and Political Character of the People. . . .* London: T. Cadell, 1824.

Chandler, Lloyd H. "The Followers of Ann Lee." *Granite Monthly* 16 (1894): 255–266, 321–323.

Chase, Daryl. "The Early Shakers: An Experiment in Religious Communism." Ph.D. diss., University of Chicago, 1936.

Chase, Eugene Parker, ed. and trans. *Our Revolutionary Forefathers: the Letters of Francois, Marquis de Barbe-Marbois, during His Residence in the United States as Secretary of the French Legation, 1779–1785.* New York: Duffield and Co., 1929.

Clark, Thomas D., and F. Gerald Ham. *Pleasant Hill and Its Shakers.* Harrodsburg, Ky.: Pleasant Hill Press, 1983.

————. *The Gift of Pleasant Hill Shaker Community in Kentucky.* [Harrodsburg, Kentucky]: Pleasant Hill Press, 1991.

Conlin, Mary Lou. *The North Union: A Shaker Society, 1882–1889.* Cleveland, Ohio: Ontario Printers, Inc., 1961.

Coombs, Elizabeth. "Shaker Colony at South Union, Kentucky. *Filson Club History Quarterly* (Louisville, Ky.) 14 (July 1940): 154–173.

Count, Jerome. "Teen-agers and the Shakers." *Shaker Quarterly* 1 (Summer 1961): 80–87.

[Cushman, Charlotte.] "Lines: Suggested by a Visit to the Shaker Settlement, Near Albany." *Knickerbocker* 9 (January 1837): 46–47.

Desroche, Henry Charles. *The American Shakers: From Neo-Christianity to Presocialism.* John K. Savacool, trans. and ed. Amherst, Mass: University of Massachusetts Press, 1971.

Dixon, W. Hepworth. *New America.* 3rd ed. Philadelphia: J. B. Lippincott and Co., 1867.

Dow, Edward F. *A Portrait of the Millennial Church of the Shakers.* Orono: University Press of Maine, 1931.

Everett, Edward. "The Shakers." *North American Review* 16 (January 1823): 76–102.

Extract from an Unpublished Manuscript on Shaker History (by an Eye-witness), Giving an Accurate Description of Their Songs, Dances, Marches, Visions, Visits to the Spirit Land, &c. Boston: E. K. Allen, 1850.

Faber, Doris. *The Perfect Life: The Shakers in America.* New York: Farrar, Strauss and Giroux, 1974.

[Felt, Mrs. Charles W.] "Among the Shakers." *Shaker Manifesto* 10 (January–March 1880): 5–6, 29–31, 56–58.

Ferguson, Richard G., Jr. "Central Themes in Shaker Thought." *Register of the Kentucky Historical Society* 74, No. 3 (July 1976): 216–219.

Filley, Dorothy M. *Recapturing Wisdom's Valley: The Watervliet Shaker Heritage, 1775–1975.* Albany, N.Y.: Albany Institute of History and Art, 1975.

Finch, Marianne. *An Englishwoman's Experience in America.* London: R. Bently, 1853.

Foster, Lawrence. *Religion and Sexuality: Three American Communal Experiments of the Nineteenth Century.* New York: Oxford University Press, 1981.

Garrett, Clarke. *Spirit Possession and Popular Religion: From the Camisards to the Shakers.* Baltimore, Md.: Johns Hopkins University Press, 1987.

Gifford, Don, ed. *An Early View of the Shakers: Benjamin John Lossing the Harper's Article of July 1857.* Hanover, N.H.: University Press of New England, 1989.

[Gilder, Richard Watson.] ["The Shaker Service at Mt. Lebanon."] *Scribner's Monthly* 2 (October 1871): 656–657.

Gooden, Rosemary D. "'In the Bonds of True Love and Friendship': Some Meanings of 'Gospel Affection' and 'Gospel Union' in Shaker Sisters' Letters and Poems." In *Women in Spiritual and Communitarian Societies in the United States,* Wendy E. Chmielewski, Louis J. Kern, and Marlyn Klee-Hartzell, eds. Syracuse, N.Y.: Syracuse University Press, 1993.

Gordon, Beverly. "Shaker Fancy Goods: Women's Work and Presentation of Self in the Community Context in the Victorian Era." In *Women in Spiritual and Communitarian Societies in the United States,* Wendy E. Chmielewski, Louis J. Kern, and Marlyn Klee-Hartzell, eds. Syracuse, N.Y.: Syracuse University Press, 1993.

Greeley, Horace. "A Sabbath with the Shakers." *Knickerbocker* 11 (June 1838): 532–537.

———. *Hints towards Reforms. . . .* New York: Harper and Bros., 1850.

Haight, Charles Sherman. "The Lebanon Shakers." *Godey's Magazine* 137 (August 1898): 177–184.

Ham, F. Gerald. "Shakerism in the Old West." Ph.D. diss., University of Kentucky, 1962.

Handberg, Ejner. *Measured Drawings of Shaker Furniture and Woodenware.* Stockbridge, Mass.: Berkshire Traveller Press, 1980.

Hawthorne, Nathaniel. *The American Notebooks.* Randall Stewart, ed. New Haven, Conn.: Yale University Press, 1932.

Haywood, Charles. *A Bibliography of North American Folklore and Folksong.* New York: Greenberg, 1951.

Held, Conrad Christopher, arranger. *Fifteen Shaker Songs. . . .* New York: G. Schirmer, Inc., 1944.

[Hill, Isaac.] "The Shakers." *Farmer's Monthly Visitor* (Concord, N.H.) 2 (August 31, 1840): 113–118.

Hinds, William Alfred. *American Communities: Brief Sketches of Economy, Zoar, Bethel, Aurora, Amana, Icaria, the Shakers, Oneida, Wallingford, and the Brotherhood of New Life.* Oneida, N.Y.: Office of the *American Socialist,* 1878.

Holland, Josiah Gilbert [Timothy Titcomb, pseud.]. *Lessons in Life: A Series of Familiar Essays. . . .* 10th ed. New York: C. Scribner, 1862.

Honeywood, St. John. *Poems . . . with Some Pieces in Prose.* New York: T. and J. Swords, 1801.

Horgan, Edward R. *The Shaker Holyland: A Community Portrait.* Harvard, Mass.: Harvard Common Press, 1982.

Howells, William Dean. "A Shaker Village." *Atlantic Monthly* 37 (June 1876): 699–710.

————. *Three Villages.* Boston: J. R. Osgood, 1884.

Humez, Jean M., ed. *Gifts of Power: The Writings of Rebecca Jackson, Black Visionary, Shaker Eldress.* Boston, Mass.: University of Massachusetts Press, 1981.

————. *Mother's First-Born Daughters: Early Shaker Writings on Women and Religion.* Bloomington: Indiana University Press, 1993,

Hutchinson, Gloria. "The Shakers of Sabbathday Lake [Maine]." *Down East* 18 (October 1971): 38–41, 66–67, 70, 75, 77.

Hutton, Daniel Mac-Hir. *Old Shakertown and the Shakers: A Brief History of the Rise of the United Society of Believers in Christ's Second Coming, the Establishment of Pleasant Hill Colony, Their Beliefs, Customs, and Pathetic End. . . .* Harrodsburg, Ky.: Harrodsburg Herald Press, [c. 1936].

Hyde, Alexander. "Shakerdom. Its History and Principles and Practical Workings." *Old and New* (Boston) 3 (June 1871): 706–716.

Jackson, Barry. *Making Shaker Furniture.* Portsmouth, England: Grosvenor Press, Ltd., 1992.

Journal of Shaker Studies (Mount Pleasant, Mich.) 1–4 (March, 1995–1998).

Joynes, Thomas. "Memorandum Made . . . on a Journey to the States of Ohio and Kentucky, 1810." *William and Mary College Quarterly Historical Magazine* 10 (January–April 1902): 145–158, 221–232.

Kern, Louis J. *An Ordered Love: Sex Roles and Sexuality in Victorian Utopias—the Shakers, the Mormons, and the Oneida Community.* Chapel Hill: University of North Carolina Press, 1981.

Klyver, Richard D. *Brother James: The Life and Times of Shaker Elder, James Prescott.* Solon, Ohio: Evans Printing Co., 1992.

Kramer, Eugene F. "Identifying Mother Ann's Picture." *New York Folklore* (Autumn 1960): 226–227.

Lane, Charles. "A Day with the Shakers." *Dial* (Boston) 4 (October 1843): 165–173.

Lassiter, William Lawrence. *Shaker Architecture: Descriptions with Photographs and Drawings of Shaker Buildings at Mt. Lebanon, New York, Watervliet, New York, West Pittsfield, Massachusetts.* New York: Vintage Press, 1966.

Lathrop, George Parsons. *A Study of Hawthorne.* Boston: J. R. Osgood, 1876.

Lawson, Donna. *Brothers and Sisters All over This Land: America's First Communes.* New York: Praeger Publishers, 1972.

Lee, Charles O. "The Shakers as the Pioneers in the American Herb and Drug Industry." *Journal of Pharmacy* 132 (May 1960): 178–193.

Lossing, Benjamin John. "The Shakers." *Harper's New Monthly Magazine* 15 (July 1857): 164–177.

Lyford, James Otis. *History of the Town of Canterbury, New Hampshire, 1727–1912.* 2 vols. Concord, N.H.: Rumford Press, 1912.

MacLean, John Patterson. "The Society of Shakers: Rise, Progress, and Extinction of the Society at Cleveland, Ohio." *Ohio Archaeological and Historical Quarterly* 9 (April 1900): 32–116.

———. *A Bibliography of Shaker Literature, with an Introductory Study of the Writings and Publications Pertaining to Ohio Believers.* Columbus, Ohio: F. J. Heer, 1905.

———. *Sketch of the Life and Labors of Richard McNemar.* [Franklin, Ohio]: Office of *Franklin Chronicle*, 1905

———. *The Shakers of Ohio: Fugitive Papers.* Columbus, Ohio: F. J. Heer Printing Co., 1907.

Manroe, Candace Ord, and Joseph Boehm. *Shaker Style: The Gift of Simplicity.* New York: Crescent Books, 1991.

Marini, Stephen A. "A New View of Mother Ann Lee and the Rise of American Shakerism." *Shaker Quarterly* 18, no. 3 (Fall 1980).

Martineau, Harriet. *Society in America.* 3 vols. London: Saunders and Otley, 1837.

Maxwell, Archibald Montgomery. *A Run through the United States during the Autumn of 1840,* 2 vols. London: Henry Colburn, 1841,

McCorison, Marcus Allen. "Amos Taylor: A Sketch and Bibliography." *Proceedings* (of American Antiquarian Society) 69 (April 15, 1959): 37–55.

McVey, Frances Jewell. "Shaker Chronicles of Pleasant Hill [Kentucky]." *Kentucky Progress Magazine* 5 (Summer 1933): 16–19, 47–50.

Meader, Robert F. "The Story of the Shaker Museum [Old Chatham, N.Y.]." *Curator* (American Museum of Natural History) 3 (Fall 1960): 204–216.

———. "The Emma B. King Library of the Shaker Museum, Old Chatham [New York]." *Bookmark* 27 (July 1968): 391–393.

————. *Illustrated Guide to Shaker Furniture.* New York: Dover Publications, 1972.

Melcher, Marguerite Fellows. *The Shaker Adventure.* Princeton, N.J.: Princeton University Press, 1941.

Mercandante, Linda A. *Gender, Doctrine, and God: The Shakers and Contemporary Theology.* Nashville, Tenn.: Abingdon Press, 1990.

Morse, Flo. *The Shakers and the World's People.* New York: Dodd, Mead, and Co., 1980.

————. *The Story of the Shakers.* Woodstock, Vt.: Countryman Press, 1986.

Moser, Thomas. *How to Build Shaker Furniture.* Rev. ed. New York: Sterling Publishing Co., 1977.

"Mother Ann Lee, the Shaker." *Illustrated Annual of Phrenology and Physiognomy* (New York) (1872): 38–41.

Neal, Julia. *By Their Fruits: The Story of Shakerism in South Union, Kentucky.* Chapel Hill: University of North Carolina Press, 1947.

————. "South Union Shakers during the War Years." *Filson Club History Quarterly* 39 (April 1965): 147–150.

Neal, Julia, and Elmer R. Pearson. *The Shaker Image: The Shakers, as They Saw Themselves and as Others Saw Them.* Hancock, Mass.: Shaker Community, Inc., 1974.

————. *The Kentucky Shakers.* Lexington: University Press of Kentucky, 1977.

Newman, Cathy. "The Shakers' Brief Eternity." *National Geographic* (September 1989): 302–325.

Nickless, Karen K., and Pamela J. Nickless. "Sexual Equality and Economic Authority: The Shaker Experience, 1784–1900." In *Women in Spiritual and Communitarian Societies in the United States,* Wendy E. Chmielewski, Louis J. Kern, and Marlyn Klee-Hartzell, eds. Syracuse, N.Y.: Syracuse University Press, 1993.

Nordhoff, Charles. *The Communistic Societies of the United States. . . .* New York: Harper and Bros., 1875.

Noyes, John Humphrey. *A History of American Socialisms.* Philadelphia: J. B. Lippincott and Co., 1870.

Oved, Yaacov. *Two Hundred Years of American Communes.* New Brunswick, N.J.: Transactions, 1988.

Patterson, Daniel Watkins. "Turtle Creek to Busro: Notes on Shaker Ballads." *North Carolina Folklore Journal* (December 1955): 31–37.

————. *Nine Shaker Spirituals.* Old Chatham, N.Y.: Shaker Museum Foundation, 1964.

————. "Inspiration and Authority in the Development of the Shaker Spiritual." *North Carolina Folklore* 13, Nos. 1–2 (1965): 111–120.

————. *The Shaker Spiritual.* Princeton, N.J.: Princeton University Press, 1979.

————. *Gift Drawing and Gift Song.* Sabbathday Lake, Maine: United Society of Shakers, 1983.

Peladeau, Marius B. "The Shaker Meeting Houses of Moses Johnson." *Antiques* (October 1970): 594–599.

Phelps, Lillian. "Reminiscences of Shaker Recreational Life": *Shaker Quarterly* 1, no. 2 (Summer 1961): 55–57.

Phillippi, Joseph Martin. *Shakerism: Or, The Romance of Religion*. Dayton, Ohio: The Otterbein Press, 1912.

Phillips, Hazel Spencer. *The Shakers: A Story of a Way of Life*. Lebanon, Ohio: N.p., 1959.

———. *Traditional Architecture, Warren County, Ohio*. [Oxford, Ohio: Typoprint, Inc., 1969].

———. *Richard the Shaker*. [Oxford, Ohio: Typoprint, Inc., c. 1972].

Piercy, Caroline Behlen. *The Valley of God's Pleasure*. New York: Stratford House, 1951.

Piercy, Harry D. "Shaker Medicines." *Ohio State Archaeological and Historical Quarterly* 63 (October 1954): 336–348.

Pike, Kermit, comp. *A Guide to the Manuscripts of the Western Reserve Historical Society*. Cleveland, Ohio: Western Reserve Historical Society [Case Western Reserve University Press], 1975.

Plummer, William. "The Original Shaker Communities in New England." *New England Magazine*, n.s., 22 (May 1900): 303–309.

Proper, David, comp. "Bibliography of Shaker Literature, [Part 1]–Part 11." *Shaker Quarterly* 4 (Winter 1964): 130–142; 5 (Spring 1965): 26–32.

Pulos, Arthur J., and Rex Moore. "The Shakers." *Flying Chips* 41 (May–June 1972): 68–73.

Purcell, L. Edward. *The Shakers*. New York: Crescent Books, 1988.

Procter-Smith, Marjorie. *Women in Shaker Community and Worship: A Feminist Analysis of the Uses of Religious Symbolism*. Lewiston, N.Y.: Edwin Mellen Press, 1985.

Randles, Raymond J. "The Shaker Harvest in Kentucky." *Filson Club History Quarterly* 37 (1963): 38–58.

A Return of Departed Spirits of the Highest Characters of Distinction, as Well as the Indiscriminate of All Nations, into the Bodies of the "Shakers," or "United Society of Believers in the Second Advent of the Messiah." By an Associate of Said Society. . . . Philadelphia: J. R. Conlon, 1843.

Richmond, Mary L., comp. *Shaker Literature: A Bibliography*. 2 vols. Hancock, Mass.: Shaker Community, 1977.

Robinson, Charles Edson. *A Concise History of the United Society of Believers Called Shakers*. East Canterbury, N.H.: Shaker Village, 1893.

Rourke, Constance. *Roots of American Culture, and Other Essays*. Van Wyck Brooks, ed. New York: Harcourt, Brace, and Co., 1942.

Sasson, Diana. *The Shaker Spiritual Narrative*. Knoxville: University of Tennessee, 1983.

Schiffer, Herbert, comp. *Shaker Architecture*. West Chester, Penn.: Schiffer Publishing Ltd., 1979.

Schroeder, Theodore. "Shaker Celibacy and Salacity Psychologically Interpreted." *New York Journal of Medicine* 113 (June 1, 1921): 800–805.

Sears, Clara Endicott, comp. *Gleanings from Old Shaker Journals.* New York: Houghton Mifflin Co. 1916.

Sellin, David. "Shaker Inspirational Drawings." *Philadelphia Museum Bulletin* 57 (Spring 1962): 93–99.

Setta, Susan M. "When Christ is a Woman: Theology and Practice in the Shaker Tradition." In Unspoken Worlds: Women's Religious Lives, Nancy Auer Falk and Rita M. Gross, eds. Belmont, Calif.: Wadsworth Publishing Co., 1989.

Shaker Historical and Biographical Register. (Old Chatham, N.Y.) (1995–Present).

Shaker Messenger. (Holland, Mich.) (1968–Present).

"Shaker Series." *Flying Chips* 41 (May–December): 74–79, 100–107, 150–155, 184–188.

"The Shaker's Bible." *Newcastle Magazine* 3 (January 1824): 18–23.

"Shakers." *Niles Weekly Register* 37 (September 18, 1829): 58–59.

"Shakers." *Penny Magazine* 6 (November 18, 1837): 445–448.

Shaver, Elizabeth. *The Watervliet Shaker Cemetery.* Albany, N.Y.: Shaker Heritage Society, 1986.

———, ed. *Fifteen Years a Shakeress. Author Unknown.* Albany, N.Y.: Shaker Heritage Society, 1989.

Shaver, Elizabeth, and Ned Pratt. *The Watervliet Shakers and Their 1848 Meeting House, Albany, New York.* Albany, N.Y.: Shaker Heritage Society, 1994.

Shea, John. *The American Shakers and Their Furniture, with Measured Drawings of Museum Classics.* New York: Van Nostrand and Reinhold Co., 1971.

[Silliman, Benjamin.] *Remarks Made on a Short Tour, between Hartford and Quebec, in the Autumn of 1819. . . .* New Haven, Conn.: S. Converse, 1820.

Skees, Suzanne. *God among the Shakers: A Search for Stillness and Faith at Sabbathday Lake.* New York: Hyperion, 1998.

Smith, Alson J. "Mother Ann's 'Work,' or History of the Shakers." *Fate* 18 (October 1965): 59–69.

South Union Messenger. (Shakertown, South Union, Ky.) (1972–Present).

Stahl, Sanda K. D. "Personal Experience Stories." *Handbook of American Folklore.* Richard M. Dorson, ed. Bloomington: Indiana University Press, 1983.

Stein, Stephen J. *The Shaker Experience in America: A History of the United Society of Believers.* New Haven, Conn.: Yale University Press, 1992.

[Stone, Horatio.] *Lo Here and Lo There! Or, The Grave of the Heart.* New York: [Burgess, Stringer, and Co.], 1846.

Sturm, Ann Black. *The Shaker Gift of Song.* Berea, Ky.: Berea College Press, 1981.

Swain, Thomas. "The Evolving Expressions of the Religious and Theological Experiences of a Community: A Comparative Study of the Shaker *Testimonies* concerning the Sayings of Mother Ann Lee; an Exploration of the Development from Oral Traditions to Written Forms as Preserved in Four Documents." *Shaker Quarterly* 12, no. 1 (Spring 1972): 3–31; 12, No. 2 (Summer 1972): 43–67.

Symonds, John. *Thomas Brown and the Angels: A Study in Enthusiasm.* London: Hutchinson, [1961].

Taylor, Frank G. "An Analysis of Shaker Education: The Life and Death of An Alternative Educational System, 1774–1950." Ph.D. diss., University of Connecticut, 1975.

Thomas, James C. "Micajah Burnett and the Buildings at Pleasant Hill." *Antiques* 98 (October 1970): 600–605.

Thomas, S. W., and J. C. Thomas. *The Simple Spirit.* Pleasant Hill, Ky.: The Pleasant Hill Press, 1973.

"Transactions of the Ohio Mob against the Shakers, August 27th, 1818." *Telescope* 2 (1825): 175–176.

True, Alida Cogswell. "Shaker Meeting." *Granite Monthly* 52 (March 1921): 122.

Tudor, Henry. *Narrative of a Tour in North America . . . in a Series of Letters Written in the Years 1831–2,* 2 vols. London: J. Duncan, 1834.

Upton, Charles W. "The Shaker Utopia." *Antiques* 98 (October 1970): 582–587.

Upton, James Merritt. "The Shakers as Pacifists in the Period between 1812 and the Civil War." *Filson Club History Quarterly* 47 (July 1973): 267–283.

Van Kolken, Diane. *Introducing the Shakers: An Explanation and Directory.* Bowling Green, Ohio: Gabriel's Horn Publishing Co., 1985.

Vanstory, Burnette. "Shakers and Shakerism in Georgia." *Georgia Historical Quarterly* 43 (December 1959): 353–364.

"A Visit to the Shakers." *Blackwood's Edinburgh Magazine* 11 (April 1823): 463–469.

[Warner, Charles Dudley.] "Out of the World." *Scribner's Monthly* 18 (August 1879): 549–558.

Webber, Everett. *Escape to Utopia: The Communal Movement in America.* New York: Hastings House, [1959].

[Weeks, Estella.] "Shakerism. Shakerism in Indiana; Notes on Shaker Life, Customs, and Music." *Hoosier Folklore Bulletin* 4 (December 1945): 59–85.

Wertkin, Gerald C. *The Four Seasons of Shaker Life: An Intimate Portrait of the Community at Sabbathday Lake.* New York: Simon and Schuster, 1986.

Whitson, Robley Edward, ed. *The Shakers: Two Centuries of Spiritual Reflection.* New York: Paulist Press, 1983.

Whitworth, John McKelvie. *God's Blueprints: A Sociological Study of Three Utopian Sects.* Boston: Routledge and Kegan Paul, 1975.

Williams, Emily. "Spirituality as Expressed in Song." *Connecticut Magazine* 9 (Autumn 1905): 745–751.

Williams, John S. *Consecrated Ingenuity. The Shakers and Their Inventions.* Old Chatham, N.Y.: Shaker Museum Foundation, 1957.

———. *The Shaker Religious Concept, together with the Covenant, Hancock, Mass., 1830.* Old Chatham, N.Y.: Shaker Museum Foundation, 1959.

Williams, Richard E. *Called and Chosen: The Story of Mother Rebecca Jackson and the Philadelphia Shakers.* Metuchen, N.J.: Scarecrow Press, 1981.

Winchell, Wallace. *The Poetry of the Shakers.* [Nashville, Tenn.: Abingdon Press, 1970]. Offprint: *Religion in Life* 39 (Winter 1970): 530–544.

Winter, Esther C., comp. *Shaker Literature in the Grosvenor Library: A Bibliography.* Buffalo, N.Y.: Grosvenor Library, 1940.

Wisbey, Herbert A., Jr. *The Sodus Shaker Community.* New York: Wayne County Historical Society, 1982.

Woodbury, Benjamin C. *An Album of Verse Written in the Antique Mood Dedicated to the Shakers of Harvard, Massachusetts.* N.p., 1947.

World of Shaker (Spring Lake, Mich.) 1, no. 1 (Fall 1971).

Zieget, Irene. "The Shakers and Their Adventures with Seeds and Herbs: A True Story of Long Ago." *Potomac Herb Journal* 8 (Spring 1972): 1–6.

SCHOLARLY STUDIES OF IMAGINATIVE LITERATURE FEATURING SHAKERS

Brooks, Van Wyck. *Howells: His Life and World.* New York: E. P. Dutton, 1959.

Cate, Herma R. "Shakers in American Fiction." *Tennessee Folklore Society Bulletin* 41 (1975): 19–24.

Cooke, Delmar Gross. *William Dean Howells: A Critical Study.* New York: E. P. Dutton, and Co., 1922.

Duffield, Holley Gene. "Brother Hervey Elkins' Shaker Short Story." *Shaker Messenger* 14, No. 4 (January 1993): 15, 20.

———. "Shakerism in Kentucky Fiction." *Journal of Kentucky Studies* 11 (September 1994): 90–96.

———. "Shakers: Education, Historical Narrative, and Narrative Fiction in the Nineteenth Century." *Journal of Shaker Studies* 3, no. 1 (April 1, 1997): 2–13.

———. "The Shakers of North Union in Two Imaginative Tales by Authors of 'the World.'" *Journal of Shaker Studies* 3, no. 2 (August 1, 1997): 2–9.

———. "The Shakers in Fictions for Young Readers of the Late Twentieth Century." *Journal of Shaker Studies* 3, No. 3 (December 1997): 2–15.

Duffield, Holley Gene, and Pamela Sue Gates-Duffield. "The Apostate Shakeress Heroine in Nineteenth Century American Short Stories by Non-Shakers." *Journal of Shaker Studies* 2, no. 1 (April 1, 1996): 2–11.

Duffield, Holley Gene, Pamela Sue Gates-Duffield, and Susan B. Steffel. "Commentary on Historical Fiction: The Case of Hawthorne's 'The Shaker Bridal.'" *Journal of Shaker Studies* 1, no. 2 (September 23, 1995): 6–14.

Farnham, James Franklin. "Hawthorne and the Shakers." *Shaker Quarterly* 6 (Spring 1966): 5–13.

Firkins, Oscar W. *William Dean Howells: A Study.* Cambridge, Mass.: Harvard University Press, 1924.

Flitcroft, John E. *The Novelist of Vermont: A Biographical and Critical Study of Daniel Pierce Thompson.* Cambridge, Mass.: Harvard University Press, 1929.

Gates-Duffield, Pamela Sue. "Shakers in Picture Books: Historical Fiction of Didactic Tutorials?" *Journal of Shaker Studies* 2, no. 3 (December 1, 1996): 2–5.

———. "Shakers in a New Picture Book [*Shaker Hearts*]." *Journal of Shaker Studies* 3, no. 1 (April 1, 1997): 14–16.

Gollin, Rita K. "Hawthorne Contemplates the Shakers." *Nathaniel Hawthorne Journal* 8 (1978): 57–65.

Gross, Seymour. "Hawthorne and the Shakers." *American Literature* 29 (1958): 457–463.

Macheski, Cecilia. "Introduction." *The Believers*, by Janice Holt Giles. Lexington: University Press of Kentucky, 1989.

McAdams, Ruth Ann. "The Shakers in American Fiction." Ph.D. diss. Texas Christian University, 1985.

Pugh, Robert Michael. "A Thorn in the Text: Shakerism and the Marriage Narrative." Ph.D. diss. University of New Hampshire, 1994.

Waggoner, Hyatt H. "Hawthorne's 'The Canterbury Pilgrims': Theme and Structure." *New England Quarterly* 22 (September 1949): 373–387.

Watkins, Dianne. "Janice Holt Giles and *The Believers*." *Shaker Messenger* 11 (Summer 1989): 5–7, 24–28.

Vanderbilt, Kermit. *The Achievement of William Dean Howells*. Princeton, N.J.: Princeton University Press, 1968.

About the Author

Holley Gene Duffield has taught at several universities. His academic bailiwicks are literary criticism and aesthetics, and his publications on these subjects include *Tolstoy and the Critics: Literature and Aesthetics* (1965) and *Problems in Criticism of the Arts* (1967). His discovery of the Shakers in short stories and novels of the nineteenth and twentieth centuries, as well as seeing their furniture being lauded in modern woodworker journals among other places, created in Duffield an immense curiosity about the Shakers and inspired him several times to visit their defunct villages and Sabbathday Lake, New Gloucester, Maine, the home of the extant Shakers. In 1994, he founded the Society for Shaker Studies, a not-for-profit organization dedicated to the acquisition, preservation, and dissemination of knowledge about the sect. During the same year, he established the *Journal of Shaker Studies*, for which he has written several articles. His publications on the Shakers have also appeared in the *Shaker Messenger* and the *Journal of Kentucky Studies*.